Innovation & Entrepreneurship

Centre for Innovation and Entrepreneurship

Centurion University of Technology & Management, Odisha, India

CONTENTS

Eleven	Innovative way towards Sustainable Business development through Corporate Social Responsibility in India	Brij Lal Mallik & Sisir Ranjan Dash
Twelve	Digital Age Pedagogy for English Language Teachers	Ajit Kumar Pradhan & Amit Kumar Singh
Thirteen	Need of Listening Skills in the Second Language Acquisition Process: An Innovation	Pradeep Kumar Sahoo
Fourteen	Impact Of Management Of Service Product Innovation On Business Success Through Organizational Culture	Satyaprakash Naik, Dr Sabyasachi Dey and Dr Sisir Ranjan Dash
Fifteen	Entrepreneurship Development Leading to Growth of MSME	Dr Sabyasachi Dey
Sixteen	The Growth and Performance of MSME Segment: A study on Odisha's Perspective	Dr.Pramod Kumar Patjoshi Dr. Girija Nandini
Seventeen	A significant role of innovative entrepreneurs in Animation and Visual Effects industry	Saban Kumar Maharana
Eighteen	Constraints in Cashew nut Entrepreneurship in India and Suggestive Measures	Kalee Prasanna Pattanayak and Chitrasena Padhy
Nineteen	Digital skills, competencies and employment opportunities	Prajna Pani
Twenty	Entrepreneurship Development Cycle and Programmes in India	Dr. Girija Nandini Dr.Pramod Kumar Patjoshi
Twenty One	A study on Locational Mobility of Entrepreneurs in India	Dr.Pramod Kumar Patjoshi Dr. Girija Nandini
	A study on Factors Affecting	

Two	**Growth of Entrepreneurs in India**	
Twenty Three	**A study on Reasons for Slow Growth and Remedies for Rapid Development of Entrepreneurship in India**	**Dr.Pramod Kumar Patjoshi**
Twenty Four	**A Study On Evaluation Of Entrepreneurial Development In India**	**Dr.Pramod Kumar Patjoshi** **Jasmeen Nisha**
Twenty Five	**Institutional Innovation in Promoting Access to Education for Children with Disabilities: A Case of Swabhiman**	**Bibhunandini Das**
Twenty Six	**Insights on Modern Communication: an allure for entrepreneurs**	**Taneeva Das**
Twenty Seven	**Institutional Intervention to Tackle Socio-economic Problems: A case of Central India Initiative and Collectives for Integrated Livelihood Initiatives**	**Madhumita Das and Bibhunandini Das**
Twenty Eight	**Opportunities and Challenges of MSME Segment: A study on Odisha's Perspective**	**Dr.Pramod Kumar Patjoshi**
Twenty Nine	**Social Entrepreneurship**	**Dr. Girija Nandini, Anindita Bosu**
Thirty	**The Other Voice: Revisiting Educational Radio during the pandemic**	*Dr. Chinu Bohidar*
Thirty one	**A Study on Gayatri Engineering Construction & Consultancy**	**Dr. Prasanta Kumar Mohanty**
Thirty Two	**A Study on Integrity Infotech Private Limited**	**R. Pradeep Patnaik Dr. Umakanta Nayak**

Thirty Three	A Study on M/s. Computer lab	Rabindra Kumar Mohanty N.D. Prasad
Thirty Four	A Study on Essar Bakery	Dr. Subhendu Mishra
Thirty Five	A Study on Shree Paschimasombhu Fuels and Lubes Pvt. Ltd	Dr. Bhagabat Barik Dr. Pramod Kumar Patjoshi
Thirty Six	A Study on Body Care Gym	Pooja Patnaik Dr. Girija Nandini
Thirty Seven	A Study on Jagadamba Retail	Dr. Prashant Chopdar Dr. Madhumita Das
Thirty Eight	A Study on Bob N Harry's	Somabhusana J. Mishra Dr. Bibhunandini Das
Thirty Nine	A Study on Maa Ugratara Food Products	Dr. Prakash Kumar Pradhan Dr. Sisir Ranjan Das
Forty	A Study on a Horticulturist	Dr. Kshitish Kumar Khuntia & Dr. Sabyasachi Dey
Forty One	A Study on Chapan Bhog	Dr. Monalika Rath Dr. Anita Patra
Forty Two	A Study on Rajamoni Foods	Shiv Sankar Das Dr. Susanta Kumar Mishra
Forty Three	A Study on Bakul Foundation	Dr. Pranaya K. Swain Dr. Umaknata Nayak
Forty Four	Green Marketing as a Prospect for Green Entrepreneurs	Dr.Girija Nandini Dr.Alaka Samantaray

CHAPTER ONE

Innovation & Entrepreneurship at the Time of Pandemic

Prof. (Dr) Susanta K. Mishra,

Centurion University of Technology & Management, Odisha

1.1. Introduction

Innovation is something new which could relate to a process, product or an idea. It could also relate to the new type of uses of a product or service. Innovation could involve any new technology, process or the use of existing technology in different way which was not used earlier. When any new innovative idea or technology is applied and adopted successfully in the business and results in a successful product or service accepted by the market it could be said that the innovation is successful. Lot of new ideas come to the mind of the innovators but not all of them result in successful products. Lot of ideas come into the mind of the innovators but all new products and services do not become successful. Despite all the efforts some of the products are not accepted in the market.

Story of Sipani Automobiles

Sipani Automobiles Ltd. Was the manufacturer of Dolphin cars in India. The first Dolphin car that arrived in the market was in the year 1982.The Car was light in weight because of a fibre body and compact in dimension. Being light and compact it was fast too. The other Car manufacturers during that period were Premier Automobiles and Hindustan Motors. Maruti cars were also entering to market during that time. However all other Competitors of Sipani were manufacturing cars with metal body. Despite the initial euphoria and bookings it could not sustain for a longer period in the market. The buyers were not confident of a car which had plastic body and two door.

Story of Hero Honda Street

Hero Honda in the year 1997 launched a new bike in the name of Hero Honda Street .It was based on the other 100cc engine models of the company. It had the advanced auto clutch technology where the rider of the bike was not required to depress the clutch of the bike while changing the gears. The bike had no clutch lever. While shifting the gears the clutch gets compressed and decompressed automatically. However the bike was not accepted much in the market due to the look of the motorcycle which had the design of a Moped and as a result had to be discontinued.

Thus in order to be successful in the market the innovation should be acceptable by the consumers and should not be way ahead of its time.

1.2. Role of Innovation in our Day-to-Day Life

According to the definition of Schumpeter an entrepreneur is a person who is willing and able to convert a new idea or invention into a successful innovation. In the last century and also during the current century some innovations have changed the way people think and act. They have also increased the size of the market. Some inventions during the last century like the invention of electricity, motor cars and aeroplanes have changed the people's lives and the way of seeing the world. These innovative products besides helping the entrepreneurs to have a name and fame for themselves has helped the Business, economy and the Society.

During the last Century combinations of innovative and highly technical products and services like computers, internet and smart phones have helped the entrepreneurs to expand their business operations beyond the boundary of a single country to a larger market .The technology closed the doors for some entrepreneurs whereas it opened the opportunity for some others. The expansion of market and the unrestricted availability of products beyond the boundaries gave the consumers more options than ever before and the consumers understood their importance. For example if we look into the automobile market during the 1970s and 1980s in India then we can see that to get a Car or a two wheeler during that period a consumer had to wait for months and sometimes the waiting period was even higher. However this is not the case in the present era. And the COVID-19 Pandemic also taught the newer ways of doing Business. A Customer willing to buy a vehicle can do all the activities like booking a vehicle and making payment online and can have a contactless delivery too.

The addition of various online payment gateways not only helped the entrepreneurs to have a better reach in the market but also helped the customers to buy products with ease without going to the physical stores. The payment gateway in addition to the high speed internet is an important innovation of the current century. Technology has played a greater role in innovation. Computers with superior computing powers and the advent of newer and better software aided by digital technology led to the advent of a number of mobile applications to be used by customers in their smart phones .This in turn created more business .With the addition of technology the concept of marketing the products and services have also changed. Through technology it is possible for the Business to get into the mind of the customers .Thus e-marketing has replaced door to door marketing.

Technology has not only helped the product market but also has helped the service sector in introducing new way of providing services. There have been a number of innovations in the service sector too. Taxi Services like Ola and Uber, food delivery services like Swiggy and Zomato, payment gateways like Phonepe and Google pay had successfully demonstrated the use of technology in the service sector.

However no innovation is permanent and there is always a better way of doing it. It today's world of constant innovation there is always a room for improvement and there is a constant threat from competitors. So entrepreneurs must keep on innovating through research & development. Because a shift in the preference of consumers can create problems for some companies. Mobile Handset sector is an example in this direction. In the beginning of this Century mobile handsets became affordable and it became a way of communication as telecom service providers created networks for communication. Keypad handsets initially ruled the market and some companies became the household name. However as soon as the touch screen phone market came into existence and a combination of platforms like Android,IOS and 4G mobile networks changed the market equations. Another set of Companies replaced the existing market leaders due to change in people's preference coupled with new technology. Change in technology also changed the equation in the mobile service providers. People preferred those companies which provided better services and additional facilities. Thus no change and innovation is permanent and those entrepreneurs who think of innovation and change as a continuous process can win over the heart of the customers.

At times change and innovation results from the action and reaction of the Government and Society. Worldwide protest against environmental pollution necessitated the decrease in the manufacturing of diesel cars. Those Companies which could not provide alternative solutions like a good petrol engine car to replace their diesel powered car saw a decrease in their market share. Similarly the Companies focussing on electric vehicles and hybrid vehicles combined with the power of gasoline and electricity gained their importance in the market.

1.3. Innovation During the time of Pandemic

At times chance factors also affect the process of innovation and it gives rise to a new breed of entrepreneurs who would not have become successful otherwise. The current worldwide pandemic resulting from COVID-19 shows how chance factors could result in successful innovations. For example take the case of education sector . It was the assumption of the people associated with education sector that class room teaching is the best way for academic delivery. However some people associated in this sector had already started the online mode of delivery of course. Those who were prepared for online delivery of courses and were ready with the course content and course material reaped the benefit during the Pandemic. Online meeting platforms like Zoom, Google Meet,Impartus also proved their market readiness as an intermediary between teachers and students, corporate and clients and showed that there is always a way if there is a will.

Thus innovation is a way of continuation of Business for an entrepreneur. The current pandemic resulting from COVID-19 is not the only challenge faced by the human race .Various wars and other calamities like natural calamities and diseases have threatened the human race time and again. We have to use our intellect to overcome these challenges. The current pandemic possess short –term challenges but also opens up some incredible opportunities for the future. Organizations and individuals those who are prepared to embrace the change and seize the opportunity will have a higher likelihood of success and market dominance.

The entrepreneurs must find the areas of opportunity. The problems faced by the human race in present time will not be there forever .But the solutions will teach us how to act intelligently in future. The following are some of the areas where the focus of the entrepreneurs will shift.

- Robotics and Automation will be the focus area
- Businesses like Mobile Payments and Online Meeting Platforms

- E-Learning is not a new concept but till now has been the secondary method of education.

1.4. Examples of Innovation in the Product and Service Market

CHIK SHAMPOO

C.K. Ranganathan, Chairman and Managing Director of Cavinkare, a Rs 500-crore cosmetics company wanted to fulfill the dreams of his father Chinni Krishnan, a school teacher by profession who wanted to make products affordable to common man.He switched to the pharmaceutical packaging business and tried innovations in it. He put talcum powder in sachets but did not succeed. But according to Ranganathan his father sowed the seed of the sachet revolution and he learnt his first business lessons from his father.

After splitting from his brothers' shampoo-manufacturing business, run under the brandname Velvette, Ranganathan bought a shampoo packaging machine and with an initial investment of Rs 15,000, launched Chik Shampoo, named after his father Chinni Krishnan. He sold 20,000 sachets in the first month, making a modest profit. According to Ranganathan the journey was bumpy and banks refused loans as I could not offer collateral.

He started the Chik India Company in 1982 and did the unthinkable by launching shampoos in rural, instead of urban areas. If MNC-bottled shampoos found shelf space in departmental stores, Cavinkare peddled its Re-1 wonder through roadside shops and grocery outlets in rural areas. Corporations soon realised the power of the sachet and launched their own products in small, affordable packages.

After capturing the Tamil Nadu market, Ranganathan organised village tours and conducted live demonstrations in movie halls on the use of shampoos. Soon enough, villagers replaced body soap for hair wash with the Re-1 sachet. Cavinkare then launched Shikakai powder, talcum powder, hair oil and fairness cream in sachets infusing beauty consciousness among rural masses, also showing a multi-crore possibility to other companies.

OYO Rooms

Ritesh Agarwal is an Indian Entrepreneur,Billionaire and founder CEO of OYO Rooms.He was born in Bisam Cuttack and brought up in Titilagarh,both places being in the State of Odisha,India.At the age of 13 he started selling SIM Cards of mobile phones.Agarwal was dropped out of College and was selected for Peter Thiel Fellowship.The fellowship is intended for School dropouts under the age of 23 and it offers them a fellowship of US$1,00,000 over a period of two years.Ritesh belongs to a family running a small local shop in Odisha.He was not good at study.So he thought if he goes to college and don't do well then his Family may not like it.So he decided to start some entrepreneurial venture instead.He founded the Company before the age of 20.Ritesh funded his entrepreneurial activity through the venture capital funds.Initially he raised a total of US$125 million in four rounds from 7 investors.OYO rooms has a network of 2,200 hotels operating in 154 cities across India with a monthly revenue of US$3.5 million and 20,000 employees.It's current valuation is US$10 billion which makes it one of the most valuable start-ups in India after financial services firm Paytm and e-commerce giant Flipkart.

3M

Minnesota Mining and Manufacturing Company was founded by Dr. J. Danley Budd, Henry. S. Bryan, William A. McGonagle, John Dwan and Hermon W. Cable in Two Harbours, MN. in the year 1902. The Company's name was changed to 3M in the year 2002.In the year 2014 3M reached an innovation milestone with the issuance of its 100,000th patent. Each year about 3,000 patents are issued to 3M worldwide, with more than 500 granted in the U.S. Post –it and Scotch Brite are amongst its well-known products. It earns revenue of more than US $ 5 billion.

Centurion University of Technology and Management

Centurion University of Technology and Management was established in the year 2010 and became the 1st Multi Sector Private University in the state of Odisha. The Promoters just did not stop there. In the year 2017 Centurion University, Andhra Pradesh was established. At present the Universities have 6 Campuses to their credit both in the state of Odisha and Andhra Pradesh. It's sister concerns include Gram Tarang Employability Training Services Pvt.Ltd., Gram Tarang Foods Pvt.Ltd, Gram Tarang Inclusive Development Services Pvt. Ltd.and Gram Tarang Technologies Pvt.Ltd. Gram Tarang Employability Training Services Pvt.Ltd. works in the field of skill building for employment and self employment in partnership with NSDC. Gram Tarang Foods Pvt.Ltd is engaged in pure and natural CO_2 extracts, select oils, oleoresins and total extracts from organic spices and herbs. Gram Tarang Inclusive Development Services Pvt. Ltd. Works in the area of banking correspondence services to 27,000 unbanked villages. And Gram Tarang Technologies Pvt.Ltd. works in the direction of making students Industry 4.0 ready by introducing advanced technologies in rural areas. By the year 2025 the promoters have the vision of skilling 1, 00,000 peoples annually.

Centurion University has recently developed a Mobile Payments App Insta Money. Through this app it is possible to have adhar based cash withdrawal, Balance enquiry and mini statement. A registered user can also use the app to go for card based withdrawal. Further this App has the advantage of digital Banking through the Bharat Bill Payments System.

CHAPTER TWO

A Conceptual Model of Social Entrepreneurship: Reflections from Gandhian Socialistic Philosophy

Dr.Subhendu K Mishra,

Centurion University of Technology & Management, Odisha

2.1. Introduction

Social entrepreneurship has been drawing specific attention among business schools since last three decades. The no of studies attempted on the discipline is testimonial to the gaining popularity. The recognition of the discipline as a powerful agent of change is visible as institutions such as Asoka foundation, Skoll foundation and Schwab foundation have initiated to cognize the efforts of the individual social entrepreneur across the globe. (Dacin, Dacin, Tracey,2011) As introduced by Dacin et al.(2010, P. 37):

"Social entrepreneurship continues to be a field of interest that crosses academic disciplines and challenges traditional assumptions of economic and business development ...some even suggest that the phenomena transcend the individual domains of entrepreneurial studies, social movement and non-profit management".

Despite the rapid growth, the discipline has aggregated a fragmented body of literature lacking of well-established theories as well as unified empirical research leads to lack of clarity and a poor definition of social entrepreneurship (Mair and Marti,2006,p.36). There is diversified opinion among the early thinkers for conceptualizing Social entrepreneurship. Nicholls (2006 b)wrote it as a new model of social change, Create novel opportunity for business(Prahalad,2005), a model of political transformation and empowerment(Alvord, Brown, & Letts, 2004; Yunus, 2008).

Perrini (2006) noted that there is a dyadic view regarding the existing definitions of Social Entrepreneurship. One view suggests Social entrepreneurship is a new phenomenon and significantly different from the Non Profit sector. The other view suggests it as a broaderand wider force for change in the society.Social Entrepreneurship consists of a multidimensional construct intended to explain a phenomena with specific assumptions and limitations.The theoretical development in social entrepreneurship largely follows an inductive approach of drawing conclusions based on observed phenomenon or evidences. (Alvord, Brown, Letts, 2004) with case studies being the most used approach (Short,Moss & Limpkin, 2009). However the relevance of case methods in theoretical development has been found in literature embedded in the grounded theory (Glaser& Strauss, 1967), further progressed by Miles & Huberman (1984) with design of procedures for analysing qualitative data. Eisenhardt (1989) in his work on building theories from case studies further extended the boundaries. Despitethere is a lack between the current understanding of case studies as a tool for research in social entrepreneurship and its methodological rigour and an enhanced knowledge could aid in researching and fostering this emerging field.

Table-2.1. Examples of Case Study Research

Study	Research Problem	Data Source	Output
Burgelman (1983)	"Management of new ventures"	Archives, interviews and observations	"Process model linking multiple organizational models"
Mintzberg and Mc Hugh (1985)	"Formulation of Strategy in an adhocracy"	Archives, Interviews	"Grassroots model of strategy formulation"
Harris & Sutton (1986)	"Parting ceremonies during organizational death"	Interview and archive	"Conceptual frameworks about the functions of parting ceremonies for displaced members"
Eisenhardt & Bourgeois(1988)	"Strategic decision making in high velocity firms"	Interview, questionnaire, archive and observation	"Mid-range theory linking power, politics and firm performance"

Gersick(1988)	"Group Development in project team"	Observation and Interview	"Punctuated equilibrium model of group development"
Leonard-barton	"Internal technology transfer	Interview, observation and archive	"Process model
Pettigrew(1988)	Strategic change and competitiveness"	Interview, archives and observation	"Linkages between change in business environment, business strategy and structure and HRM policies of the firm"

Adapted from Eisenhardt(1989) Examples of Inductive case study research

2.2. Early Socialist Schools of Thought

Socialism is considered to be an older ancestral origin than democracy in the sense that the debate about equality and inequality is as old as civilization itself. In his earlierdiscourses, Plato indicates that societies consists of the rich and poor and he cautioned on the revolution is an effect of the persistent inequality. After the French revolutions the first indication of socialism was in the writings of Francois Noel 'Gracchus'Babeuf,(1760-97) and Fillipo Michel Buonarroti(1761-1837) who were inspired by the writings of J. Rousseau (1712-78) and the utopians of the enlightment.(Mukherjee,Ramaswamy, 2000, 15). Socialism essentially arose as a moral and humanitarian critique of early liberalism. The socialist have accepted industrialisation but not capitalism because of its focus on injustice, exploitation and inequality. Socialism promised a humane, democratic free and equal society. The motivation and passion of equality led the early socialists argued on equal right of individual to the wealth of the earth. In a metaphorical sense socialism is seen as a broad river which contains many different currents. From a distance the river may seems to have a continuous flow in one direction but upon close inspection each current assume greater significance. The currents thus refer to particular groups of socialists such as Marxism, Leninism, revisionism, Fabianism and anarchism.(Lovell,2005). The ideological differences spurred distinctions between socialism and communism and between libertarian and authoritarian socialism which still confronts socialists of today. Parallel to interpretative criticality in socialism, R.N.Berki (1975) made an attempt to listfour normative tendencies in socialist ideology, egalitarianism, moralism, rationalism and libertarianism. His contributions helps in the understanding of modern socialism and its relevance in the 20th century and its impact on societies.

2.3. The Gandhian Socialistic Philosophy

The Socialistic philosophy pronounced by MK Gandhi was influenced by the distinct ideas of socialists of the west and subsequently scouring the philosophical and spiritual doctrine from Bhagvad Gita, Vedas and Upnishads. It advances Gandhi's socialist philosophy following a separate discourse from his western counterparts of Karl Marx and Lenin.His vision of socialism consists of a higher moral order and where all members of the society are equal. He believed to achieve socialism it requires pure crystal like means and with impure means results impure ends. According to him truth cannot be established by untruthfulness. He further advocated for the embeddedness of non-violence in truth and vice versa. Therefore only truthful, non-violent and pure hearted socialists will be able to establish a socialistic society. Gandhi Wrote,

"To my knowledge no country in the world is purely socialist. Without the means described above the existence of such a society is impossible. *(Harijan, 13-7-47)*

He also emphatically declares that real socialism has been handed down to us by our ancestors who *taught "all land belongs to gopala; where then is the boundary line? Men are the maker of that line thus they can unmake it". Gopala literally means shepherd; it also means God. In modern language it means the state, i.e. the people. (Harijan,21-1-37)*

He further said socialism was not born with the discovery of the misuse of capital by capitalist and contended that the idea of socialism,even communism is explicit in the first verse of Isa Upanisad

"Isavasyam idam sarvam yat kim ca jagatyam jagat

Tena tyaktena bhunjitha, ma gradhah kasyasvid dhanam"

Whatever moves in the moving world is enveloped by god. Hence an individual should aim for renunciation because that can bring pure enjoyment, and restrain from coveting what is not yours.

His keen observations resulted in to deep understanding of the economic and socio-cultural diversity and the colonial regime exists in India and thus carving a path to free India from the grip of the inequality and exploitation. His principles of Swaraj and Sarvodaya has ignited masses and created a revolution the free India movement.

The Sarvodaya movement started in the early 20th century in India. Mahatma Gandhi used the nomenclature by borrowing it from a Jain text by Acharya Samantabadra. The meaning of the word 'Sarvodaya' is upliftment or welfare and good of all. Gandhi Ji was greatly influenced by the text published by Western philosopher Ruskin "Unto This Last" The writings has a deep impression on Gandhi Ji while conceiving his ideas on Sarvodaya. He summarized the essence under three doctrines of truth,

- *The good of the individual is contained in the good of the all.*
- *A lawyer's work has the same value as the barber in as so much as all have the same right of earning their livelihood from their work*
- *A life of a labour, that is the life of the tiller of the soil and the handicraftsman is the life worth living.*

It is not only the freedom movement that has driven MK Gandhi, there are a plethora of issues including the glitches and evils of the society, which alerted him such as the villages of India, democracy and the states, empowering the labour and establishing industrial harmony, the revival of village industries, education, untouchability, health, hygiene and diet. The foremost focus was on the villages of India and its role and its constructive role in the post independent India.

The theory of trusteeship is enunciated at a time when the popular socialist theory was placed on the possessions of the wealthy. Gandhi Ji's call for the wealthy to outgrow greed and obsession with possession and consider themselves as trustees. Under the system, the trustee will retain what is necessary for a decent standard of living and the rest will be used for social welfare. The basic idea was to bring a parity in income inequality. Gandhi Ji believed that Trusteeship as an ideal means to create a true socialist society. However theory of trusteeship calls for a conviction and self-determination for the individual and driven by highest moral and ethical principles and hence its practice may seem difficult.

Gandhi Ji's doctrine gave the impetus to many of his disciples and the result of which there has been a rapid growth of Gandhian Non Profit Organizations (NPO) in the post- independence era (Sen, 1993) for promoting development works on behalf of the Government. Since there is visible transformation of the nature of not for profit sector worldwide including India. The nature of the initiatives and their interventions were a major area of interest.

Among theHodge Podge of characterizing the Social organizations, an initiative came from the Schwab foundation founded in 1998. The foundation indicated on three organizational forms of Social enterprises, the first group as leveraged non-profit, the second as hybrid non-profit and the third type are social business ventures. As social entrepreneurship falls in the broad spectrum ranging from social purpose organizations and private enterprises, it necessitates the need to explore in detail the status of Social entrepreneurship in relation to traditional socially oriented organizational forms(Nicholls & Cho, 2006). It is also a matter of study to understand and describe the role of social entrepreneur as different from business entrepreneur.

The social entrepreneur creates social value, adopts a mission to create and sustain social value; recognizing and relentlessly pursuing new opportunities to serve that mission; engaging in a process of continuous innovation, adaptation and learning;acting boldly without being limited to resources currently available and exhibiting a heightened sense of accountability to the constituencies served and for the outcomes created (Dees et al.2001). In addition to the description given above the Gandhian socialistic philosophy and its two major principles, Sarvodaya and Trusteeship, can have a profound impact on the way social entrepreneurship can be conceptualized and help it become operationally sustainable. Sarvodaya and trusteeship can become significant constructs in advancing the study of Social entrepreneurship research.The framework will discuss on the impact of the principles on two dimensions of social entrepreneurship, the social entrepreneur and his/her intentions in creating social value and governance of social enterprises.

2.4. Objective of the study

The study aims to achieve the following objectives,

- To propose a conceptual framework of Social Entrepreneurship based on Sarvodaya and Trusteeship principles of Mahatma Gandhi.
- To analyse the case history of two reputed social enterprises in India, SEWA and SELCO for validation of the concept

2.5. Methodology

The study will case based method for developing the conceptual framework. The case studies of two successful social enterprises in India, SEWA and SELCO has been taken and data were collected by using methods such as Interviews, published material and anecdotal references, websites. The author further searchedthe conceptual literature surrounding Gandhian Socialistic Philosophy and its basic propositions as Sarvodaya and Trusteeship and use it as a platform for building a conceptual framework of social entrepreneurship.

Figure-1.Conceptual Model of Social Entrepreneurship

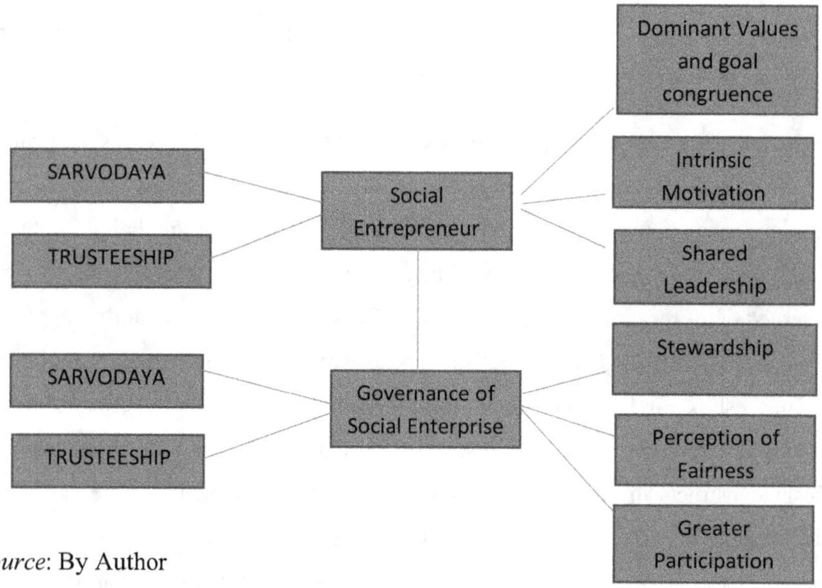

Source: By Author

2.6. Conceptual Model of Social Entrepreneurship

In the discussion, I have illustrated the cases of SEWA and SELCO and made an attempt to apply them in the conceptual framework proposed in the paper.The principles and its impact on the entrepreneur as well as the governance of the social enterprise has been focused. Keeping the basic premises of the principles of Sarvodaya and Trusteeship and its objectives of equality, equity,truthfulness, purity of means, preservation of basic human values,and the paper will reflect how it affected Social Entrepreneurs e.g. Dr. Ela Bhatt and Dr.Harish Hande by preserving the dominant values and aligning it successfully with the organization goals, being intrinsically motivated and displayed a shared form of leadership. In addition, the discussion will reflect on the governance mechanism of the enterprises through a structure supporting stewardship, perception of fairness from the system and participatory functioning.

Case-1. Dr.Harish Hande, The man with a mission of alleviating poverty through sustainable energy

It was 1991 and Dr. Harish Hande as a Ph.D Scholar at MIT. He was travelling to Dominican Republic in relation to his thesis. During his trip he observed a unique model of supplying solar power to households. He was convinced on the applicability of the model to bring respite to the energy woes of Indian hinterlands. The trip happened to be a life changing event for him.In 1995 he along with Neville Williams cofounded SELCO in Bangalore with a mission to enhance the quality of life of undeserved households and livelihoods through sustainable energy solutions and services. Selco was founded as a for profit enterprise with a social objective and it has proven to finely balance both objectives. It has through its unique model reached 1.2 million customers. Besides its activities of solar electrification and financial inclusion. It has further credited in establishing centres to create a favourable climate for entrepreneurs and organizations. The SELCO foundation, SELCO centre for innovation and SELCO Incubation are some of the extensions for achieving the mission of poverty alleviation, livelihood generation through sustainable energy solutions across India. Dr.Harish Hande has been conferred with the Ramon Magsaysay's award in 2011, Schwab foundation Social entrepreneur of the year 2007, Ashoka fellowship in the year 2008, Ashden award for sustainable energy in the year 2005 and many more.

Dr.Harish Hande believes the fortune for those at the bottom of the pyramid can be transformed if they have access to electricity which in turn can improve their livelihood potential. The efforts by Dr.Harish Hande to provide energy access to millions of rural undeserved households through renewable energy stands testimony to the principle of Sarvodaya which calls for 'welfare for all' and as an entrepreneur his actions suits the principle of trusteeship. Though formally he is the founder and the chairman of the organization in spirit he is actually acting as a trustee. SELCO is a live example of a for profit organization following a trusteeship approach. After two decade of the journey with SELCO It can be established that Dr.Hande has been uncompromisingly following the values which has been a part of the Sarvodaya and Trusteeship philosophy. He has further aligned these values with the goal of SELCO which has been driving SELCO as an institution of excellence. As a leader he is able to attract likeminded individuals to be a part of the team who have internalized and committed themselves to the pursuit of the mission.

As a Social Entrepreneur Dr. Harish Hande is motivated intrinsically. Intrinsic motivation refers to the engagement with an activity for its inherent satisfaction. (Deci & Ryan, 2000) In this case the inherent satisfaction is derived from the association with a noble purpose and its perceived meaningfulness. In addition it also reflect on the degree of choice/autonomy, self-efficacy and progress made towards fulfilling the purpose (Thomas, 2009). So when reviewing both the success and failures of SELCO, it reminds intrinsic motivation as a self-renewal tool for the social entrepreneur to persistently undertake the mission.

Great organizations goes beyond its founders. In SELCO, Dr. Harish Hande prefers a shared form of leadership. He calls SELCO as an 'open source organization' and believes in the form of sharing and not hiding. He does not believe in micromanaging and emphasizes on the selection of leaders within the organization and among his peers. A shared leadership approach generates a climate of trust and equality and accountability. It further departs from the notion of individual to organizational and societal.

Case-2. Dr. Ela Bhatt, Empowering Self-employed Women in the Unorganised Sector

While beginning a discussion to find the commonalities between M.K. Gandhi and Dr.Elaben Bhatt, it can be found that both belong to Gujarat, lawyers by education and profession and associated with textile labour association(TLA).Working with Gandhi ji has offered Dr. Elaben a platform for learning and practicing the values and principles enumerated by Gandhiji. The Inspirations drawn has driven Dr. Elaben to initiate the lead to establish Self Employed Women's Association(SEWA) as a recognized union in 1972. Since its inception SEWA has been committed to achieve 2 major goals to offer full employment and ensure self-reliance for the self-employed women members.

Being a member driven organization the necessities and priorities of the members are vital and governs the activities of the organization. Hence the list of activities undertaken aims to increase the income and assets of the members, provide them with adequate healthcare, nutrition, child care and housing. It also ensures the workers leadership, education and organizational strength.

The total membership is more than two millions and in Gujarat it has a membership strength of more than one million. SEWA believes that, by the unity and solidarity of the members their collective strength and bargaining power can be increased and they can be free from the clutch of exploitation and injustice. It has followed 2 distinctive approaches for organizing them through unions and cooperatives. It thus can help in building a just and equitable society as quoted in the principle of Sarvodaya.Gandhi Ji and his principles drawn from the spiritual Sarvodaya Philosophy encompasses simplicity, nonviolence, dignity of labour and preserving basic human values. These principles are driving SEWA since inception. SEWA has successfully aligned these guiding principles to the organization's goals. Dr.Elaben has been committed and intrinsically motivated to the purpose and ensures the empowerment of women through grassroot entrepreneurship. Her efforts were recognized worldwide and she is the recipient of the Indira Gandhi prize for peace in 2011, Niwano peace prize in 2010, Padma Bhushan in 1986, Padma Shri in 1985, Ramon Magsaysay award in 1977 and many more.

2.7. The Governance of Social Enterprises: A Gandhian socialism perspective

Corporate governance as a field of study gathered attention due to inappropriate managerial practices and frauds involved in private multinational organizations Including Enron, Satyam and many more. The Organization for Economic Cooperation and Development(OECD) has given a definition for Corporate Governance and calls it as a set of relationships between a company's management, board, shareholders and stakeholders. It also provide the structure through which the objectives of the company are set and the means of achieving the objectives and monitoring performance are decided. In the context of Governance of social enterprises there is a growing interest among practitioners and academia to understand the nuances of how they are governed.(Mason, Kirkbride& Bryde, 2006)

The conceptual framework proposed in the paper and the Gandhian Socialistic principles Sarvodaya and Trusteeship can thus provide useful directions in the governance of social enterprises through a stewardship approach, create perceptions of fairness and participatory governance.

Stewardship approach has been accepted as a basis of governance for social enterprise (Low,2006). The Steward act in the best interest of their principal and their behaviour is pro-organizational than individualistic (Davis, Schoorman & Donaldson, 1997). Looking it from the angle of Gandhian socialistic perspective, by following the principles of Sarvodaya and Trusteeship, the pro-organizational and collectivist behaviours can be reinforced in social enterprises. The cases of SELCO and SEWA also validate the assertion made above. Each member in the team act collectively as stewards and serves in their best interest to the organization.

The governance system of an organization results into the perception of fairness among its members. (Beugre, 1998) has found that, when men perceive fairness as equity, women perceive fairness as equality. The perceptions of unfairness may lead to under appreciation, lack of respect and recognition and lower engagement with the task. In organizations presence of rigid hierarchical structures and cliques increases the potential for perception of unfairness as it blocks communication. (Axelrod,2000). For SELCO and SEWA both organizations have through their governance ensures fairness for its members and especially through the shared leadership approach people from inside are assigned with higher responsibilities and became the part of the executive committee.

The participatory form of governance is evident in SEWA. For the union elections are held for its executive committee and office-bearers every three years. 200 members of SEWA choose one representative called a "Pratinidhi". The representatives then elect the 25 members of the executive committee. The latter, in turn, elect their office-bearers. All 25 members are worker-leaders. Over the last forty years, mostly worker-leaders are chosen as the office-bearers. In the case of cooperatives, each share-holder has a vote, and elections are conducted as per the bye-laws of the cooperative. Every three years, elections are held at the Annual General Meeting of the cooperative, and the Board of Directors is elected. Here too, the majority of directors elected are worker- leaders. The trusteeship approach is best suited to a participatory form of governance where each member is crucial as well as accountable.

2.8. Conclusions

At its early stage, social entrepreneurship means different things to different people. With a broad range of institutional forms it evokes set of questions related to social enterprise, social entrepreneurs and Social Entrepreneurship. The quest for a theoretical foundation, methodological rigour, contextual orientation and clear definition are few areas which drives researchers. The paper highlights a contextual dimension of social entrepreneurship and presented two principles of Gandhian socialistic philosophy and its relevance for social entrepreneurship research. The principles of Sarvodaya and Trusteeship as presented by MK Gandhi can be a useful constructs and help in advancing the field of research. The objective of the paper is to establish the applicability of the construct in social entrepreneurship by using two different forms of social enterprises and find how it affects the social entrepreneur and the governance of the enterprise. However in future an empirical examination of the construct is necessary for its validation.

---

*Note: SEWA and SELCO has been recognized by Schwab Foundation and Dr. Ela Bhatt, the founder of SEWA is recognized as Schwab Fellow of the World Economic Forum and Harish Hande the founder of SELCO awarded with Schwab Social entrepreneur of the year 2007.

*SELCO has its operations in Gujarat in collaboration with SEWA.

References

Alvord, S. H., L. D. Brown, C. W. Letts. (2004). Social entrepreneurship and societal transformation: An exploratory study. J. Appl. Behav. Sci. 40(3) 260–282.

Anderson, B. and J.G. Dees. (2008). Rhetoric, Reality and Research: Building a Solid Foundation for the practice of Social Entrepreneurship. In Nicholls (ed.) Social Entrepreneurship: New Models of Sustainable Social Change, Oxford University Press

Axelrod, R. (2000). Terms of engagement: changing the way we change organizations. San Francisco, CA: Berrett-Koehler Publications.

Berki, R.N. (1975) Socialism. London : John Dent and Sons

Beugre, C. (1998). Managing fairness in organizations. Westport, CT: Quorum Books.

Bornstein,D.,(2004).How to change the world:Social Entrepreneurs and the power of New Ideas.Oxford: Oxford University Press.

Choi, N. and S. Majumdar.(2014).Social Entrepreneurship as an essentially contested concept: Opening a new avenue for systematic future Research. Journal of Business Venturing (29) 363-376

Dacin, P.A., M.T.Dacin and M. Matear., (2010) Social Entrepreneurship: why we don't need a new theory and how we move forward from here. Academy of Management Perspective 24(3), 37-57

Davis. J.H.,Schoorman.F.D., Donaldson.L. (1997) 'Towards a stewardship theory of management' Academy of Management Review.Vol.22 (1), 20-47

Dees, J.G. (1998) Enterprising Non-profits. Harvard Business Review

Dees, J.G. (1998) The Meaning of Social Entrepreneurship

Dees, J. G., & Anderson, B. B. (2006). Framing a theory of social entrepreneurship: Building on two schools of practice and thought. In R. Mosher-Williams (Ed.), Research on Social Entrepreneurship: Understanding and Contributing to an Emerging Field. ARNOVA Occasional Paper Series, 1(3), 39-66.

Dees, J.G. and P. Economy (2001).Social Entrepreneurship. In G.J Dees, J. Emerson and P. Economy (eds), Enterprising Non-Profits: A toolkit for Social Entrepreneurs. New York: John Willey & Sons,pp.1-18

Denzin,N.K., and Y.S.Lincoln.,(2011). Introduction: The Discipline and Practice of Qualitative Researh. In N.K.Denzin and Y.S.Lincoln (eds.) The Sage handbook of Qualitative Research. USA: Sage

Eisenhardt, M.K.,(1989). Building Theories from Case Study Research. Academy of Management Journal. Vol.14 (4), 532-550

Gandhi, M.K., (1947) India of My Dreams. Ahmedabad: Navajivan Publishing

Gandhi, M.K., and (1951) Sarvodaya: Its principles and Programme, Ahmedabad: Navajivan Publishing

_ _ , (1957) My Socialism, Ahmedabad: Navajivan Publishing

_ _ , (1962). Ruskin Unto This Last: A paraphrase, Ahmedabad: Navajivan Publishing

Glaser, B., & Strauss, A. (1967) The discovery of grounded theory: Strategies of qualitative research. London: Wledenfeld and Nicholson.

http://www.schwabfound.org/entrepreneurs

http://khemkafoundation.in/index.php?option=com_k2&view=item&id=73:podcast-harish&Itemid=259

http://iveybusinessjournal.com/publication/the-four-intrinsic-rewards-that-drive-employee-engagement/

Lichtheim, G. (1975) A short History of Socialism. Glasglow: Fontana

Lovell, D.W., (2005) Socialism and Communism Vol.II

Low, C., (2006). A framework for the governance of Social Enterprise" Int Journal of Social Economics. Vol.33, 376-85

Lumpkin, G.T. and J.G. Dees (1996).Clarifying the entrepreneurial Orientation construct and linking it to performance. Academy of Management review 21(1), 135-172

Lumpkin, G. T., Cogliser, C. C., & Schneider, D. R. (2009). Understanding and measuring autonomy: an entrepreneurial orientation perspective. Entrepreneurship Theory and Practice, 33(1), 47-69.

Mair, J. and Marti, I. (2006). "Social entrepreneurship research: a source of explanation, prediction, and delight", Journal of World Business, Vol. 41 No. 1, pp. 36-44.

Mason.C. Kirkbride. J., Bryde.D. (2007) "From stakeholders to institutions: the changing face of social enterprise governance theory" Management Decision, Vol.45, 2 pp.284-301

Miles, M., & Huberman, A. M. (1984) Qualitative data analysis. Beverly Hills, CA: Sage Publications.

Mukherjee, S and S.Ramaswamy. (2000). A History of Socialist Thought: From the precursors to the Present. New Delhi: Sage

Narayanswamy, S., (2003) The Sarvodaya Movement: Gandhian Approach to peace and Non-violence. New Delhi: Mittal Publication

Nicholls, A. and A.H. Cho. (2006). Social Entrepreneurship: The structuration of a Field. In Nicholls (ed.) Social Entrepreneurship: New Models of Sustainable Social Change, Oxford University Press

OECD (2004). Principles of Corporate Governance, Organisation for Economic Cooperation and Development, Paris

Perrini, F., C. Vurro. 2006. Social entrepreneurship: Innovation and social change across theory and practice. J. Mair, J. Robinson, K. Hockerts, eds. Social Entrepreneurship. Palgrave Macmillan, Basingstoke, UK, 57–86.

Ryan, M.R., Deci, L.E., (2000). Intrinsic &Extrinsic Motivation: Classic definition and New Directions. Contemporary Education Psychology.Vol.25, 54-67

Seymour,R.G. (2012).Researching Social Entrepreneurship. In R.G.Seymour (ed.) Handbook of research Methods on Social Entrepreneurship, UK, Edward Elgar

Shane, S. and S. Venkatraman (2000).The promise of entrepreneurship as a field of research. Academy of Management Review 25(1), 217-226

Short, J.C., Moss, T.W. & Lumpkin, G.T., (2009) "Research in social entrepreneurship: Past contributions and future opportunities", Strategic Entrepreneurship Journal, 3, 2, pp. 161-194.

www.sewa.org

www.selco-india.com

CHAPTER THREE

A Study on Role of Self Help Groups for Empowering Women

Dr. Girija Nandini, Dr.Pramod Kumar Patjoshi

Centurion University of Technology & Management, Odisha

3.1 Introduction

Women empowerment and gender equality are two most important factors for the development of our economy and also for society. This is a major challenge for every Government. Government has started many schemes for women. Self -help groups are voluntary associations which are taken major role in women empowerment and gender equality. It helps poor, rural, underprivileged women for getting income and social recognition. Self -help groups increased to 3927, in which 39272 women are getting benefit in Odisha as on 31st March 2019 (Ministry of Women and Child Development, GOI). Child sex ratio is low as per 2011 census. According to Odisha Economic Survey 2018-19, maternal mortality ratio is very high. Bank deposits and savings of women is very low as per RBI,2018. Therefore the study is analyzing the role of SHGs for empowering women in Odisha. SHGs are helping women in discussing their common problem and solving it in groups. So they must aim at changes in the income generation activities; improve savings potential, borrowing capacity and their standard of living. SHGs are the potent tools of women empowerment in rural areas. After a lot of effort also SHGs are not able to do the expected result. Women are the major part of the society. In the developing country like India women are the most vulnerable part of our society. So now Government, researchers, academicians all are trying to do a lot of study and analysis on this problem. It can increase the social and economic condition of women.

In India women are suffering a lot due to financial and social problems. They are one of the important parts of every economy. All around development of India can be possible when this important part will be considered as equal to men. Women can get freedom and strength when they are financially strong. Poverty is the major problem for the development of the women. It is very important to make them independent and to fulfil their need by using their own skill. Even so many problems are there, today women are better than men in many sector. They need more motivation and support from family and society. To achieve all these targets SHGs have taken a major role in India. SHGs are not only giving credits to poor, they are giving strength to poor by giving support, training and motivation. When poor women earns money through the help of SHGs, it gives them status and decision making power in the family. Overall it helps women for empowerment. Very less study has been conducted in this area. This study will through some light in this area. Rural poor women do not have knowledge on banking and financial services. Because of their ignorance they do not save. They cannot take loan from bank or financial institutions to start their own business. If they can avail the benefit of financial system by the help of SHGs, they can more economically independent.

Women should be given equal importance in our society for the actual development of our country. A society cannot be developed without gender equality. Women are considered as inferior to men as their income is low for which their confidence is also low. Self-help group (SHGs) have taken a major role for giving employment and income to women. Women are starting their own business and getting income by the help of SHGs. Increasing income is increasing the confidence and their decision making capacity in family and society. This continuous effort will increase the gender equality in our society. This chapter will particularly focus on the role of SHGs for women empowerment in the state of Odisha and also to study the Mission Shakti initiatives of the Government of Odisha.

3.2. Review Of Literature

Many studies have been done related to women empowerment and the problems associated with this. Some of the significant studies are discussed here.

Pattnaik (2003) analysed in the study that SHGs are trying to empower the tribal women so that they can take decision in their life and they can be more independent financially. But there are many problems like exploitation, gender inequality, torture to women, household problems which are the major constraints in women empowerment. So even SHGs are trying to do, they are not successful. Manimekalai (2004) analysed in his research that SHGs should take the help of different NGOs to increase income of the poor women. Banks also should take part in the activities. They can guide the rural poor women, to start some business where income generation is more. He also found that income generation and confidence of rural women is increased due to SHGs. Sahu and Tripathy (2005) tried to analyse in their study that seventy per cent of the poor in the world are women. They do not have access to banking service. It is very important for the development of the economy. SHGs have important role for the development and women empowerment. The rural poor women are the weaker section of the society for their low income.

They have lot of problems. They are poor and backward for a long period of time. They can upgrade themselves with the help of SHGs and microfinance.Vinayamoorthy and Pithoda (2007)done their analysis to study the women empowerment in Tamil Nadu through SHGs. They have taken 398 members from 20 SHGs from 3 villages. They tried to find mainly the income, savings and expenditure of the members who joined in SHGs. They also analysed how the SHGs are helping in getting credit by the members. They analysed that SHGs are quiet successful in their activities to empower women. Sobha (2008) studied on the problems faced by self-employed women. He has taken a sample of 400 self-employed women in Coimbatore Municipal Corporation. He found that the problem is less for those who are the receivers of Prime Minister's RozgarYojana than those who are not the beneficiaries. Kumararaja (2009) done the study to find how the self -help groups are working in Tamil Nadu. He found from the study that there is an increase in number of SHGs and the loan sanctioned in Tamil Nadu. He concluded that if there is a regular and time to time check of micro credit given by SHGs ,it will increase the development of rural women. Preema ,Nichlavose (2017) done the research on SHGs. They have taken a sample of 16 SHGs from Kerala state. They found from their research that there is a need of proper programme and individual training of SHG members to increase the self-improvement and enterprise skills. Nithyashree, Veena and Rekha (2016) did the research of individuals in SHGs in Karnataka. They have taken a sample of eight diferent areas consisting of 400 SHGs with 6338 members in it. They tried to get the reasons of individual joining in SHGs. Most of the members given the reason that they joined to get monetary help in advance, to start their start-ups and also to pay their credits. Very few members said that they joined for salary.

Malhotra (2016) done the research on self-help groups in Chandigarh. He has taken the sample as women members from different SHGs. He tried to find the actual problems and the circumstances. He has also taken information from the banks to understand it more clearly. SHGs are trying hard to empower women in those areas. They are also associated with government and non-government organisations. Women are also getting more benefit in the whole process.Manohar (2015), studied on different self-help groups in Haveri locale in Karnataka. He tried to find how the women are getting monetary benefits by joining in SHGs. He has taken 240 ladies from the SHGs for examination. He also analysed the effect of money given by the SHGs to the ladies. How the SHGs are increasing the monetary empowerment of women is analysed very thoroughly. Prabhavathy(2011) analysed on SHGs working in the state of Tamil

Nadu. She found that SHGs are working effectively in certain areas and in some areas they are facing problems. SHGs are helping women to increase their financial strength which will increase their confidence for decision making in family and society. Ladies can get salary also can use reserve fund in different SHGs. They are now self-motivated and can work for their own development and also for the development of country.Venkatesh, Kala (2010) examined on self-help groups in South Tamil Nadu. He found that in South Tamil Nadu the income of the women increased after joining in SHGs. Their family income also increased. SHGs in those areas are very successful in empowering women. Venkateshmurthy, Dinesh (2009) are tried to find women empowerment after joining in SHGs. He found that SHGs are doing remarkable job in motivating women for earning money by using their skills. SHGs are playing the important role for women empowerment. They increase the confidence and social status of the women in the society.Lakshmikandan (2000) examined on self-help groups. He tried to find how SHGs are changing the life of rural people. He found that most of the members in the SHGs are little landlords and farming works. The poor people are getting the benefit at the lower level. They are not getting much benefits in market study, purchasing assets or general creation. The ability and skills of the people who are in SHGs increased to 90 % from 5%. Manimekalai ,Rajeswari (2000) done their research on Self Help Groups and how they are empowering women. They did their analysis in the rural villages of Tiruchirappalli District. They found that non-Government organisations like "Society for Education and Village Action and Empowerment (SEVAE)" isoperating in 362 different cities. One lakh women are getting help to earn income and get financial independence.

3.3.Importance of SHGs for Women Empowerment

A self-help group is consisting of group of people with same economic and financial condition. They usually make the groups to help each other by solving their problems. It is basically a small group of poor people who makes the group voluntarily to improve their social and economic status. Usually more than twenty people can be there in SHGs. It can come under law in India. It can be formal by registration or informal. The group generally meet with each other to reduce their crisis by helping each other. They save money in a common fund with mutual agreement and also can use that money as loan by giving low rate of interest as decided by the group. They usually give the money to needy people. Banks and microfinance institutions also lend money to members of the SHGs in one account instead of having different accounts for all the members. It reduces the work of banks and financial institutions. The rural people are weak due to many reasons like low income, low education, low motivation and low economic condition. They are mostly socially backward. They are not only backward, they also don't have information regarding the financial institution, how to save or how to take loan which are the most important things in today's world. But when they are in a group, they can overcome from many of these problems by helping each other.

Both national and state governments have undertaken various policy measures for the improvement of women empowerment. It is very important that women should empower economically, politically, socially and also in legal matters. In this context this research will give a focus mainly on the rural women who are more deprived in our country. The analysis on SHGs is required for the Government and also for the planner. The policy makers can make proper plan after finding the strength and weaknesses of the SHGs. SHGs can also know their weak areas and can take action on that. Overall improvements of SHGs are also required for the development of economy. SHGs can be motivated to work more for the social and economic development of women. Factors which are important for the good performance of SHGs should be taken into consideration. In Odisha number of steps has been taken to encourage the women entrepreneurship. The"MahilaVikasSamabaya Nigam (MVSN)"is helping in selling the different products of Women's SelfHelp Groups (WSHGs) in "PallishreeMelas" and "SisirSaras" organized in different parts of the state including Bhubaneswar. It gives fund to the rural poor women to develop their training skills to produce different products. "MukhyaMantriMahilaSashakti Karana Yojana (MMMSY)"also trying to increase the economic condition of the rural poor women of WSHGs which are under MissionShakti. They are forming new WSHGs which will work on training, skill development, capacity building, of the poor women by linking them with banks and financial institutions.

3.4. Role of SHGs

There are many roles of SHGs. Some of them are;

- To organize the funds of individual members for the overall benefit of all the members to develop their economic conditions.
- To increase the habit of savings among members.
- To increase the skills of members to earn money.

- To aware people about their rights.
- To discuss individual problems in groups and solve them by helping each other.
- To play the role of mediator for the overall socio- economic development of the community and village.
- To help in getting back the loan amount.
- To motivate the members which increase their self-confidence.
- To encourage people for working in team.
- To increase the leadership qualities among members.
- To make a proper system for giving credit to the rural poor people

3.5. Increasing access to Finance through Self Help Groups

Odisha adopted SHGs model to increase financial inclusion in the state. It increased banking services in the rural areas where many people do not have any banking access. SHGs which are under the"Odisha Livelihood Mission (OLM)"are giving banking services. OLM has agreement with different banks to increase financial inclusion in the state. 70% of the Gram Panchayats (GP) is without mortar bank branches. Three lakhs SHGs will work under OLM as banking correspondent. First these SHGs will work as banking correspondent in 1000 Gram Panchayats where there are no banking facilities. Gradually they will work in another 4000 GPs. They will work so as to cover the whole state in financial inclusion. Government is giving interest subsidy to the WSHGs which are working under OLM, NULM, NRLM or Mission Shakti. A very low interest is charged at 1% whose loan accounts are regular.

3.6. Role of Mission Shakti for Women Empowerment

Odisha is promoting Women Self Help Groups (WSHGs) to empower women through "Mission Shakti". It is trying to increase socio economic activities for the women. The mission is started on 8th March 2001 which is celebrated as International Women's Day. It has an objective to empower women through lot of socio economic activities by giving credit. Till now 70 lakh women are divided into 6 lakh groups in different blocks and urban areas. Mission Shakti is helping to increase the activities of WSHGs and also helping in creating new WSHGs. They are handholding and helping women throughout the year. Directorate of Mission Shakti is specially created under separate department. It is under "Women and Child Development" and "Mission Shakti". Mission Shakti is a great achievement in Odisha with 6,02,013 WSHGs consisting of

70,00,010 women. When it started the objective was to form 2 lakh groups in 2 years. It reached to 2,48,689 WSHGs by 2006-07. It increased to 3,14,646 by 2016-17.

Progress of WSHGs under Mission Shakti

Progress of Women SHGs

Year	WSHGs
2001-02	41475
2006-07	248689
2016-17	314646
2018-19	602013

Source : Women and Child Development Department and MS, Odisha

3.7. SHG Federations and WSHGs

Financial help is agreed to WSHGs and SHG Federations for differenteventslike:

- For giving credit facilities
- Help to improve Bank Linkage
- It help the SHG and their Federations for starting new livelihood activities and for financial requirements
- Helps to arrange their requirements and investment plans

3.8. SHG Bank Linkages

SHG-Bank Linkage Programme is a major activity of Mission Shakti to increase financial inclusion. The main objective is to give credit to the Women Self Help Groups to increase their livelihood. This will increase self confidence among the women. They can save and lend from their own WSHGs fund.

3.9. Mission Shakti Loan

The "Mission Shakti Loan (State Interest Subvention Scheme)"is giving the benefit to those WSHGs who are paying the loans regularly. Those WSHGs working in rural and urban areas of

Odisha are getting the benefits. In this scheme the WSHGs are repaying the loans as per Bank lending and saving. The Government is repaying the interest by the respective banks. To motivate the women in SHGs for entrepreneurship Government started Interest Subvention Scheme for WSHGs from 2013. They have to pay 2 % interest on loans up to 3 lakhs. To include more women into entrepreneurship the interest rate is reduced to 1% for WSHGs in Odishafrom 2015. This loan rate is reduced to o% from 2019 to increase the bank linkage programme. Overall it will increase the livelihood of women in the society. Mission Shakti increased the self-employment of women in the state of Odisha. Women are using their skills to earn money. They are also doing different activities like pisciculture, poultry, mushroom farming and vegetable cultivation. They are working with Government Departments, which is giving benefit to nearly18,000 WSHGs in the state.

3.10. Conclusion

The most important thing in the SHGs is that women should save in a group. Earlier it was only men who earn and save. Research says that men are more defaulters while paying loan than women. Because of which Government of India started making women's groups linked to different credit facilities for the developmental strategy from early 1990s. SHGs are getting more powerful for making women empowerment in the rural poor villages. In Odisha also state Government started many schemes to give the benefit to the rural poor women so that they can start economic activities to earn money. The needs of the women are not only to earn money but to get overall socio-economic development. It can be a developed country only if both the men and women workforce will contribute to the economic activities. In the earlier period women were usedto work only in home doing their household work. But now with the help of SHGs they are working and earning money as men. Women are getting a distinguished position in home due to their earning capacity and self-confidence to take decision. The SHGs are working in the right direction but again they have to do lot of things. It is very important to empower women, financially, socially, culturally, economically and politically for the development of society and so also for the nation.

SHGs are the potent tools of women empowerment in rural areas. Though SHGs are working hard to achieve their goal, they are not totally successful for different reasons. SHGs have given women a place to discuss and solve their problems.So they must aim at changes in the income generation activities, improve savings potential, borrowing capacity and their standard of living.Mission Shakti has been a flagship programme of Govt of Orissa initiative for women empowerment. It has been riding through women Self Help Groups (WSHGs) towards its mission goal. Achieving women empowerment in a state like Odisha suffering from regular calamities is a great challenge before Government of India and Odisha both. There has been multi prong approaches to make women prominently visible in development scene of Odisha. However it is again another gigantic task before Government, corporate, academies and NGOs.Women are the major part of society. So, till this part will not develop the overall society cannot be developed. The present situation does not allow women to actively take part in the decision making. Even the government is started so many schemes, it is not reaching to the poor women. So here there is a major role of SHGs to reach those benefits to the poor women. Then only women empowerment and overall development of the society can be possible.

References

- Ahmed, W.S.; Nilofer and Parveen, G. 2008. Women's Political Participation and Changing Pattern of Leadership in Rural Areas of U.P., The Indian Journal of Political Science, Vol. LXIX, No. 3, July-Sept., pp. 661- 671.

- Anbalagan, M., Amudha, R., &Selvam, V. (2005). Micro Credit to Self-Help Groups: A Boon for Economic Empowerment of Rural Women.

- Christopher, D. S., &Senthilkumar, C. B. (2018). Dimensions of preference towards organic products: An empirical study on consumer's perspective. Indian Journal of Public Health Research & Development, 9(11), 1950-1956.

- Christopher, D. S., Senthilkumar, C. B., &Nallusamy, S. An Assessment of Consumers Attitude in Organic Products Usage Purposes and Dominant Groups.

- Jose, S., Chockalingam, D., &Velmurugan, D. (2019). Problems of Women Self Help Group Members in Ernakulam District. Journal of Critical Reviews, 7(1), 2020.

- Krishnaveni, V., Haridas, R., Nandhini, M., &Usha, M. (2013). Savings And Lending Pattern Of Help Groups An Overview. i-Manager's Journal on Management, 8(1), 49.

- Lakshmikandan, K. R. (2000). Self-help groups in the life of Rural Poor—A Philibhit Case Study‖. Women‟ s Link, 9-14.

- Malhotra, S. (2016). Contribution of Self Help Groups in The Socio Economic Development of The Women. International Journal of Research in Social Sciences, 6(8), 333-344.

- Manimekalai, N., &Rajeswari, G. (2000). Empowerment of women through Self-Help Groups (SHGs). Margin, 32(4), 74-87.

- Malhotra, Meenakshi (2004), Empowerment of Women, Isha Books, Delhi.

- Manimekalai, K. (2004), "Economic Empowerment of Women through Self-Help Groups", Third Concept, February.

- Nandhini, M., Usha, M., &Palanivelu, P. Women Empowerment through Self Help Groups: A Study in Coimbatore District.

- Nichlavose, P. R., & Jose, J. (2017). Impact of SHG Initiatives on Socio-Economic Status of Members. Asian Journal of Research in Business Economics and Management, 7(6), 209-216.

- Odisha Economic Survey 2018-19.

- Palanivelu, P., Nandhini, M., Usha, M., &Krishnaveni, V. (2011). Poverty Eradication: Women's Self Help Groups. SCMS Journal of Indian Management, 8(2), 52.

- Pratheep, S., &Dharmaraj, A. (2016). An empirical study on stress levels among working women in export oriented units of Tirupur district. Man In India, 96(9), 3079-3087.

- Pattnaik, Sunanda, (2003) "Smaranika, 2003", Empowerment through SHG: A Case Study of Gajapati District.

- R. Prabhavathy (2011)-An Empirical Study of SHGs and Rural Development in Tuticorin

- S. Venkateshmurthy and G.M, Dinesh (2009) -Women Empowerment through SHG – An Analysis.

- Sahu and Tripathy (2005), Self-Help Groups and Women Empowerment, Anmol Publications Pvt. Ltd., New Delhi.

- Shiralashetti A S and Hugar S S (2008), "Micro Finance: A Study of SHG and Bank Linkage", Journal of Business Studies, Vol. 5, No. 9, pp. 31-37.

- Shobha, K. (2008), "Problem of Self Employed Women: An Analysis", Southern Economist, Vol. 47, No. 6, pp. 24-26.

- Sankaran, A. (2009), "Trends and Problems of Rural Women Entrepreneurs in India", Southern Economist, Vol. 48, No. 4, pp. 11-12.

- Suriyamurthi, S. Christiana, Sheela. andUmarani, T. S. (2009), "Globalisation: Challenges Faced by Women Entrepreneurs", Journal of Management, Vol. 11, No. 3, pp. 34-47.

- Sathiyabama, N. Rural Transformation through Self Help Groups (Shg) In Mayildathurai, Nagapattinam District. Akshaya International Journal of Management, 64.

- Senthilkumar, C. B. (2019). Antecedents of Customers Loyalty towards Organic Products a Study with Reference to Hedonic Consumption and behaviour.

- Sharad, M. (2016). Contribution of self-help groups in the socio economic development of the women. International Journal of research in social sciences, 333-344.

- Shree, D.A., Chandavari, V., &Rayanagoudar, R. (2016). A study on the profile of SHGs and their members in Karnataka. Agric International, 3(2), 97-101.

- Sivakumar, M.V., &Prabakaran, G. (2012). Review on Financial Prospects and Problems of Women's Self Help Groups (SHGs) with Special Reference to Dharmapuri District, Tamil Nadu. Management, 1(12).

- Suganthi, S., Senthilkumar, C.B., &Nallusamy, S. (2018). Study on Factors Affecting the Physical and Mental Health by Stress and emotional Crisis of Working Women. Indian Journal of Public Health Research & Development, 9(3), 335-340.

- Sureshkumar, D. (2010). Self-help groups and micro credit-an analytical study with special reference to Coimbatore city. Osmania Journal of International Business Studies, 5 (1and2), 135-144.

- Tom, T.R., &Selvam, V. (2010). A Study and Fostering Rural Growth through Micro Insurance. Global Management Review, 4(2).

- Venkatesh, J. & K. Kala. 2010. Empowering rural women all the way through self-help groups. International Journal of Management 1(2): 156-63.

- Vasanthakumari, P. (2008), "Women Empowerment through Micro Enterprise Development", Southern Economist, Vol. 47, No. 15, pp. 31-34.

- Vinayamoorthy, A. and Pithoda, Vijay. (2007), "Women Empowerment through SHG: A Case Study in North Tamil Nadu", Indian Journal of Marketing, Vol. 37, No.11.pp 32-35

CHAPTER FOUR

Opportunities and Challenges in Social Entrepreneurship

Mr.Kalee PrasannaPattanayak,

Centurion University of Technology & Management, Odisha

4.1. Introduction

Now the society needs leaders who have the passion tosolve social problems while dealing with many challenges which may crop up in that effort. There are always some problems within the society which needs someone's attention. Social entrepreneurship has emerged as a platform for such leaders who have unwavering commitment towards solving social problems.The importance of Social entrepreneurship is growing as it attempts to solve multiple social problems that are not solved by the government and commercial enterprises. There is a need to build a supportive environment for their growth. Most of these enterprises operate in resource poor areas, depend on volunteering work, face acute financial constraints and normally rely on funding from external sources. This chapter evaluates the concept of social entrepreneurship in the light of opportunities and challenges that are present.

Social entrepreneurship has emerged as a potent tool for framing solutions to various societal problems being faced by the world today (Konda, Starc and Rodica, 2015). Ithas appeared as an answer to the problems faced by the poor and excluded people which went unanswered by the state as well as the private sector (Zahra et al., 2008). Dacin et al. (2010) considers SE is an unselfish activity for achieving social welfare. Dees (2007) describes Social entrepreneurship as "new engines for reform" (Dees, 2007). Social entrepreneurship is imbibed with certain characteristics which are always present: importance to value creation, innovation, sustainable solutions and empowering of participants in the value chain. Instead of aiming at profiteering, social enterprises aim at creating value by targeting a social problem. They may offer a variety of products or services but the underlying motive always remains to be social welfare (Konda, Starc and Rodica, 2015). Social entrepreneurs usually work for issues which are local in nature but global in relevance (Zahra et al., 2008). The local problems on which social entrepreneurs are working may give rise to certain innovations which may be replicated in different geographical regions with similar settings and can trigger global industries (Zahra et al., 2008).Social entrepreneurs can also be called as social investors who decide on the best possible way to use the resources available to them through business activities and constructive methods which help the poor and marginalised people economically. Such entrepreneurs are able to create a social impact by using sound principles of business, strategy and management (Sijabat, 2015).

Mueller et al. (2014) points out some reasons as to why social entrepreneurship is a very popular research topic. First, although social entrepreneurship mainly belongs to management discipline it receives contributions from other disciplines also (Dacin, Dacin and Tracey, 2011). Second, social entrepreneurship offers a lot of scope for scholarly research thereby facilitating publications in a range of journals. Third, the developed countries provide a lot of research funding in this area as they view social entrepreneurship as a sort of universal remedy for a majority of social problems. Finally, many people view SE as a good way of engaging in philanthropic activities.Many people justify social entrepreneurship as good, as the underlying motives are social causes and not profiteering. But should it imply that profiteering organisations are bad and not social? Mueller et al. (2014) mentions about three issues which are often overlooked. First, many not for profit organisations have started projecting themselves as social enterprises. But, normally organisations are not labelled as social enterprises because of absence of profit motive. Second, now most of the corporations are not solely based on profit maximisation principles. They strive to gain the support of their stakeholders by engaging in a variety of activities. That is why we have seen the popularity of the corporate social responsibility (CSR) concept among the corporations in the last two decades. Third, what are seen as social problems varies from place to place and time to time. Although there are some universal social problems like hunger, illiteracy and health etc., but there are some social problems whose definition, meaning and scope varies from place to place.

Social entrepreneurship includes both profit oriented and non-profit oriented enterprises and delivers business solutions for problems of society. They seek benefits even for those individuals who are not a part of activities of their organisation (Santos, 2012). Studying various definitions of social entrepreneurship given by different authors highlights two key components: entrepreneurial activity and social goals (Sijabat, 2015).The main aim behind social entrepreneurship is to decrease vulnerabilities and social disparities on the earth (Barki et al., 2015). Yunus (2010) believes that social businesses have the social impact as their main objective and that all profits should be reinvested in the organization. For Yunus (2010) there is another type of social business: the one owned by the poor and the profitability of which goes to pooras a means to alleviate their poverty (Barki et al., 2015).Yunus (2010) mentions that social business should become economically sustainable by ploughing back all profits back into the organisation.

4.2. Social entrepreneurship structure

Rahim and Mohtar (2015) have suggested a model of social entrepreneurship (Figure 1). In this model social entrepreneurship has been divided into two broad headings; non-profit and hybrid. Hybrid organisations have a profit motive in addition to the social motive. Contributions of traditional NGOs (Non-governmental organisations) have been considered under non-profit heading. These organisations, also sometimes called as civil societies are neither government organisations nor purely business commercial businesses. These organisations are usually made by ordinary citizens and may be funded by different organisations and individuals like government, charities, corporates and individuals. Some of the NGOs never receive any funding from any sources and operate from the contributions made by the volunteers.

The Hybrid type of social enterprises is further segregated into social hybrid and economy hybrid. These two types of organisations have a common dual goal of social service and profit generation. The main distinction between these two types of organisations lies in their primary motive, either more inclined towards social service or profit generation. Social service is the primary motive of social hybrid organisations while profit generation is their secondary motive. Social service organisations have a secondary motive of profit generation so that they can be financially sustainable to extend their service to more and more people over longer periods. Economy hybrid organisations aim to have higher profits but are however, constantly engaged in social activities. Many of the socially responsible business fall under this group.

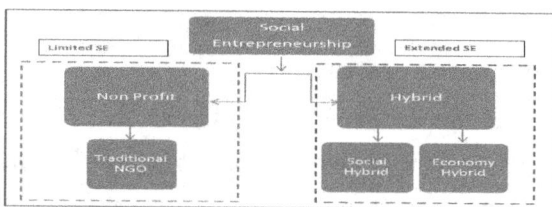

Figure 4. 1. A model of social entrepreneurship (Source: Rahim and Mohtar (2015))

4.3. Economic upliftment through social enterprises

Sijabat (2015)describes threeprominent roles played by Social Enterprises in bring about an improvement in economic conditions of people which are discussed below:

   i.   **Access to Financial resources:**

As most of the poor and marginalised people work in informal sector, lack of access to formal financial institutions proves to be a major impediment to their financial security. So the benefits of financial institutions must be extended to the informal sector. The terms of such benefits to informal sector should be different than those extended by conventional banking system which demands collateral before disbursing loans. One such effort was made by MuhammadYunus in 1976 through creation of Grameen Bank in Bangladesh. Grameen bank offers loans to poor people without asking for any collateral (Yunus, 2011). This method is quite different than the method adopted by the conventional banking system. Grameen bank disburses loans to people on the principles of trust, accountability, contribution and originality. There are three main features of lending by the Grameen bank which distinguishes it from other banks: 1) loan repayment terms are adjusted according to the convenience of the borrower so that they can easily repay the loans; 2) loans are given only to very poor and landless borrowers; 3) women are given the priority while considering loan approvals.Grameen bank model has proved that microcredit targeted at poorest of the poor and women, who are active in the informal economy, has the potential to pull them out of dire poverty.

ii.   **Social Innovation**

Social innovation is closely linked to social entrepreneurship. The social entrepreneur acts as a medium through which social innovation happens. Social innovation also refers to social changes, indicating the process and the outcome of changes which happens.Recently social innovations have taken a prominent role in framing social development plans, which are mostly based on sustainability principles (Konda, Starc and Rodica, 2015). Even though there has been a shift in perception about innovations lately, innovation principles are still based on economic outcomes rather than social outcomes. Recently the view that innovations should spread to economic as well as social aspects of life of people involving both the public as well as private sector is gaining ground. Companies which are oriented towards sustainable development should leverage on technology and social innovations which are the outcomes of entrepreneurial efforts (Konda, Starc and Rodica, 2015).

A study was undertaken by Groot and Dankbaar (2014) in Netherlands where they have studied twenty social enterprises to conclude that social innovation is very vital for solving social problems.Their study was mainly concentrated around three main issues: 1) what is the social impact created by these twenty enterprises? 2) Is the impact created by these enterprises higher than normal enterprises operating in the same market? 3) Are these enterprises financially sustainable? An enterprise cannot be consideredas a social enterprise if it does not create any social impact even after being financially stable. An enterprise which aims to create high social impact but is not financially stable would cease to exist as an enterprise. They have concluded that focus on social impact is more important than intention and that the enterprises having social goals should also make all efforts to stay financially stable otherwise they would cease to exist. They have also opined that social enterprises should also allow themselves to be compared with normal enterprises as far as creation of impact is concerned. If they are genuinely working for social problems they would definitely score well above the normal enterprises on impact creation criteria. They are of the view that normal entrepreneurs also should think about social innovations without thinking social innovation as a domain to be looked after only by governments, NGOs, foundations and charities.

iii.   **People Empowerment and Job Creation**

Empowerment is vital to social entrepreneurs as they have to work under severe resource constraints when solving social problems. Creation of jobs is one of the social impacts of the social entrepreneurs. The labour market operates on a very competitive principle. People who do not have the required skills fail to secure a job in the organised market. This is called as skill mismatch. Skill mismatch is the greatest problem of the poor in securing a job. Although they possess the skills, they are unable to use them in absence of a proper recognition of these in the form of certifications. Our institutional and policy mechanisms are also accountable for this problem (Yunus, 2011). So the social enterprises can contribute significantly to this problem by absorbing those people who are unable to get jobs in the organised and competitive job market. Empowerment missions created by social enterprises can concentrate on the following aspects: 1) enabling people to solve their own problems through capacity building programs; 2) facilitating the linkage of the informal economy with formal sources of finances; 3) Community development can be encouraged through creation of a cooperative network between central, state and local governments; 4) a cooperative network can also be created between societal groups, charity organisations and NGOs, both locally and internationally.

4.4. Environmental elements of social entrepreneurship

The major stakeholder of social entrepreneurship is the social entrepreneur. Other stakeholders include those persons and organisations who work closely with social entrepreneur like government, communities, consumers, workers, traders etc. (David, 2017).David (2017) mentions about some environmental elements of social entrepreneurship which interact among themselves in meeting the objectives of social entrepreneurship:

1. **Social entrepreneurs**: Persons with a vision to solve problems within society.
2. **Environmental problems and needs**: Value system imbibed in citizens due to societal environment throws a variety of challenges for social entrepreneurs.
3. **Culture**: The type of culture prevalent in the concerned society also challenges the motivation of social entrepreneurs.
4. **Social Capital**: Within the social capital there are social networks which are interrelated, reliable and collaborated.
5. **Ideas**: Innovative and unique ideas are considered central to social entrepreneurship as they are the basis of framing solutions to societal problems.
6. **Expertise**: It is the ability of individuals to adapt to physical and social environments.

7. **Knowledge**: Refers to proper understandings of data and facts relating to an area to conduct social entrepreneurial activities successfully.
8. **Innovation**: Innovation is a new way of solving a problem. Social entrepreneurs are also called social innovators as they are always discovering new ways of solving societal problems.
9. **Resources**: Every social entrepreneurial activity requires some resources like funding, human resources, and infrastructural facilities etc. for their successful completion.
10. **Collaboration**:there should be proper communication between staffs and volunteers who work on projects to make them successful. Light (2006) stresses on the need for a collaborative approach where the vision and mission of the individual social entrepreneur should recognize other social entrepreneurial efforts put forward by individuals and organisations across the globe.
11. **Technologies**: The social entrepreneurs must be conversant with various information technology tools and social networking sites for better accomplishments for their enterprises.

The basis of social entrepreneurship lies in the fact that in addition to personal benefits, the individuals should also recognise the importance of benefits to others. (Sijabat, 2015).

4.5. Challenges

Social entrepreneurship is meeting multiple challenges mainly due to the premature stage of the field (Snellman, 2016). There are several limitations stemming from theoretical as well as empirical concerns. Such limitations are regarded to jeopardize the full development of social entrepreneurship as a distinct field which, in turn, may hinder the full development of frameworks and specific approaches allowing application of methods aimed at solving concrete social problems such as poverty, discrimination, and social exclusion (Estrin et al., 2013). Mueller et al. (2014) points out some lacunas that are holding back the theoretical advancement in this field. Firstly, there is no consensus on the scope, boundaries, meanings and definitions of Social Entrepreneurship (Short, Moss, and Lumpkin, 2009) which is leading to confusion among academics, practicenors and policy makers. The absences of clear cut boundaries of the field are making it difficult for scholars to set a research agenda and explore the area further (Gartner, 2001). Second, a dearth of proper research methods (Short, Moss, and Lumpkin,2009) is limiting the development of this field. Third, the understanding of the role of social entrepreneurship is somewhat unclear in relation to traditional economic assumptions (Santos,2012).Kiradoo (2019) lists some further problems associated with social entrepreneurship which is given below:

1. Social Entrepreneurship is sometimes confused with social work. People start questioning the need for revenue generation when the organisationis involved in social work. What they fail to understand is that they are not charity organisations with funding support from various sources. They fail to realise that in order to be financially sustainable and serve the needy people in a better way, it is essential for them to have sound financial support through its own sources of revenue generation.

2. Social innovations are difficult to come by as social enterprises mostly operate in resource constraint areas. Most investors are wary of funding to social enterprises as they do not see any attractive returns. Commercial enterprises too do not take up the cause because of similar reasons.

3. Social enterprises face the crunch of committed and reliable workforce. As social enterprises are mostly working towards social causes, their remuneration structure is not very rewarding for the employees due to poor revenue generation. There are only a few people who come forward for receiving lowerremuneration while working for social causes.

4. Social enterprises always work under a moral framework, giving high priority to solving societal problems while revenue generation remains as a secondary objective. It is sometimes difficult for the people working with the social enterprises to resist the temptation to achieve higher financial gains at the expense of solving societal problems.

5. Social enterprises are unable to maintain proper organisational and financial structure due to insufficient funds and low workforce. They often fail on these criteria which are considered important by funding agencies.

It is really a daunting task to monitor social enterprises in relation to their genuineness and commitment to solving social problems. MuhammedYunus, a well-known personality in social entrepreneurship has condemned several micro financing institutions for prioritizing revenue generation over the aim of social value creation (Dacin, Dacin, and Tracey, 2011). So the overarching problem for social enterprises is to remain true to the original mission which is social welfare (Seda and Ismail,2019). Social entrepreneurs create value by adhering to the enterprise's mission for discovering unique ways of solving social problems through unorthodox thinking (Konda, Starc and Rodica, 2015).There is also a problem in the manner in which SE is promoted now. Some social entrepreneurs advertise their individual achievements in an interesting way to attract funding and publicattention. Such an act, however, overlooks the contributions of the organisations (Light, 2006), groups and of different stakeholders, there by projecting a narrow view of this field(Seda and Ismail, 2019). Such wrong promotion could also hinder the evolution of this field.

Another challenge is that many innovations are made locally to solve the local problems, but they never travel outsidethat particular community as the problem is specific to that particular place (Seda and Ismail, 2019). Another issue is absence of profit motive in social entrepreneurship. Why should someone start a social business when they could earn good profits by opening commercial ventures? Even though there are people with purely service motive, such proportion of people is very less. Moreover, the percentage of people becoming successful social entrepreneurs is also less. This is how social enterprise is and will remain different from philanthropic and charitable institutions. The only point of difference is that social enterprises look for a level of profit just sufficient to keep the organisation running. In doing so their aim is to help as many needy people as possible (Seda and Ismail, 2019). It is always difficult to convince the investors to invest in social ventures as they fail to see any investment-return equation unlike the business markets. Business markets have a track record of investment and returns over a period of time which helps investors arrive at a decision. Unfortunately, social entrepreneurship sector is yet to provide such security to investors for securing funds from them (Seda and Ismail, 2019). It has been found that most of the social enterprisesoperate in resource poor areas. Gradually the pressure on theses constrained resources is increasing due to competition among non-profit and for-profit enterprises. So there is need for social enterprises to adopt some professional business practices and marketing techniques in order to remain competitive against commercial ventures in order to continue to offer their services to the community. Moreover, even though social enterprises are considered indispensible for the society, there are no proper standards for measuring the impact that is created by these enterprises on the society.

4.6. Opportunities

The presence of opportunities is vital for entrepreneurship (Snellman, 2016). According to Venkataraman (1997), opportunities for entrepreneurs are always present, regardless of the ability of the entrepreneurs for identifying and exploiting them. It has been widely accepted in entrepreneurial sphere that the will and the intention to identify and capitalize on the opportunities is what distinguishes entrepreneurs from normal individuals (Perrini, 2006). Entrepreneurs continuously engage themselves in various activities through which they experiment, learn and come out with innovative solutions and this has been considered as the way entrepreneurs should conduct themselves (Snellman, 2016). Entrepreneurs are accustomed to the risks and uncertaintiesthat arise out of their endeavours. Social entrepreneurs use innovation as tool to combine resources most efficiently and discover new ways of solving most daunting social problems (Steyaert and Hjorth, 2006).Although social entrepreneurs face numerous challenges while trying to solve societal problems, they have the ability and the vision to perceive them as opportunities as they particularly aim at solving such problems even though it may require unique and unknown steps to solve them. It has been aptly noted by Dees (1998) that the an issue which commercial entrepreneurs see as a problem becomes an opportunity for social entrepreneurs as they always try to find new solutions to existing problems while others see it as a trouble. This comes out from some personal attributes which they possess as opposed to other entrepreneurs like internal motivation, originality, action orientation and resolution to solve societal problems(Martin and Osberg, 2007).

The biggest opportunity for social entrepreneurs that exists is that the world has a host of social problems that need urgent action (Kiradoo, 2019). Social enterprises could be an excellent option for solving these problems along with gaining some financial benefits. The plethora of social problems can be picked up by many social entrepreneursacross the world and converted into meaningful solutions.Another opportunity for social enterprises exists in those areas where the commercial enterprises are reluctant to enter because of investment-return equation (Kiradoo, 2019).These areas normally referto areas with poor endowment of resources.There is a general impression that entrepreneurs always drive themselves for higher profits in order to be known as successful enterprises and that most of the research in the entrepreneurial area is taking place by keeping in mind the economic value and wealth creation aspects (Dacin et al., 2010). Recently researchers have observed that it is not necessary for entrepreneurs to always limit themselves to financial gains and remain within the ambit of their own businesses (Dacin et al., 2010).

It has been observed that a society depends upon an array of support systems in order to operate and grow successfully (Joshua et al., 2019). Some of them are: healthcare, education systems, infrastructure, information and communication technology and so on. It is very unlikely that a single social entrepreneur can provide all these services to a community. So social entrepreneurs should target any one of these areas based upon the need and urgency of such service to the community concerned and develop their business models accordingly (Joshua et al., 2019).The use of the term social entrepreneurship should not be used only to mean non-profit organisations with a social cause. An organisation can be called as a social enterprise without having a purely social objective. The only things that should be considered are that the entrepreneurs demonstrate entrepreneurial behaviour and his/her organisation has a social mission, irrespective of their organisation being a non-profit organisation or hybrid organisation (organisation with social and financial goals). So it should be understood that an organisation can conduct social entrepreneurship activities, also while pursuing financial goals. This would encourage many profit oriented businesses to adopt social goals and transform into hybrid organisations that care for the society (Rahim and Mohtar, 2015).

4.7. The Way Ahead

Many social entrepreneurs are working in many parts of the country without a proper understanding of the market and technical knowledge. Various sensitisation programs need to be planned and conducted by the authorities and policy makers to bring them to public eye (Pathak, Poudel and Acharya, 2018).In connection with this, Kiradoo (2019) extends some suggestions which are as follows:

1. The government should consider making some boards or associations for looking after the problems of social enterprises just the way it is done for commercial enterprises.
2. The educational institutions and universities of each country should collaborate with each otherto offersocial enterprises courses as compulsory subjects in their syllabus so that young minds could be sensitised towards solving various social problems facing their countries.
3. There is a need to create mass awarenessprograms about social entrepreneurship so that people can understand that they can be involved in various social entrepreneurship activities and also get financial gains through them.

4. Governments should consider offering various infrastructural facilities for establishment of social enterprises like working spaces, meeting rooms etc., so as to attract people into establishing social enterprises.

5. Governments should organise some social entrepreneurship development programs at regular intervals to continue motivating the visionary social entrepreneurs.

6. Financing support should be extended to social enterprises on easier terms than compared to commercial enterprises so as to motivate more and more people to establish social enterprises.

7. Governments should prefer offering its social improvement projects to social entrepreneurs as they are a set of local visionaries with a unique interest in solving their local problems. So they are likely to carry out the execution of the projects more seriously than any other agencies or organisations.

4.8. Conclusions

Social entrepreneurship has facilitated easy access to financial resources, stimulated social innovations as a tool for solving social problems, created employment opportunities and empowered people with social inclusion. Intricate and universal societal problems that are seen as complex or inconvenient by governments and private businesses are creating ample of opportunities for social enterprises in order to find and solve social problems which are local as well as universal in nature. So social entrepreneurship is all about finding opportunities and executing them through innovative practices and processes for creating social value, and, particularly increasing public wellbeing. Social entrepreneursshould aim to create social value through unique business models, organisational structures and unique strategies as they are faced with severe resources constraints to support traditional entrepreneurship. Contextual factors like legal, institutional and social environment factors are deciding factors for judging the efficacy of the social entrepreneurial initiatives as these factors could either aid or stand as barriers to such efforts. Since social entrepreneurship is considered indispensible for bringing positive change in society, there is a need to identify ways in which they can be supported through policy and other measures.

References

1. Barki, E., Comini, G., Cunliffe, A., Hart, S., &Rai, S. (2015). Social entrepreneurship and social business: Retrospective and prospective research. *Revista de Administração de Empresas*, *55*(4), 380-384.

2. Dacin, M. T., Dacin, P. A., & Tracey, P. (2011). Social entrepreneurship: A critique and future directions. Organization science, 22(5), 1203-1213.

3. Dacin, P., Dacin, M., &Matear, M. (2010). Social entrepreneurship: Why we don't need a new theory and how we move forward from here. Academy of Management Perspectives, 24(3), 37-57.

4. David C. Chou, Applying design thinking method to social entrepreneurshipproject, Computer Standards & Interfaces (2017).

5. Dees, J. G. (2007). Taking social entrepreneurship seriously. *Society*, *44*(3), 24-31.

6. Estrin S., Mickiewicz T., & Stephan U. 2013. Entrepreneurship, Social Capital,and Institutions: Social and Commercial Entrepreneurship Across Nations.Entrepreneurship Theory and Practice, 37, 3, 479 –504.

7. Gartner, W. B. (2001). Is there an elephant in entrepreneurship? Blind assumptions in theory development. *Entrepreneurship Theory and practice*, *25*(4), 27-39.

8. Groot, A., &Dankbaar, B. (2014). Does social innovation require social entrepreneurship? Technology Innovation Management Review, 17.

9. Joshua Pearce, Lonny Grafman, Thomas Colledge, Ryan Legg. Leveraging Information Technology,Social Entrepreneurship, and Global Collaboration for Just Sustainable Development. 2019. hal-02120513

10. Kiradoo, G. (2019). Social Entrepreneurship and their Roles and Responsibility. Towards the Society and Challenges Faced in Profitable Organization. *International Journal of Management*, *10*(3).

11. Konda, I., Starc, J., &Rodica, B. (2015). Social challenges are opportunities for sustainable development: tracing impacts of social entrepreneurship through innovations and value creation. *Economic Themes*, *53*(2), 211-229.

12. Light, P. C. (2006). Reshaping social entrepreneurship. *Stanford Social Innovation Review*, *4*(3), 47-51.

13. Martin, R. L., &Osberg, S. (2007). Social entrepreneurship: The case for definition.

14. Mueller, S., D'Intino, R. S., Walske, J., Ehrenhard, M., Newbert, S. L., Robinson, J. A., &Senjem, J. C. (2014). What's Holding Back Social Entrepreneurship? Removing the Impediments to Theoretical Advancement.

15. Pathak, R. R., Poudel, B. R., &Acharya, P. E. (2018). Social enterprise and social entrepreneurship: conceptual clarity and implication in Nepalese context. NCC Journal, 3(1), 143-152.

16. Perrini, F. (Ed.). (2006). The new social entrepreneurship: what awaits social entrepreneurial ventures?. Edward Elgar Publishing.

17. Rahim, H. L., &Mohtar, S. (2015). Social entrepreneurship: A different perspective. *International Academic Research Journal of Business and Technology*, *1*(1), 9-15.

18. Seda, A., & Ismail, M. (2019). Challenges facing social entrepreneurship. *Review of Economics and Political Science*.

19. Sijabat, R. (2015). The role of social entrepreneurship in enabling economic opportunities for the poor: A synthesis of the literature and empirical works. International Journal of Business and Social Science, 6(11), 35-41.

20. Santos, F. M. (2012). A positive theory of social entrepreneurship. *Journal of business ethics*, *111*(3), 335-351.

21. Short, J. C., Moss, T. W., & Lumpkin, G. T. (2009). Research in social entrepreneurship: Past contributions and future opportunities. *Strategic entrepreneurship journal*, *3*(2), 161-194.

22. Snellman, L. (2016). Social Entrepreneurship: Making change in the world. *Journal of Logistics, Informatics and Service Science*, *3*(1), 1-25.

23. Steyaert, C., &Hjorth, D. (2006). Entrepreneurship as Social Change: a Third Movements in Entrepreneurship Book.

24. Venkatraman, S. (1997). The distinctive domain of entrepreneurship research. *Advances in entrepreneurship, firm emergence and growth*, *3*(1), 119-138.

25. Yunus, M (2010). Building social business: The new kind of capitalism that serves humanity's most pressing needs. Public Affairs.

26. Yunus, M. (2011). Vision 2050: A Poverty-Free World. Social Business – A Step toward Creating New Global Economic Order. *Journal of Social Business. Social Business and New Economics Paradigm, 1*(1), 7-23.

27. Zahra, S., Rawhouser, H., Bhawe, N., Neubaum, D. and Hayton, J. (2008) 'Globalization ofsocial entrepreneurship opportunities', Strategic Entrepreneurship Journal, Vol. 2, No. 2, pp.117–131.

CHAPTER FIVE

Women Entrepreneurship in the Rural Environment

Mr.N. Durga Prasad

Centurion University of Technology & Management, Odisha

5.1. Introduction

Women represent 50percent of the world population but they are receiving only 10percent of the world income and 1percent of worlds assets. Women shoulders the burden of the worlds poverty. This poverty level is worsen than that men as clear gender disparities in education , decision making power, society regulations and employment opportunities while women constitute half of worlds population . They have been deprived for too long from participating in the opportunities and benefits of economic growth and globalization.

Rural entrepreneurship is considered as one of the most important factors contributing to the economic development of the rural society . promotion of entrepreneurship among rural women is a major step to increase women participation in rural and economic development . Rural entrepreneurship is today buzzword in the changing rural economy. It is purposeful activity initiating, promoting and maintaining economic growth. Rural entrepreneurship is not new to our culture. What it needs today is to nurture this spirit and instil it in the present and coming generations of both men and women. It is said that if a man starts a business venture he only becomes the entrepreneur , while when a women takes to entrepreneurship the whole family becomes entrepreneurial in its behaviour and outlook. Therefore, if women gain economic strength, they gain visibility and voice. With the economic restructuring and societal acceptance in the modern days , women have started establishing and running enterprises successfully.

Though women entrepreneurship is in its infancy and transition period , it is all set to go a long way.

Today rural women entrepreneurs represent a group of women who have broken away from the beaten track and exploring new avenues of rural and economic development . The number of women entrepreneurs have grown over a period of time and it is clear that the percentage is increasing every year

5.2. Driving forces for women entrepreneurs:

- To attain economic independence.
- To establish their own creativity.
- To establishing their own identity.
- To achieve excellence.
- To developing risk-taking ability.
- To attain equal status in society.
- To have greater freedom and mobility.
- To earn additional income to the family.
- To achieve women empowerment.
- To make use of unutilized and underutilized local resources.

5.3. Indian perspective

India has the world's largest number of professionally qualified women. It has more female doctors, surgeons, scientists and professors than in U.S. It also has successful women entrepreneurs. India has more working women than any other country in the world.But, the women who are highly qualified, skilled, take-up good jobs and are very successful as entrepreneurs are confined to urban areas and their contribution towards the generation of National income and economic growth is not adequate. In India the rural area contributes to 72 percent and among that 50percent are women, who are not having adequate opportunities to educate, develop, get good opportunities or start their own business by which they can stand on their own feet. Thus they are not given an opportunity to contribute for national income, growth and development.

In India we face the problems of unemployment, disguised employment, under employment and poverty. Rural women entrepreneurship can be a good answer to all these problems as it not only provides employment and source of income to the major neglected sector of the country but also to all those who become associated with the business concern.

5.4. Bottlenecks for the development of women entrepreneurs:

In spite of their important contribution to socio-economic development, women suffer from various constraints, which inhibit them from fully realizing their potential for development. Some of the reasons are as below:

> Rural women are also unaware of the legal provisions and legislative systems that help them to take initiative and avail opportunities to become entrepreneurs. Their understandings as well as their capacity to identify unjustified application of the regulation are weak.
> Increase in the crime rate and lack of security to women is also not permitting them to come out and participate in the business activities at par with men.
> Complex regulatory requirements and lengthy licensing process and costly operations often discourage rural women to start a business.
> Furthermore, their reproductive role in family and the community puts women in a disadvantaged position to engage in entrepreneurial activities.
> Cultural values and social norms hinder the equal participation of women in the society.
> One of the major constraints women face as entrepreneurs is the unequal access to productive resources and services, including finance and skill upgrading opportunities.

Some other problems which our rural women entrepreneurs face today are:

> Small investment.
> Tough competition.
> Lack of awareness of marketing techniques.
> Lack of women entrepreneur role models in rural areas.
> Business not in the area of interest.
> Lack of confidence.
> Lack of motivation.

> Lack of family support.
> Inability to dream.
> Lack of Computer Knowledge and access to internet

5.5. Government Initiatives

The Government of India has been encouraging self-employment and has started several schemes to promote entrepreneurship among women. Various income generating schemes like Support to Training and Employment Programme (STEP), Swavalambana Socio-Economic Programme, Pradhan Mantri Gram SwarozgarYojana, Pradhan Mantri Shahri SwarozgarYojana, Jana Shikshan Sansthan (JSS) etc. have been launched to this end. Women are encouraged to organize and form Self Help Groups (SHGs) and Cooperatives which undertake activities to generate income for the most vulnerable groups of women. Rastriya Mahila Kosh (RMK) was set up to provide loans to these women who could then become self employed by establishing their own business or small scale enterprises. Women's Development Corporations, operating in a few States in India are promoting entrepreneurship among women at the gross root level. In this way, women at the grassroots and other levels, who are managing small-scale industries and enterprises, are becoming economically empowered.

5.6. Measures to remove the bottlenecks and overcoming the problems:

- Women human resource should develop in such a way to increase their competitive entrepreneurship, technology absorbing capacities and control over asset management.
- To respond to the needs of women to materialize their economic potential and thereby to improve their standard of living, it is necessary to design programmes by applying mainstreaming strategy.
- Necessary measures have to be devised to integrate women as decision-makers, participants and beneficiaries in all relevant development activities, irrespective of the sector or type of activity.
- It is also necessary to address the totality of problems rural woman face as entrepreneurs, due to wide spectrum of elements effecting the equitable participation in development.

- A bottom-up growth strategy has to be planned which focuses on the transformation and diversification of micro and small scale enterprises run by rural women to growth-oriented activities and on increasing the productive capacity in order to enable them to participate in the main stream economy of the nation.
- A plan or strategy must be designed and implemented in close collaboration with various development partners in different specialized areas, notably education, health, human rights as well as environment and energy.

By organising themselves in groups and associations, rural women entrepreneurs can voice their specific concerns and advocate change through formal policy making process. This entrepreneurial group capacity helps to plan and implement common projects and keep motivation going. They can establish common projects such as:

- Collective marketing.
- Bulk purchasing.
- Group lending and group oriented enterprises.
- Common facilities like sharing machines and equipment, a warehouse or a vehicle or office furniture.

Top level and successful women entrepreneurs in urban areas and country wide should help, involve and encourage rural women entrepreneurs in mainstreaming their activities at national level. For example; women involved in textile and garments business in urban areas and well developed areas can give orders in bulk to rural women entrepreneurs involved in crochet lace business and saree embroidery works. Strong rules and measures should be taken and implementation of severe punishments should be made to bring down crime rate and to eradicate sexual harassments on women.

5.7. Conclusion

Scope and need for rural women entrepreneurs is high in India. Hence the development of Rural Women Entrepreneurship is the need of the hour. Not only that they also help in producing eco-friendly and pollution free products which are necessary as pollution an global warming are a very serious and burning topics today. Business opportunities are not created by external intervention - they arise from market and entrepreneurial capabilities. The issue is to enable rural women entrepreneurs to take advantage of market opportunities.

Many government policies, reservations and opportunities are being exploited and are used by males making their wife or mother as instruments in the process i.e., business will be run in his wife's or mother's name but the ropes will be in his hands. Reducing Urban – Rural inequalities and gender inequalities is essential for the development of any Country. Mobilizing the potential productivity of rural women by developing them as entrepreneurs is one of the best solutions and is indispensable to achieve the resilient economic growth that will pull people above the poverty line.

We can come to a conclusion that overall literacy and gender equality is a prerequisite for development because of the contribution women make and the role they play in society and in the economic well-being of the family and community.Be it in rural or urban area, be it micro or medium or large enterprise, women must be an integral part of development not only as beneficiaries but also as decision-makers and agents of change.

One thing is clear that, whatever may be the suggestions, whatever may be the rural women entrepreneurship development programmes and projects undertaken and whatever may be government policies for encouraging rural women entrepreneurs, no change comes unless and until the rural women they themselves have a strong desire and passion to develop. Change should come from within. They have to be educated and made clear that "Nobody can make them feel inferior without their concern". And once they are strongly determined and has a desire to become entrepreneurs, nothing and nobody can stop them. In such process the hurdles and difficulties in their way becomes negligible.

Finally as a strong, unavoidable and standard measure overall literacy rate and awareness regarding the concern should increase irrespective of men and women. Because, though women are educated, motivated, aware and ready to grab the opportunities, men should be in a position to accept equality in gender and to encourage their mother, sister, wife and daughter to become an entrepreneur.

References

1. AmartyaSen and Jean Dreze, India Economic Development and Social Opportunity, Oxford University Press, 1996.

2. Anil Kumar S, Poornima S.C, Abraham M.K and Jayashree K, Entrepreneurship Development, New Age International (Pvt.) Ltd, New Delhi, 2004.

3. Anil Kumar, Financing Pattern of Enterprises owned by Women Entrepreneurs, The Indian Journal of Commerce, Vol.57, No.2, April-June, 2004, pp 73 and74.

4. Anand Neeta, Working Women: Issues and Problems, Yojana, March 2003, pp.11-14.

5. Aravinda.C, and Renuka S, Women Entrepreneurs: An Exploratory Study, SEDME Journal, September, Vol.28, No.3, 2001,pp. 1-7.

6. BeharaSreenivasa R and Niranjan K.(2012), Rural Women Entrepreneurship in India, IJCEM International Journal of Computational Engineering & Management, November.Vol. 15, Issue 6.

7. Business Today, September 26, 2004, p.85.

8. Business Today, April 14-17, 2003, p.64.

9. Business Line, Saturday, April 27, 2002, p.1.

10. Chandar S. and Arora D (2013), Study of Financial Problems of Women Entrepreneurs, IJSSIR, Vol. 2(4). April.

11. Dubhashi M., Women Entrepreneurship in Asia-Ventures of Experiences of Asian Women, SEDME Journal, Vol.30, No.4, 2003, pp.21-24.

12. George P.A., Women Entrepreneurship in India, Pranjan, Vol.2, No.1, Jan-June 1998.

13. Government of India, Economic Survey, 2003-2004.

14. Government of India(2001-02), Third All India Census of SSI, DC(SSI), Ministry of SSI, New Delhi, 2002.

15. Gupta C.B and Khanka S.S, Entrepreneurship and Small Business Management, Sultan Chand, New Delhi, 2003.

16. Heggade O.D, Development of Women Entrepreneurs – Problems and Prospects, Economic Affairs, 1981, pp. 39-50.

17. Hanuman Prasad and B.L. Verma, Women Entrepreneurship in India, The Indian Journal of Commerce, Vol.59, No.2, April-June, 2006.

18. Kondaiah C, Entrepreneurship in the New Millennium-Challenges and Prospects, Tata McGraw-Hill Publishing Company, New Delhi, 2002

19. Manimekalai N. and Ganeshan R., Global Women entrepreneurs Profile: An Analysis, Southern Economist, July 15, 2001, pp.12-16.

20. Mittal K.C, Indsutrial Entrepreneurship in India, Deep and Deep Publications, New Delhi, 2003.

21. Peter F. Drucker, Innovation and Entrepreneurship, Harper & Row, New York, 1986, pp.27-28.

22. Planning Commission, Report of the Committee on India Vision 2020, Academic Foundation, New Delhi, 2003, pp.23-24.

23. Punitha M, Sangeetha S and Padmavathi, Women Entrepreneurs: Their Problems and Constraints, Indian Journal of Labour Economics, 42(4), 1999, pp 701-706.

24. Robert D. Hirsch and Michael P. Peters, Entrepreneurship, Tata McGraw-Hill Publishing Company Ltd, New Delhi, 2003.

25. Rajendran.N, Problems and Prospects of Women Entrepreneurs, SEDME Journal, 2003, Vol.30, No.4, pp.39-42.

CHAPTER SIX

Entrepreneurial Communication Skills

Dr.Girish Prasad Rath

Centurion University of Technology & Management, Odisha

6.1 Introduction

Entrepreneurs are trying to maintain goodwill of their company by communicating all the time with their investors, employees, and clients; however entrepreneurs don't have enough time to hone their communications skills. One of the most important parts of running an organization in any level is effective communication. An entrepreneur needs lots of skills to run a business. He/she needs to persuade customers to purchase your product or service, convince investors of the advantage of your idea, or motivate a top candidate to work for you, communication skills are essential to success in a number of ways, Besides all these, communication skills are important at the time of presentations, project explanation, training, as well as many other situations where the entrepreneur has face to face conversation with people from different levels. A person becomes entrepreneur after communicating effectively with people by telling the story of the idea he/she has. The entrepreneur may have a brilliant idea, a business model but if he/she fails to tell his/her story to communicate the vision, there is hardly any chance of conversing the idea into reality. To give a tangible body to the idea communication plays a vital role, to keep the vision alive in person's communication with people and him/herself communication is the key. The idea gets envisioned with communication, otherwise the idea remains in its abstract form and in due course of time it may vanish.

6.2 Communication for Team building

To turn the idea into reality the entrepreneur has to convince the partners with adequate communication; and if he succeeds then he has to build a team, so that he/she can assign the task so, for a building a team proper and effective communication is a vital. Idea must be shared among the team so that the team can work for the common goal. Many a time we have seen that team fails to reach to the goal because there is a miscommunication, they don't know where they are leading to. The entrepreneur plays s the role of a leader and gives proper guidelines and instruction to reach to the goal. He must communicate with members to know the difficulties, problems and must solve them to get succeed.

6.3 Listening Skills

Listening is basic to all incredible correspondence. Without the ability to listen satisfactorily, messages are helpfully misconstrued. In this way, correspondence isolates and the sender of the message can without a doubt get baffled or troubled. In case there is one correspondence capacity you ought to hope to expert, by then listening is it. Listening is fundamental to the point that many top supervisors give listening capacities planning to their agents. This isn't amazing when you consider that extraordinary listening aptitudes can incite better shopper dependability, more critical benefit with less stumble, and extended sharing of information that accordingly can provoke more innovative and imaginative work. Various productive pioneers and business visionaries credit their thriving to incredible listening capacities. Extraordinary listening capacities moreover have benefits in our own lives, including:

A more noticeable number of buddies and casual networks, created certainty and conviction, higher assessments at school and in academic work, and amazingly better prosperity and general thriving. Studies have shown that, while talking raises beat, careful listening can chop it down.

6.3.1. Listening Vs Hearing

Listening is basic to all or any incredible correspondence. Without the power to concentrate satisfactorily, messages are helpfully misconstrued. during this way, correspondence isolates and therefore the sender of the message can without a doubt get baffled or troubled. just in case there's one correspondence capacity you need to hope to expert, by then listening is it. Listening is prime to the purpose that a lot of top supervisors give listening capacities getting to their agents. This is not amazing once you consider that extraordinary listening aptitudes can incite better shopper dependability, more critical benefit with less stumble, and extended sharing of data that accordingly can provoke more innovative and imaginative work. Various productive pioneers and business visionaries credit their thriving to incredible listening capacities. Extraordinary listening capacities moreover have benefits in our own lives, including:

A more noticeable number of buddies and casual networks, created certainty and conviction, higher assessments at college and in academic work, and amazingly better prosperity and general thriving. Studies have shown that, while talking raises beat, careful listening can chop it down.

6.3.2. Listening is the most key part of relational abilities.

Listening isn't something that essentially happens (that is hearing), listening is a working cycle wherein a perceptive decision is made to check out and fathom the messages of the speaker.

Crowd individuals should remain unbiased and non-basic, this infers putting forth an attempt not to support one side or structure assessments, especially first thing in the conversation. Full focus is also about tirelessness - stops and brief occasions of calm should be recognized.

Crowd individuals should not be allured to bounce in with questions or comments each time there are a few snapshots of calm. Full focus incorporates giving the other individual occasion to research their insights and feelings, they should, thusly, be given adequate time for that.

Full focus infers focusing in totally on the speaker just as adequately giving verbal and non-verbal signs of tuning in. Overall speakers need crowd individuals to delineate 'full focus' by responding appropriately to what they are expressing.

6.3.3. Indications of Active Listening

Non-Verbal Signs of Attentive or Active Listening

This is an ordinary once-over of non-verbal signs of tuning in, toward the day's end client/customers who are listening will undoubtedly show most likely a bit of these signs. In any case these signs may not be legitimate in all conditions and over all social orders.

a) Smile

Little smiles can be used to show that the crowd is zeroing in on what is being said or as a technique for agreeing or being lively about the messages being gotten. Gotten together with offers of the head, smiles can be astonishing in declaring that messages are being fixed on and fathomed.

b) Eye to eye connection

It is average and for the most part encouraging for the crowd to look at the speaker. Eye to eye association can at any rate be terrifying, especially for more humble speakers – check how much eye to eye association is appropriate for some irregular situation. Join eye to eye association with smiles and other non-verbal messages to help the speaker.

c) Stance

Position can edify an extraordinary arrangement concerning the sender and beneficiary in social coordinated efforts. The careful crowd will when all is said in done lean barely advance or sideways while sitting. Various signs of full focus may join a slight tendency of the head or laying the head on one hand.

d) Reflecting

Modified reflection/reflecting of any outward appearances used by the speaker can be a sign of careful tuning in. These clever explanations can help with demonstrating empathy and compassion in more energetic conditions. Attempting to purposefully imitate outward appearances (for instance not customized impression of explanations) can be a sign of absentmindedness.

e) Interruption

The mindful individual won't be involved and thusly will do without wriggling, looking at a clock or watch, doodling, playing with their hair or picking their fingernails.

Most by far, as a general rule, belittle tuning in, it's something that just happens. It is exactly when you stop to consider tuning in and what it includes that you begin to comprehend that listening is really a critical capacity that ought to be continued and made. Listening is perhaps the most critical of each and every social ability. Effective listening is routinely the foundation of strong relationship with others, at home, socially, in preparing and in the workplace.

6.3.4. General Listening Types:

The two fundamental kinds of tuning in - the establishments of all listening sub-types are:

i) Discriminative Listening

Discriminative listening structures through youthfulness and into adulthood. As we become more prepared and make and get useful experience, our ability to perceive different sounds is improved. Not solely would we have the option to see different voices, anyway we also develop the ability to see inconspicuous differences in the way that sounds are made – this is major to finally understanding what these sounds mean. Differentiations fuse various subtleties, seeing obscure tongues, perceiving common accents and clues to the emotions and assumptions of the speaker.

Having the alternative to perceive the subtleties of sound made by somebody who is happy or forlorn, enraged or centered, for example, finally builds the estimation of what is truly being said and, clearly, helps discernment. Right when discriminative listening aptitudes are gotten together with visual enhancements, the ensuing ability to 'tune in' to non-verbal correspondence engages us to begin to fathom the speaker even more totally – for example recalling that somebody is hopeless regardless of what they are expressing or how they are expressing it.

ii) Extensive Listening

Broad listening incorporates understanding the message or messages that are being conferred. Like discriminative tuning in, complete listening is fundamental to all listening sub-types.

In order to be fit use broad tuning in and thus increment understanding the crowd first needs fitting language and language aptitudes. Using exorbitantly tangled language or particular language, thusly, can be an obstruction to broad tuning in. Complete listening is also tangled by the way that two interesting people checking out something fundamentally the same as may understand the message in two particular habits. This issue can be copied in a social occasion setting, like a homeroom or gathering where different ramifications can be gotten from what has been said.

Thorough listening is adulated by sub-messages from non-verbal correspondence, for instance, the way of talking, movements and other non-verbal correspondence. These non-verbal signs can phenomenally support correspondence and thankfulness anyway can similarly dumbfound and perhaps lead to misinterpretation. In many listening conditions it is significant to search for clarification and use capacities, for instance, reflection help understanding.

iii) Explicit Listening Types

Discriminative and broad listening are basics for express listening types. Listening types can be portrayed by the target of the tuning in. The three basic kinds of listening commonly fundamental in social correspondence are:

a) **Educational (Listening to Learn)**

Accommodating or Empathetic (Listening to Understand Feeling and Emotion)

A wide scope of listening is dynamic. Informative listening is less powerful than countless various kinds of tuning in. Right when we're checking out learn or be told we are taking in new information and real factors, we are not censuring or analyzing. Illuminating tuning in, especially in formal settings like in work get-togethers or while in preparing, is routinely joined by note taking – a strategy for recording key information with the objective that it will in general be reviewed later.

a) **Basic (Listening to Evaluate and Analyze)**

We can be busy with fundamental listening when the goal is to survey or research what is being said. Fundamental listening is an essentially more powerful direct than informative tuning in and customarily incorporates a kind of basic reasoning or dynamic. Fundamental listening is like essential scrutinizing; both incorporate assessment of the information being gotten and game plan with what we unquestionably know or acknowledge. In spite of the fact that informational listening may be commonly stressed over tolerating real factors just as new information - essential listening is connected to separating determination and making a judgment.

Exactly when the word 'fundamental' is used to depict tuning in, scrutinizing or figuring it doesn't generally infer that you are ensuring that the information you are checking out is somehow flawed or defective. Or on the other hand perhaps, fundamental listening suggests participating in what you are checking out by asking yourself requests, for instance, 'what is the speaker endeavoring to state?' or 'what is the standard conflict being presented?', 'how does what I'm hearing difference from my feelings, data or evaluation?'. Essential listening is, thusly, head to real learning. Various regular decisions that we make rely upon some kind of 'fundamental' assessment, whether or not it be essential tuning in, examining or thought. Our assumptions, characteristics and feelings rely upon our ability to deal with information and plan our own feelings about our overall environmental factors similarly as weigh up the potential gains and drawbacks to make a good choice.

It is routinely critical, when listening on a very basic level, to have an open standpoint and not be uneven by speculations or suspicions. By doing this you will improve as a group of people and broaden your knowledge and impression of others and your associations in the association.

b) Remedial or Empathic Listening

Empathic listening incorporates trying to fathom the opinions and sentiments of the speaker – to put you into the speaker's point of view and offer their contemplations.

Sympathy is a technique for significantly connecting with another person and remedial or empathic listening can be particularly trying. Compassion isn't equal to empathy, it incorporates more than being sympathetic or feeling disappointed about someone else – it incorporates a more significant affiliation – an affirmation and perception of another person's viewpoint.

Counsellors, masters and some various specialists use healing or empathic checking out understands and finally helps their clients. Such a listening does exclude settling on choices or offering direction yet gently consoling the speaker to explain and clarify their assumptions and emotions. Aptitudes, for instance, clarification and reflection are routinely used to help avoid misguided judgments. We are generally prepared for empathic tuning in and may practice it with buddies, family and accomplices. Demonstrating compassion is an appealing quality in various social associations – you may well feel more incredible talking about your own notions and sentiments with a particular person. They are likely going to be better at listening thoughtfully to you than others, this is habitually established on relative perspectives, experiences, feelings and characteristics – a representative, a client , an old pal, your mate, a parent or kinfolk for example.

6.3.5. Boundaries to Effective Listening

To improve the pattern of ground-breaking tuning in, it might be valuable to turn the issue on its head and look at limits to convincing tuning in, or deficient tuning in. For example, one typical issue is that instead of tuning in close to what someone is expressing, we routinely get involved after a sentence or two and rather start to consider what we will say in answer or think about detached things. This infers that we don't totally check out the rest of the speaker's message.

This issue is credited, somewhat, to the qualification between ordinary talk rate and typical planning rate. Typical talk rates are some place in the scope of 125 and 175 words for each moment however we can quantify on ordinary some place in the scope of 400 and 800 words each second. It is a regular penchant for the crowd to use the additional time while checking out stray in dream land or think about various things, rather than focusing in on what the speaker is expressing.

Clearly the clearness of what the speaker is expressing can in like manner impact how well we tune in. Generally we feel that its easier to focus if the speaker is familiar with their talk, has a characteristic feature, and talks at a fitting uproar for the condition. It is more problematic, for example, to focus in on somebody who is talking fast and unpretentiously, especially if they are passing on complex information. We may moreover get redirected by the speaker's own special appearance or by what someone else is expressing, which sounds furthermore captivating. These issues impact you, yet you are likely going to show your nonappearance of thought in your non-verbal correspondence. Generally, we imagine that it's significantly harder to control our non-verbal correspondence, and you are presumably going to show your interference and also nonattendance of energy by nonappearance of eye to eye association, or position. The speaker will distinguish the issue, and likely quit talking, most ideal situation. At more awful, they may be uncommonly aggravated or upset.

Right when we talk about 'correspondence', we consistently imply 'what we express': the words that we use. In any case, social correspondence is considerably more than the express significance of words, and the information or message that they pass on. It moreover consolidates got messages, if deliberate, which are conveyed through non-verbal practices.

Non-verbal correspondence joins outward appearances, the tone and pitch of the voice, movements appeared through non-verbal correspondence (kinesics) and the physical detachment between the communicators (proxemics).

These non-verbal signs can give clues and additional information and essentialness a long ways past spoken (verbal) correspondence. Unquestionably, a couple of evaluations prescribe that around 70 to 80% of correspondence is non-verbal!

6.4. Utilizing Non-Verbal Communication

Non-verbal correspondence/communication causes individuals to:

a) Strengthen or alter what is said in words.

For example, people may signal their heads vigorously when saying "Yes" to stretch that they agree with the other person. A shrug of the shoulders and a forsaken enunciation when saying "I'm fine, much valued" may truly propose that things are not commonly fine in any way shape or form!

b) Pass on data about their enthusiastic state.

Your outward appearance, your manner of speaking, and your non-verbal communication can regularly tell individuals precisely how you feel, regardless of whether you have barely said a word. Consider how frequently you have said to somebody,

"Is it true that you are OK? You look a clamped down."

We realize how individuals feel from their non-verbal correspondence.

Characterize or strengthen the connection between individuals.

In the event that you have ever watched a couple sitting talking, you may have seen that they tend to 'reflect' each other's non-verbal communication. They hold their hands in comparable positions, they grin simultaneously, and they go to confront each other all the more completely. These developments fortify their relationship: they expand on their compatibility, and help them to feel more associated.

If you have ever watched a couple sitting talking, you may have seen that they tend to 'mirror' each other's non-verbal correspondence. They hold their hands in practically identical positions, they smile at the same time, and they go to defy each other even more totally. These advancements invigorate their relationship: they develop their similarity, and help them to feel more related.

c) Give criticism to the next individual.

Grins and signals tell someone that you are tuning in and that you agree with what they are expressing. Advancement and hand signs may show that you wish to talk. These unnoticeable signs give information softly anyway obviously.

d) Direct the progression of correspondence

There are various signs that we use to inform individuals that we've completed the method of talking, or that we wish to speak . A determined gesture and firm shutting of the lips demonstrates that we do not have anything more to state, as an example. Visually connecting with the seat of a gathering and gesturing marginally will show that you simply wish to speak.

6.5. Guide to Effective Presentations

If you would like to enhance your presentation capacities promptly, arranging is that the main little bit of making a strong presentation. you would like information before you'll really start to plan your presentation and pick what you'll say. the most points consolidate the target of the presentation, the topic , and therefore the group.

Free of whether the function is formal or easygoing, you ought to reliably hope to offer a wise, all around composed transport. To try to therein capacity, you would like to make your presentation material. You'll either do that in your psyche, or use a technique like mind eager to assist you with recognizing associations and incredible stream.

At the purpose once you come to make your presentation, you ought to know exactly what you've got to state and therefore the solicitation during which you've got to state it. You'll got to use one among the quality presentation structures, as an example , 'What, Why, How?'. You'll similarly feel that its steady to think about the way to describe your story most suitably, and to use stories in first experience with show centers. You similarly got to pick your presentation methodology. Acquaintances range from the formal with the easygoing. Your choice of presentation strategy will depend on various factors, including the group, the setting, the workplaces, and your own tendencies.

Visual aids can add estimation to your presentation, helping with holding your group's thought, and besides go probably as a badge of what you expected to state. Regardless, they have moving cautiously. Perhaps use visual aids if they're imperative to stay up interest and help appreciation. If visual aids aren't used well, they will wreck a presentation.

A particular example of visual aids is that the use of knowledge during a presentation.

There are times while using data during a presentation can genuinely assist you with describing the story better. It is, in any case, critical to not stun your group with bits of data. You furthermore may get to review that various people find numbers hard to fathom.

6.6. Effective Writing

Successful entrepreneurs will design out their organization's procedures and propose complex thoughts continually. In the event that you are bad at business arranging, there is a high possibility you need authoritative aptitudes. In any case, there is more. On the off chance that you don't design in like manner, you are presumably a helpless essayist.

Pause for a moment to consider business arranging, and envision how significant composing abilities are in any business visionary's life. When arranging your business, you are:

Pondering approaches to fund-raise and build up your business – so as to fund-raise for growing your business, you should record a solid business methodology with convincing contentions for your speculators. Being a decent author is a ground-breaking advantage in this circumstance, as individuals will be additionally ready to put resources into your business once they completely comprehend a big motivator for it and how it impacts the market.

Imparting thoughts and offering to partners – Important partners won't meet you from the beginning. You should send them an outline of your organization's exercises first. Subsequent to perusing your organization's arrangements, they choose whether or not they'd prefer to meet you and examine further subtleties. Having helpless composing aptitudes is disadvantageous in this setting too, as less speculators may meet you consequently.

Planning notices and zeroing in on special systems – If you are an entrepreneur, there is a high possibility you can't manage the cost of a promoting examiner now. In the event that that is the situation, planning ads and advancement procedures can be an agony in the bum without great composing abilities.

6.7. Another incredible special system is contributing to a blog.

Customers are bound to get to your blog first, and afterward your site. Consequently, having a capable composing style and legitimate language is an unquestionable requirement in this unique circumstance. Writing for a blog is the most productive technique to building a huge online crowd. Furthermore, a practical business with faithful clients and submitted purchasers will develop quickly. Another extraordinary favorable position of advancing your business through publishing content to a blog is that it makes you a field master. Continually expounding on your items requires steady statistical surveying. Along these lines, you are continually going to be on head of the game on the off chance that you blog. Yet, how might you blog appropriately without great composing abilities? Growing dependable associations with different organizations requires great relational abilities and astounding composing characteristics.

Introducing real reasons with regards to why accomplices should pick you over your rivals can significantly affect your organization's future turn of events. Since there are countless organizations present in the online market, a large portion of the present correspondence is done recorded as a hard copy. Being not able to adequately communicate your arrangements and splendid thoughts may keep your business from developing.

Other than taking a gander at the business part of the condition, make a stride back and take a gander at the different various reasons why composing is so significant. One of the most impressive contentions is that composing is restorative. Envision going through 15 minutes consistently spreading out concerns and relinquishing antagonism.

Showing all that is at the forefront of your thoughts on a bit of paper will expand your efficiency level by delivering the pressure and outrage aggregated for the duration of the day. After you compose, you begin seeing things all the more obviously; you begin interfacing the lines, and you understand things you've scarcely seen previously.

On the off chance that composing isn't your most grounded expertise, it is a fascinating method to expand your assurance and test your cutoff points. The more you compose, the simpler it becomes – however so as to get to that level, you should continually rehearse. Tenacious practice will clean up your mind and get you out of your usual range of familiarity. You'll discover that surrendering is certifiably not a decision.

On head of that, you're talking aptitudes may improve as well! Composing requires association, center, and organization. Building up these characteristics recorded as a hard copy would improve your talking abilities also. What's more, we as whole expertise significant verbal relational abilities are for business visionaries.

References

Business English with Distance Support. (1999). URL : http :// www.tonys.net/support/distance-business.html

Dudley-Evans, Tony and Maggie Jo St. John. (1998). Developments in ESP : A Multi-disciplinary Approach. Cambridge : Cambridge University Press. Pp. 53-73.

Karinik, P, Mehta P P, and Kulkarni P V. (1977).Comprehensive Business Communication. Hyderabad: orient Longman. Pp. 1-3.

Robinson, Pauline C. (1980). ESP (English for Specific Purpose): the present position. Oxford: Pergamon Press. Pp. 6.

Business English Course. (1999). URL: http: // www. Wordcentre. Co.uk/ plain13.htm

Ellis, M., N. O'Driscoll and A. Pilbeam.(1984). Professional English.Oxford : Oxford University Press.

Ellis, M and Christine Johnson. (1994). Teaching Business English. Oxford : Oxford University Press.

Express Course Business English. (1999). URL : http :// www.qmultimedia.com/business/express.htm

Hanks, Patrick and Jim Corbett.(1986). Business Listening tasks.Cambridge : Cambridge University Press.

Hutchinson, Tom and Alan Waters.(1985). ESP at the Crossroads. In John Swales Episodes in ESP. Oxford :Pergamon Press.

Karinik, P, Mehta P P, and Kulkarni P V. (1977).Comprehensive Business Communication. Hyderabad: orient Longman. Pp. 1-3.

Kruse, B. and B. Kruse. (1986). English for Business: Marketing. New York: McGraw Hill.

Kumar, K.J. (1982). Business Communication : A Modern Approach. Bombay :Jaico Publishers.

Lesikar, R. (1979). Basic Business Communication. Homewood, Illinois : Richard D. Irvin, Inc

CHAPTER SEVEN

Growth and Performance of MSME Segment: A study on Odisha's Perspective

Dr. Girija Nandini, Dr.Pramod Kumar Patjoshi

Centurion University of Technology & Management, Odisha

7.1 Introduction:

Micro, Small, and Medium Enterprises (MSME) segment plays an important role in the economic growth of the country. MSMEs are apparent as extremely vibrant for sustained economic development and job creation. They provide to economic growth as well as decreasing poverty by creating jobs, invention, maximising the production capacity in addition to better communal parity. Over the past few decades, the MSME segment has developed as an extremely self-motivated segment in the Indian economy. The MSME segment not only plays a vital part in facilitating huge job creation at reasonably lesser capital cost besides assistance in the development of industries in rural as well as backward regions. The MSME segment is balancing to big scale manufacturing units as subsidiary units also provide tremendously in the area of socio-economic growth of the nation.

MSME Segment consists of thirty-six million units and has provided employability of around eighty million persons in India. The MSME Segment with more than six thousand products provided around eight percent to GDP also forty-five percent to the total manufacturing industry production in addition to the growth of forty percent in exports. The MSME segment has the potential to boost the manufacturing unit's development around the nation then provides a vital supporting role as guide for comprehensive development.

On "9th May 2007", following towards a modification in the "Government of India (Allocation of Business) Rules, 1961", former "Ministry of Small Scale Industries" then the "Ministry of Agro and Rural Industries" had combined and come together to create the "Ministry of Micro, Small and Medium Enterprises (M/o MSME)". This Ministry is currently formulating strategies as well as encourages enables packages, schemes as well as arrangements in addition to televisions their application with an intention to supporting the MSME segment besides assistance them to grow in production capacity. The main accountability of up-gradation, as well as growth of the MSME segment, is the responsibility of the "State Governments". Nevertheless, the "Government of India" complements the contribution of the "State Governments" by means of numerous initiations. Therefore the MSME segment plays an important part and their administration is to contribute the States by its hard work to inspire entrepreneurship, job creation, and livelihood prospects as well as improve the attractiveness of the MSME segment in the transformed economic situation (Msme at a Glance, 2016).

As per "Odisha MSME Development Policy, 2016", "Odisha located in the eastern region of India, has a traditional past, a vibrant present then an enormous possibility for MSME segment. Odisha is correspondingly a treasure trove for natural resources. Odisha is finely associated through superficial transport, air as well as water. Odisha has a widespread rail in addition to the road system connecting numerous development epicenters. The State admittance to wide-reaching markets, existence of accomplished human resources, superior logistics, and well infrastructure in addition to an optimistic commercial atmosphere creates Odisha a preferred station designed for the corporate sector. Odisha's Gross State Domestic Production (GSDP) has improved at a Compound Annual Growth Rate (CAGR) of 10.23% from Rs.281450 crore to Rs.330200 crore between 2011-12 and 2015-16. Cumulative FDI inflows in Odisha from April 2010 to March 2016 stood at Rs.1027 crore. State Government has proclaimed strategies to smooth development in the manufacturing segment by means of year on year growth of 15% till 2020. Rendering to the Ministry of Commerce and Industry, total exports from Odisha in 2015-16 were valued at Rs.19746 crore. The value of exports from the state improved at a CAGR of 2.5% between 2006-07 and 2014-15. Odisha ranks high in the country in terms of the total value of mineral output. Throughout 2015-16, the total production of minerals in the state noted down at 239.45 million tonnes. The mineral resources of Odisha establish an arduous share in national deposits of Chromite 98%, Nickel 93%, Graphite 71%, Pyrophyllite 65%, Manganese 67%,

Bauxite 59%, China Clay 31%, Fire Clay 25%, Dolomite 18%. Odisha is the fourth biggest producer of Coal as well as the fifth biggest producer of Iron ore in India".

As per "Odisha MSME Development Policy, 2015, Draft for Discussion", "Odisha has large reserves of 45,000 MT power grade coal deposits in Mahanadi Coal Field and Talcher Coal Field area. Odisha is the home to some of the leading public sector enterprises like HAL, and private companies like Tata Steel, Vedanta Aluminum, Aditya Birla, Jindal Steel, etc. Odisha receives unprecedented investments in steel, aluminum, power, refineries, and port. This opportunity a perfect platform and presents a huge opportunity for downstream and ancillary industries and for the MSME sector."

As per "Odisha MSME Development Policy, 2015, Draft for Discussion", "The MSME sector in Odisha has made a substantial contribution to the economic development in general and generation of employment and contribution to the exports in particular and has positioned itself only next to the agricultural sector in the State in terms of employment generation. MSME in Odisha has witnessed an increasing trend in respect of the number of MSME units set up, the quantum of investment made, and employment generation over a period of time".

As per "Odisha MSME Development Policy, 2016", "The State has notified Industrial Policy Resolution, 2015, which lays down policy framework and fiscal incentives for industries including MSMEs. However, the MSME sector suffers from intrinsic disadvantages in availing priority in infrastructure, credit linkages, and marketing and needs extra support especially in industrially backward districts. With a view to providing a conducive eco-system for promoting the growth of MSMEs in a focussed manner commensurate with the present scenario and anticipated future, the State is declaring."

It is identified from the review of literature that the MSME segment is finding numerous issues and difficulties. Then also different researchers observed that MSME segment is finding numerous issues and difficulties in connected to MSME segment used to face difficulties in the area of bank credit conveniences, accessibility of appropriate equipment and technology, difficulties in the marketing of their products, obtainability of incomplete possessions, unavailability of proper human resources, etc.. Apart from the above, the MSME segment is also finding great difficulties due to changing external environment erection. Das, (2008) revealed in his study that numerous difficulties are facing by the SME sector that are connected to funding availability, technology enhancement, insufficient infrastructure facilities, improper transportation conveniences, etc. While Fridah Muriungi Mwobobia (2012) expressed that the SME segment facing lots of issue and difficulties in Kenya in the part to financing and availability of funds, various tasks occupied by women, improper impartiality, absence of education, struggle, absence of a proper plan, absence of managerial skill, etc. And also Mukund Chandra Mehta (2013) indicates that the main problems faced by means of the availability of funding, lower on producing product unavailability of proper human resources, lack of infrastructure facilities, improper of manufacturing estate conveniences etc. Correspondingly Ishu Garg and Suraj Walia (2012) had also found in their research and highlighted that the "Small Scale Industries (SSI)" segment finds several difficulties connected towards the procurement of finance, recognizing upgrade technologies as well as skills, industrial exercise, excellence control etc. SSI segment is finding regular difficulties from large as well as medium subsidiaries in facets of producing product capacity besides marketing strategies of the products. Similarly, Garg (2014) exposed the various opportunities, issues as well as difficulties found by the MSME segment in India. His research revealed that numerous difficulties in outside factors, which are faced by the MSME segment, are mostly in funding their infrastructure and working capital besides subsidies granted by Government. Subsequently, after globalization, getting bank financing and credit facilities, upgradation in technological advancement, proper skill improvement, national industrial inexpensive databases, export elevation in addition to the growing infrastructure facilities, etc. Similarly, Sangita Patil and Chaudhari (2014) in their research found that the development of the MSME segment has improved over the year by means of an increase in the number of MSME establishments. They recognized small scale segment found various problems mostly in skilled human resources, unavailability of bank finance and support, well-developed marketing, insufficient infrastructural facilities, competitiveness, improper planning, management expert, transportation amenities, unavailability of power, unavailability of godown conveniences, unavailability of information as well as data, etc. Whereas Aruna (2015) revealed that the MSME segment is mostly finding difficulties in connecting to bank credit availability, obtainability of appropriate technology, difficulties in the selling of their products, improper skilled human resources, etc. The researcher recognized that bank finance as well as fund availability restrictions besides challenges connecting to power as well as unavailability of proper human resources, lack of proper raw material, etc. However, Mathai (2015) depicted the various difficulties found in the SME segment in India are mainly difficulties connected to unavailability of bank financing accommodations, infrastructure accommodations, lack of raw materials, unavailability of proper technology, unavailability of training, unavailability of skilled labour, and potential human resources, unavailability of rules relating to labour, competitiveness from large businesses, etc. Whereas Tripathi (2016) et.al designates main six difficulties as well as articulated obtainability of relaxed bank credit in addition to funding tools, complex monitoring strategies for establishing a commercial organisation, lack of upgrade as well as reasonable technology, unavailability of infrastructural conveniences, nonappearance of high-class marketing stands plus delivery channels, uncompromising labour laws then lack reasonably accomplished manpower.

Odisha is a state of dreamland for natural resources. Despite being rich in resources; it is still one of the backward States and has huge potential for further industrialization, especially for the MSME segment. The ratio of gross capital outlay to GSDP has not been encouraging over the years. Odisha has observed that the credit which flows to the MSME segment is quite unproductive due to the lack of credit immersion capacity of this sector. MSME segment is facing many challenges in related to different areas of production and operation process, marketing of their products, an arrangement of funds, shortages of skilled manpower, and many other outside challenges. In other words, the MSME segment is finding difficulties connecting to availability credit from banks and financial institutions, obtainability of appropriate technology, problems in marketing of products, accessibility of resources, the nonexistence of skilled human resources etc. Consequently, this study is related to analyse the growth and performance of MSME in Odisha.

Therefore it can find from the above that the MSME segment in Odisha has made considerable effort to the economic growth in overall further creation of job opportunities in the state as well. This sector also contributes to the exports in precise over and above this segment also placed it merely following to the agricultural segment in Odisha in positions of employment creation. The

MSME segment in Odisha has perceived a growing inclination with regard to the amount of MSME units' establishment, significant improvement in investment in addition to job creation during the past few decades. Although the MSME segment has made remarkable contributions, simultaneously it has faced numerous challenges for its development in Odisha. The MSME segment suffers from the shortage of finance as well as the timely arrangement of funds. MSMEs are facing many challenges related to different areas of production and operation process, marketing of their products, an arrangement of funds, shortages of skilled manpower, and many other outside challenges. In other words, the MSME segment used to face difficulties in the area of bank credit conveniences, accessibility of appropriate equipment and technology, difficulties in the marketing of their products, obtainability of incomplete possessions, unavailability of proper human resources, etc. Though, the depiction is less blushing in the eastern part of India. To discourse, the different type of arrangements as well as for the growth of the MSME segment has been started by the central government's as well as state government's agencies. Different central as well as state organizations deliver wide-ranging assistance aimed at the progress of the MSME segment in eastern India. Therefore this research is related towards analysing the development and performance of the MSME segment in Odisha.

The objectives framed for the Study are: to study of growth and performance of the MSME segment in Odisha. And to examine the effect of the growth of the MSME segment, the investment made then employment generation in Odisha.This research is related to convinced shreds of evidence than the secondary information, which has composed from the different bases for a span of five years from 2012-13 to 2016-17. The data collected from the secondary sources comprise "Annual Report of MSME", "Economic Survey of Odisha", "MSME Department, Govt. of Odisha" and "RBI Website" and related articles. The regression analysis has been used for examining the effect of the growth of the MSME segment, the investment made then employment generation in Odisha.

7.2 Opportunities and Potentialities in MSME Segment in Odisha

The openings of development inside the MSME segment is massive by reason of the most important determinants alike are lesser amount Capital Intensive, Widespread reaching Promotion and Support by Government, Arrangement for High-class Production through small scale segment, Funding and Grants, Raw Material Locating, Human Resource Exercise, Cluster agenda meant aimed at growth in technical as well as entrepreneurial skills, Arrangement for fashionable purchase by Government, As a result of export growing, Increasing of demand inside the national market scope.

7.3 Challenges Faced by MSME Segment in Odisha

MSME Segment is finding problems in funding in addition to credit restraints then not getting the obligatory backing from the Government Subdivisions, Corporate sector, Financial Institutions and Banks. MSMEs find a number of difficulties as well as restraints in their track of development. They are as Absence of adequate as well as timely financing/Credit, Inadequate capital besides information, Non-availability of appropriate technology, Lower production, Nonexistence of marketing possibility, Globalization impression, competitiveness through large segments, Unavailability of extremely skilled manpower at a realistic cost, etc.

Even though many competitions by means of growth, the MSME segment has attained tremendously healthy in addition to allow our nation to accomplish an extensive range of industrial development. SSI segment has aided significant assistance to employment creation then correspondingly to rural industrialization. Thus MSME segment has backed to shape on by strengthening our outdated skills in addition to knowledge, through fermentation of technology supports, capital as well as advanced marketing strategies.

7.4 Odisha's MSME Development Policy – 2016

The major remarks of the Odisha MSME Development Policy – 2016 have elaborated below.

7.4.1 Objectives

The foremost purposes of the policy comprise

- Inspire new industrial volume related to better attractiveness.
- Deliver a favourable ecosystem aimed at promoting besides development of the MSME segment as a prospective segment.
- Deliver openings to indigenous entrepreneurship capacity.
- Make the most of the generation of employability opportunities for the younger generation.
- Enable MSME segment for retrieving national as well as international markets.

- Prepare concentrated efforts for revitalization of sick units.
- Formulate concentrating exertions for maintainable, comprehensive & composed development.

7.4.2 Ease of Doing Business

The major point's in ease of doing business of the policy includes

- The "District Industrial Centres (DIC)" intends to perform by means of a nodal intervention to upgrade of MSME segment inside the region.
- "Single Window Clearance & Online Combined Application Form (CAF)" towards enable time assured permissions for the investment.
- "District Level Single Window Clearance Authority" should evaluate and endorse the prerequisite of land.
- The "DICs" be about to strengthen as well as revitalize to remove the current blockages as well as simplify evenly make operation towards the requirements of the entrepreneurs.
- An online payment of incentives apparatus intends to be enforced in addition to the appropriate incentives mean to be granted within a time frame
- Online stage should likewise be introduced for the entrepreneurs to lodge complaints. and proper steps should be taken on the complaints
-

7.4.3 Infrastructure Development
The major points in infrastructure development of the policy includes

- MSME segment setup and frame in the Regions. "OSIC" as well as support for the implementation of the setup.
- Provision aimed at "Ancillary as well as Downstream" Initiatives Enable connections among entrepreneurs with big industries.
- Importance land portion for parklands/entrepreneurship.
- "Plant Level Consultative Committee" should frame aimed at great industries as well as "Plant Level Advisory Committee (PLAC) of CPSUs" in addition to "State PSUs".
- "Ancillary & Downstream Enterprise Cell" should frame inside of "Directorate of Industries".

7.4.4 Marketing Assistance
The major point's in marketing assistance of the policy includes

- "MSME e-Bazaar" intends to frame s deliver a stage near entrepreneurship development.
- MSME national fair means to remain prearranged by means of "OSIC".
- Obligatory procurement facilities as of Micro as well as Small entrepreneurs inside the Region.

7.4.5 Export Promotion
The major points in export promotion of the policy includes
- "Directorate of EP & M" to make in addition to inform a product country medium
- Provide support on Raw Material Provision.
- "OSIC/NSIC" towards starting "Raw Material Banks" straight or as "PPP" manner.
- "CPSUs, State PSUs, and large industries" towards source raw material towards "OSIC" through importance at the lowermost probable price.

7.4.6 Technology Upgradation
The major points in technology up-gradation of the policy includes
- Upsurge consciousness about the "Credit Linked Capital Subsidy Scheme (CLCSS)", "Quality Management Standards (QMS) and Quality Technology Tools (QTT)".
- Preferment of "Clusters".
- "Cluster Development Cell" means to frame in "Directorate of Industries" to meet resources besides merge finance aimed at cluster expansion
- Novel clusters of "Ancillary & Downstream" units intend to promote on main industrial centres
- Provide Financial Inducements

7.5 Progress of MSME Segment in Odisha

The Progress of MSME Segments in Odisha have discussed below

7.5.1 MSME Segment in Odisha from the Year 2012-13 to 2016-17

The table 1 has explained the MSME segment in Odisha from 2012-13 to 2016-17.

Table 7.1: MSME Segment in Odisha from "2012-13 to 2016-17".

Year	Numbers of MSME	MSME Established	Investment (Rs.in Crore)	Employment (persons)
2012-13	123292	5931	432.9	27104

2013-14	130301	7009	669.41	32136
2014-15	160167	29866	2267.24	107011
2015-16	214087	53920	2679.64	166731
2016-17	271870	57783	3034.64	175221
Total	271870	154509	9083.83	508203

Source: Odisha Economic Survey 2017-18

MSME segment displays a collective trend over the years by increasing the number of MSME enterprises established, the investment made over the years as well as the creation of employment opportunities. It can depict from table 1 that the MSME segment in Odisha has accomplished the greatest development by setting up 57783 numbers of units. MSME segment in Odisha has recorded an investment made of Rs.3034.64 crore then created employment opportunities of 1.75 lakh persons in the financial year 2016-17.

7.5.2 Numbers of MSME and their Growth Rate in Odisha from 2012-13 to 2016-17
The table 2 displays the numbers of MSME and their growth rate in Odisha from 2012-13 to 2016-17.

Table 7.2: Numbers of MSME and their Growth Rate in Odisha from 2012-13 to 2016-17

Year	Numbers of MSME	Growth Rate in Number of MSME
2012-13	123292	
2013-14	130301	5.68%
2014-15	160167	22.92%
2015-16	214087	33.66%
2016-17	271870	26.99%

Source: Odisha Economic Survey 2017-18

Graph 7.1: Numbers of MSME and their Growth Rate \ in Odisha from 2012-13 to 2016-17

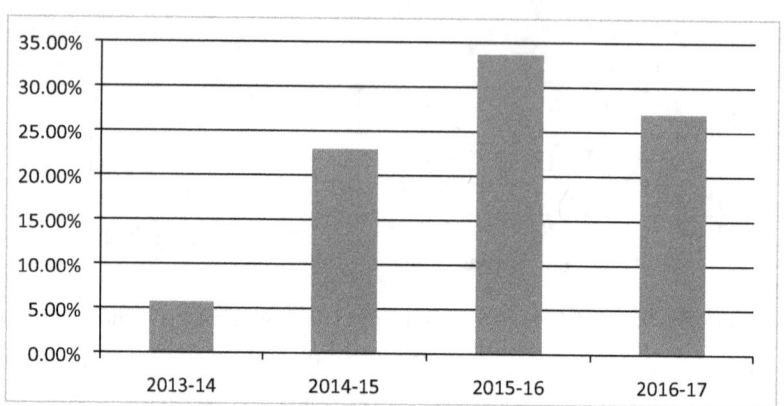

This one is clear from the above table that the numbers of MSME have gone up cumulatively from 123292 units to 271870 units over a span of 5 years from "2012-13 to 2016-17".

It can observe from the above table and graph that the numbers of MSME growth have shown an increasing trend over a span of 4 years from 2012-13 to 2015-16 and have shown a declining trend during the last year of study 2016-17. The numbers of MSME have documented the growth rate of 5.68%, 22.92%, 33.66%, and 26.99% respectively for the four years 2013-14, 2014-15, 2015-16, and 2016-17.

7.5.3 MSME units Established and their Growth Rate in Odisha from 2012-13 to 2016-17
The table 3 shows the MSME units established and their growth rate in Odisha from 2012-13 to 2016-17.

**Table 7.3: MSME units Established and their Growth Rate
in Odisha from 2012-13 to 2016-17**

Year	MSME Established	Growth Rate of MSME Established
2012-13	5931	
2013-14	7009	18.18%
2014-15	29866	326.11%
2015-16	53920	80.54%
2016-17	57783	7.16%

Source: Odisha Economic Survey 2017-18

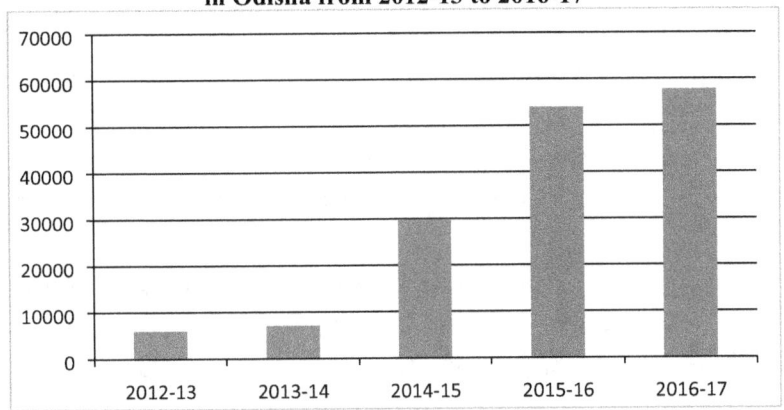

It can clearly find from the above table and graph that the numbers of MSME units established have shown a growing trend for the study period from 2012-13 to 2016-17. The numbers of MSME units established were 5931 units, 7009 units. 29866 units, 53920 units, and 57783 units respectively for the five years 2012-13, 2013-14, 2014-15, 2015-16, and 2016-17. Whereas it has observed from the above table and graph that the numbers of MSME units established a logged growth rate of 18.18%, 326.11%, 80.54%, and 7.16% respectively for the four years 2013-14, 2014-15, 2015-16 and 2016-17.

7.5.4 MSME units Established, Investment Made and Employment Generated in Odisha from 2012-13 to 2016-17

The table 4 appearances the details of established the numbers of MSME units, investment made and employment generated in Odisha from 2012-13 to 2016-17.

Table 7.4: MSME Established, Investment Made and Employment Generated
in Odisha from 2012-13 to 2016-17

Year	MSME Established	Investment (Rs.in Crore)	Employment (persons)
2012-13	5931	432.90	27104
2013-14	7009	669.41	32136
2014-15	29866	2267.24	107011
2015-16	53920	2679.64	166731
2016-17	57783	3034.64	175221

Source: Odisha Economic Survey 2017-18

For the period of five years from 2012-13 to 2016-17, the numbers of MSME units established were 154509 then logged Rs.9083.83 crores of investment by means of creation of employment opportunities of 5.08 lakh persons in Odisha. It also can be observed that at the end of 2016-17, total numbers of 2.72 lakh MSME units were operating in Odisha. In the same time, it has made an investment of Rs.13726.40 crore in addition to creating 11.87 lakh employment opportunities.

It is also clarified from the above table that the number of MSME units established has shown an increasing trend for the study period 2012-13 to 2016-17. The number of MSME units established was 5931 units, 7009 units. 29866 units, 53920 units and 57783 units respectively for the five years 2012-13, 2013-14, 2014-15, 2015-16, and 2016-17. Similarly, the investment made has also shown a growing trend from 2012-13 to 2015-16. The investment made was 432.90 crores, 669.41 crores. 2267.24 crores, 2679.64 crores, and 3034.64 crores respectively for the five years 2012-13, 2013-14, 2014-15, 2015-16, and 2016-17. As a result of the above, this one also can clarify from the above table that the numbers of employment generated in persons have shown a mounting trend for the study period 2012-13 to 2015-16. The numbers of employment generated in persons were 27104, 32136. 107011, 166731, and 175221 respectively for the five years 2012-13, 2013-14, 2014-15, 2015-16 and 2016-17.

7.5.5 Regression Analysis for Investment as Dependent Variable and MSME units Established as Predictors

The table 5 displays regression analysis for investment as dependent variable and MSME units established as predictors.

Table 7.5: Regression Analysis for Investment as Dependent Variable andMSME units Established as Predictors

Particulars	Coefficients	t Stat	P-value
Intercept	376.3632	1.4477	0.2435
SSI/MSME units Established	0.0466	6.8144	0.0065

Table-7.5 reflects the regression analysis among for investment as dependent variable and numbers of MSME units established as independent variables. The above table stated that MSME units established has a positive coefficient of 0.0466 and is a statistically significant association among investment made and numbers of MSME units established with a p-value of 0.0065 (Sig. < 0.01). 0.01).

7.5.6 Regression Analysis for Employment as Dependent Variable and MSME units established as Predictors

The table 6 shows regression Analysis for employment as dependent variable and MSME units established as predictors.

Table 7.6: Regression Analysis for Employment as dependent variable andMSME units Established as Predictors

Particulars	Coefficients	t Stat	P-value
Intercept	13368.8961	3.1435	0.0515
SSI/MSME units Established	2.8565	25.5280	0.0001

Table-7.6 reproduces the regression analysis between for employment created as dependent variable and numbers of MSME units established as independent variables. The above table specified that MSME units established have a positive coefficient of 2.8565 and is a statistically significant association among employment created and numbers of MSME units established with a p-value of 0.0001 (Sig. < 0.01). 0.01).

7.5.7 MSME units established, investment and employment created in Odisha of different Segments at the ended of 2016-17

The table 7 displays the MSME units established, investment and employment created in Odisha of different Segments at the ended of 2016-17.

Table 7.7: MSME units established, investment and employment created in Odisha of different Segments at the end of 2016-17

Category	MSME Established	Category	Investment (Rs. in crore)	Category	Employment (persons)
Livestock & Leather	619	Livestock & Leather	14.58	Livestock & Leather	3060
Electrical & Electronics	1945	Electrical & Electronics	109.94	Electrical & Electronics	9917
Rubber & Plastics	2066	Paper & Paper Products	177.18	Rubber & Plastics	12558
Chemical & Allied	3854	Forest and Wood based	200.48	Paper & Paper Products	19962

Paper & Paper Products	3940	Rubber & Plastics	285.99	Chemical & Allied	26980
Glass & Ceramics	10326	Chemical & Allied	317.00	Forest & Wood based	61748
Forest & Wood based	13124	Textiles	351.84	Misc. Manufacturing	69544
Textiles	15109	Glass & Ceramics	752.48	Textiles	73247
Misc. Manufacturing	16450	Misc. Manufacturing	753.87	Engineering &Metal Based	111972
Engineering & Metal Based	16603	Engineering & Metal Based	1219.68	Glass & Ceramics	148312
Food & Allied	35246	Food & Allied	2018.45	Food &Allied	179115
Repairing & Services	152588	Repairing & Services	7524.91	Repairing &Services	471026

Source: Odisha Economic Survey 2017-18

It can observe from the above table that Repairing & Services segment has contributed maximum numbers of MSME whereas the Livestock & Leather segment has contributed lesser numbers of MSME as compare to other segments. It can be observed that the top three better performer categories which have established maximum numbers of MSME are Engineering & Metal Based (16603), Food & Allied (35246), and Repairing & Services (152588). On the contrary, the bottom three categories that have established minimum numbers of MSME are Livestock & Leather (619), Electrical & Electronics (1945), and Rubber & Plastics (2066).

Similarly, in the case of investment made in different categories, it can see from the above table that investment made is higher in Repairing & Services segment but the investment made is lower in the Livestock & Leather segment as compared to other segments. It can be witnessed that the top three categories where maximum investment made are Engineering & Metal Based (1219.68 corers), Food & Allied (2018.45 corers), and Repairing & Services (7524.91 corers). On other hand, the bottom three categories where minimum investment made are Livestock & Leather (14.58 corers), Electrical & Electronics (109.94 corers), and Paper & Paper Products (177.18 corers).

As a result of the above, it can find from the above table that Repairing & Services segment has generated maximum numbers of employments whereas the Livestock & Leather segment has generated lesser numbers of employments as compare to other segments. It can be observed that the top three better employment generation categories which have generated maximum numbers of employments are Glass & Ceramics (148312), Food & Allied (179115), and Repairing & Services (471026). On the contrary, the bottom three categories that have generated minimum numbers of employments are Livestock & Leather (3060), Electrical & Electronics (9917) and Rubber & Plastics (12558).

7.6 Conclusion:
This study displays that there is constant progress in the area of the number of MSME units established. The development section of these segments improves employment opportunities in addition to the investment of Odisha also for India. By way of the primary objective of this study is to analyse the growth and performance of the MSME segment in Odisha. It is found that the MSME segment displays a collective trend over the years by increasing the number of MSME enterprises established, the investment made over the years as well as the creation of employment opportunities. From the regression analysis, it is established that MSME units established has a positive coefficient and is a statistically significant association among investment made as well as employment created. It has observed from the different Segments that the top better performer categories are Engineering & Metal Based, Food & Allied, Repairing & Services and Glass & Ceramics in establishing of MSME, investment and creating employment. On the contrary, the bottom three segments in establishing of MSME, investment and creating employment are Livestock & Leather, Electrical & Electronics and Rubber & Plastics and Paper & Paper Products.

References:
1. Annual Report, Government of India, Ministry of Micro, Small and Medium Enterprises, www.msme.gov.in; 2017-18
2. Das, K. (2008), _SMEs in India: Issues and Possibilities in Times of Globalisation', in Lim, H. (ed.), SME in Asia and Globalization, ERIA Research Project Report 2007-5, pp.69-97.
3. Financing for MSMEs The eastside story- CII Report, 2013, https://www.pwc.in/assets/pdfs/publications/2013/msme.pdf
4. Fridah Muriungi Mwobobia (2012) —The Challenges Facing Small-Scale Women Entrepreneurs: A Case of Kenyal, International journal of business administration, Vol 3, issue 2, PP 112-121.
5. Gisha.P.Mathai (2015) —Challenges and Issues in Micro, Small and Medium Enterprises (MSMEs) in India: A Current Scenario of Economic Growthl, Vol 4, Issue 7, PP 162-163 in Malaysial, Asia pacific business review, vol.12, no.4, PP 465-485.
6. https://investodisha.gov.in/odisha-MSME-policy/
7. Ishu Garg & Suraj Walia (2012) —Micro, Small & Medium Enterprises (Msmes) in Post Reform India: Status & Performancel, Vol 1, No 3, PP 134-141.

8. Mishu Tripathi, Mr. Saurabh Tripathi, Mr. RikinDedhia (2016) —Challenges faced by Micro, Small and Medium Enterprise (Msme) Sector In India‖, International Journal of Science technology and management, Vol 5, Issue 3, PP 69-77
9. MSME AT A GLANCE 2016, http://msme.gov.in/sites/default/files /MSME_at_a_GLANCE_2016_Final.pdf
10. Mukund Chandra Mehta (2013) —Challenges and Opportunities in Micro, Small and Medium Enterprises in India‖, 2nd International Conference on Management, Humanity and Economics (ICMHE'2013) May 6-7, 2013 Kuala Lumpur (Malaysia), PP 134-136
11. N. Aruna (2015) —Problems Faced By Micro, Small and Medium Enterprises – A Special Reference to Small Entrepreneurs in Visakhapatnam‖, IOSR Journal of business and management, Vol 14, issue 4, PP 43-49
12. Neeru Garg (2014) —Micro, Small and Medium Enterprises in India: Current Scenario and Challenges‖, Paripex - Indian Journal of Research, Vol 3, Issue 9, PP 11-13.
13. Odisha Economic Planning and Convergence Department, Survey, Directorate of Economics and Statistics, Government of Odisha, March 2018
14. Odisha MSME Development Policy – 2016, http://www.msmeodisha.gov.in/PDF/FINALbyDI(O)-Odisha_MSME_Dev._Policy.pdf
15. Odisha MSME Development Policy 2015 – Draft for Discussion, http://www.osicltd.in/Content/images/PDF/Draft%20-%20Odisha%20MSME%20Dev%20Policy%202015.pdf
16. Odisha MSME Development Policy, Micro, Small & Medium Enterprises Department Government of Odisha, 2016
17. Sangita G.Patil & P.T.Chaudhari (2014) —Problems of Small Scale Industries in India‖, International Journal of Engineering and Management Research, vol 4, Issue 2, PP 19-21

CHAPTER EIGHT

Sustainable Development of Social Enterprises

Dr Susanta Kumar Patnaik

Centurion University of Technology and Management,Odisha

8.1. Introduction:

Social enterprises facilitate business to improve the life of a community. They make a difference amongother private enterprisesasmost of their business activities are undertaken with an aim of achieving community benefit, not private profit. In the present time, where many people run after the glittery and luxurious world of corporates, one can witness a conflicting world with a right vision to work for the wellness and betterment of the society. This task can be accommodated through various ways, but the sole purpose always remains the same i.eput an impact on lives of people either directly or indirectly.Social enterprise activities in India are developing fast and in a fruitful way. India has got ample scopes where the social enterprise community can get into discussion, form network and engage closely with other stakeholders. This permitsbig and reputed organisations to share update information, opportunities, and challenges across different sectors and locations. This chapter briefly states the socio-political-economic scenario in India, to give an overview of the environment where social enterprises operate. It mainlyfocusespresent research on social enterprise in the country, and then details existing organisations which support social enterprise to grow in a wider range.

Social enterprises are revenue-generating businesses with a twist. Whether operated by a non-profit organization or by a for-profit company, a social enterprise has two goals: to achieve social, cultural, community economic and/or environmental outcomes; and, to earn revenue. In India, the central and state governments have not given legal identity to social enterprises. What has been achieved until date is the provision of registering companies under Section 8 (previously, Section 25) of the Companies Act, 1956. Section 8 companies can promote 'commerce, art, science, religion, charity or any other useful object', under the condition that all income and profit, if made, is re-invested for the objectives of the company, and not to be paid as dividend to board members. This does not explicitly talk about social enterprise as a legal identity for the Indian context. This situation, coupled with multiple stakeholder approach towards the meaning of the phenomenon in the Indian context, as discussed earlier, stimulated the authors to explore the meaning of social entrepreneurship in the Indian context, so that the suggested framework can come to aid for social entrepreneurship researchers, academicians, practitioners, and policymakers.

8.2. Present status of Social enterprises

On the surface, many social enterprises look, feel, and even operate like traditional businesses. But looking more deeply, one discovers the defining characteristics of the social enterprise: mission is at the centre of business, with income generation playing an important supporting role *(from The Centre for Community Enterprise).*

India is ranked the seventh-largest country in the world in terms of land mass and has 17.5% of the world's population, making it the second most populous country after China. It is also the youngest country within the world in terms of demography with approximately two-thirds of the population aged below 35.

If we look back the previous decade, India has seena very significant growth in its social enterprise events and activities. Many innovative ideas and business plans has improved in a large numberdue toincreasing awareness drives, support, and quality training and workshops that are available for social entrepreneurs as well as social enterprise leaders.

It is seen that the social enterprise network has grown in a huge number with support organisations catering direct, indirect, advisory and financial assistance to all social enterprises which is not less a noteworthy achievement.

Traditional business ideas can also come from identifying a social need but the difference between a social enterprise and a traditional business is the motivation of the entrepreneur. The primary motivation for a traditional entrepreneur is more-often-than-not a desire to make money whereas a social entrepreneur is driven fist and foremost by a passion to solve a social problem. Setting up as a business or using market principles (i.e. selling products or services) is used as a mechanism to solve the social or environmental problems they seek to impact.

Thoughan improving ecosystem and esteemed potential of the world , the literature on social enterprises in India is still lagging .Thegrowing number of social enterprises in India, their contribution to India's GDP and workforce, and hence the features of social enterprise leaders aren't in the least clear. Moreover, a universal understanding of the prevailinggovt policies and regulations that need to support the social enterprise sector in India is deficient.

Successful social enterprises increase the financial health of a community by providing community members with sustainable sources of income. As the enterprise grows and its workforce increases, the overall financial health of the community increases.A social enterprise that employs locally provides its employees with benefits beyond sustainable incomes. Many also offer stable schedules, employee benefits, and interest-free loans that employees can use to launch their own enterprises. Creating new enterprises locally allows the community to boost employment and economic power because they decrease their reliance on powerful international corporations and traditional intermediaries that provide basic services such as utilities, healthcare, and food.

8.3. Different Social enterprises and its contribution to India

There are few organisations which came to limelight by providing their service to social enterprises and start-ups. *Villgro,DasraIntellecap, Germany's GIZ, UnLtd, Shujog, , the Asian Development Bank, British Council, and Okapi* have contributed immensely to the understanding and growth of social enterprise in India. *UnLtd India and Villgro as* Social enterprise incubators provide financial and advisory support to budding social entrepreneurs who are looking to develop and lead their social impact ideas. *Villgro*is further involved in evolving social enterprise ecosystems in Tier-II and Tier-III cities through its 'Unconvention' initiative.

According to Jeremy et al stated that social entrepreneurship as a growing research stream, faces issues that are common to early strategic management and entrepreneurship research such as the lack of construct lawfulness and indeterminate theoretical content. The research on social entrepreneurship is shifting from having a key specialise in public policy concerns to travel on to be a more central topic within the business literature. There is extensive variance within the measurement of social entrepreneurship having measurements range from qualitative assessments like the character of innovation, the fit of opportunity with the community's objectives, and the implementation strategies to the more easily quantifiable targets like the total contribution and the size of donation. The research in non-profit organizations has traditionally been concerned with reducing social ills, providing social goods that the marketplace won't adequately supply, and supplementing government activities through the actions of private citizens. When entrepreneurship and public/non-profit research collaborate, they form social entrepreneurship by including activities that contribute to new social value creation to meet unfulfilled social needs and/or create social values. It also creates an innovative process during which opportunities are exploited through bringing together a singular package of resources within the context of a non-profit or public sector organization.

There are number of events and competitions organised by reputed companies that successfully promote innovation as well as social entrepreneurship in India. Events like *Tata Social Enterprise Challenge, NASSCOM's 10,000 Start-Ups, and Schwab Foundation's Social Entrepreneur of the Year Award, Unconvention by Villgro, the Manthan Award, and therefore the Seed Initiative Award.*

The *'Makerspace' movement,* during which entrepreneurs and other incubators get together to make, explore, learn, and brainstorming, has gained momentum. Some events include *Kerala Startup Mission's Fablab,* and therefore the *Workbench Project* in Bengaluru.

8.4. Social Entrepreneurship and its function

Social entrepreneurship has emerged over the past several decades as a way to identify and bring about potentially transformative societal change. A hybrid of government intervention and pure business entrepreneurship, social ventures can address problems that are too narrow in scope to spark legislative activism or to attract private capital.

To succeed, these ventures must adhere to both social goals and stiff financial constraints. Typically, the aim is to benefit a specific group of people, permanently transforming their lives by altering a prevailing socioeconomic equilibrium that works to their disadvantage. Sometimes, as with environmental entrepreneurship, the benefit may be extended to a broader group once the project has provided proof of concept. But more often the benefit's target is an economically disadvantaged or marginalized segment of society that doesn't have the means to transform its social or economic prospects without help.

A number of social enterprises in India run within the skills development sector – providing skills training to producers, artisans, and unskilled/semi-skilled labourers. We may note otherimportantfields like *education, agriculture, fisheries, and dairy, financial services, energy and clean technology and healthcare.*

When most of the Business Houses are busy in manufacturing products, there are always some people or group of people who keep themselves behind the scene and work sincerely towards a noble cause. *Mahindra* has taken a powerful step by creating a platform called *Spark the rise* where entrepreneurs across India, who are considered change makers, get to tag themselves to at least one another, exchange, share ideas and compete.

Indian social entrepreneurs rushed into this event with innovative ideas and therefore the best ones that are creating an impression within the country were awarded as winners. Here are the list of these social impact makers and what they are doing.

In order to safeguard the livelihood of girls and therefore the youth community in *Belda, in Narayangarh Block,* West Bengal and **HastashilpiGurukul**gives attention on being a learning and production centre in its locality. This said project incorporates technology, nature and other people and has an aim to tap over *400 villages during this region of West Benga*l . Over a period oftime, it plans to impart training in dyeing and merchandise development, market linkages, skill up gradation and also plans to introduce modern technologies. *Bamboo craft, Mat making, Pottery, Sabaii Grass, Weaving and Blacksmithery* are the areas which *HastashilpiGurukul* targets. This initiative by *HastashilpiGurukul* would help 80 artisans in three crafts each in first year i.e. *total 240 people from this community would be ready to run their household within the primary year.*

There is another organisation named*Mentor Together* looks at providing committed caring and trust worthy volunteers to destitute girls and youth from low-income families. During this programme, volunteer mentors struggle a 1-year commitment to satisfy with their mentee 2-3 times a month and it also provides a feature to correspond with them online also . Mentors and mentees are given an inventory of activities on *English skills, Career, Life skills and Academic planning,* which they utilize to structure their meetings.

This initiative is supported by some big giants that include *IBM, Starbucks and IIM-B*. It boasts of getting matched and mentored over 150 youths within the last three years. *Mentor Together* strives towards a social cause. It helps two sorts of youth between the age bracket of 18 and 21. It extends its helping hand to girls who are orphans, destitute, abused or neglected, from single parent families or below poverty level families. It also helps youth from low income group who don't have any access to the newest technology, information and opportunities

One organisation like *ERC-affordable eye care* facilities focuses on providing inclusive, affordable, accessible and sustainable eye look after all. It provides eye care services and consulting at 50 and therefore the optical retails starting at 99. It also provides cataract surgery for a really nominal rate of 3500. It's to start out off *4-5 satellite centers* providing basic eye care in rural areas. This organization has the plans to increase its supplementary benefit but looks for external funding because the setup involves cost. *ERC* features a primary objective of providing affordable eye care to all or any. It's products that are accessible and affordable to all or any regardless of varied economic backgrounds.

Ummeed Child Development Center may be a nonprofit organization that appears at developing who are at a risk of probable disability. It provides direct assistance in terms of therapy and assessment and reachescommunities which contains economically backward class. *Ummeed* features a strong and determined team that consists of *developmental pediatricians, occupational therapists, physiotherapists, autism therapists, speech therapists, special educators and counselors.* It intends to succeed in bent 100,000 children in danger and their families through building capacities of other NGO's to deal with the problemsThe direct beneficiaries of this project would be children and families from the lower income group of society, living in villages in rural India and therefore the urban slums.

In another example, _mothers2mothers_ trains "mentor mothers" to monitor HIV-positive pregnant women. Such help has been shown to increase the latter's adherence to the demanding treatment regimens required to increase their chances of delivering healthy, HIV-negative babies. As an added benefit, m2m's mentor mothers leverage the international community's enormous investment in antiretroviral drugs and other medicines to combat AIDS.

Snehadeep takes two causes at an equivalent time. It's at *helping the differently abled* along side providing them *computer knowledge*. It provides residential computer training to the dim-sighted by teaching them the *fundamentals of computer Ms Office, internet and independent scanning* of their study materials. *Snehadeep* has taken an excellent initiative by supporting 30 students with hostel facilities and it also supports.

It provides assistance to *1235 special children* at the highschool who differently abled, these students include the physically challenged, mentally, visually and hearing impaired. *Snehadeep* trains these groups of scholars to assist them get suitable jobs.

sms4blood may be a mobile *SMS* based application for Blood seekers & Blood Donors. The appliance was developed keeping in mind the knowledge of commoner and hence it's a simple thanks to access the mobile SMS to seek out donor and blood seekers. We don't need any internet connectivity to use this service. Services are going to be available for all Indian mobile operators' users.Those in need of blood during any emergency can find a donor around their locality by sending an SMS to the given number and get units of blood. It's important to note here that Indian Red Cross Scoiety too has given complete focus on Bood donation camps to be organised in different colleges and univeresities. It'S a volunteer organisation which helps ample number of people in society.

Aravind Eye Care is one of the earliest examples of a social enterprise model at work. This renowned Indian organization is designed to let people pay what they can. Aravind provides cataract surgery and other eye care services to any one who comes for it regardless of their ability to pay. Those who can afford to pay market price, do, and those who can't, don't. Amazingly, the number of patients who chose to pay covers the cost of providing care to the entire client base, allowing for wholistic care for all who need it.

8.5. Tribal entrepreneurship

With a population of over 10 crore, tribal groups or *Adivasis* form an outsized community in

India. Largely confined to forests and villages of central, south, and northeast India, the tribal population has been hooked in to the jungle and its produce for his or her livelihood. *"Tribal groups have always shared a singular relationship with nature and follow sustainable practices of livelihood. With religious practices of worshiping nature and land laws that give collective rights to communities, the tribal way of life is exclusive.*

But turning problems into opportunities, there's *an increase in entrepreneurship across tribal* groups of India. By connecting agriculture and forest produce with markets using technology, creation of self-help groups, empowering women, and creating self-sustainable enterprises, variety of tribal entrepreneurs are changing the face of tribal India. To celebrate these entrepreneurs and build greater dialogue round the problems of tribal India, alongside their methods and approaches, NITI Aayog organised India's first Global Tribal Entrepreneurship Summit in Dantewada, Chhattisgarh, recently. The summit aimed toward addressing poverty, malnutrition, low literacy and poor health using the facility of enterprise and technology.

Celebrating the tribal ways of life and therefore the rise of entrepreneurship in tribal India, we present an inventory of tribal entrepreneurs and enterprises, who are using indigenous ways to create social enterprises in India. The list, by no way is exhaustive, but represents the trends and innovations at large.

A group of over 3,500 women from 127 tribal hamlets in Kandhamal, Sambalpur, Angul Deogarh entered into a proper agreement with Leaf Democracy, a German compan provide one lakh siali leaf plates monthly. The plates, commonly referred to as pattals, ar high demand in European countries, and act as a biodegradable alternate to plastic Styrofoam. These women, who earlier sold minor forest products like siali leaves, sal s mohua flowers and tamarind locally, are today working as a women's self-help group galvanizing many other women to imitate ".

8.6. Top Social enterprises in India with Community service

8.6.1. *ALC India*: empowering 65,000 women by turning them into entrepreneurs The Hyderabad-based organisation has incubated 54 social enterprises across five Indian states, providing livelihood to over 65,000 women. These women belong to tribal groups, *small and marginal farming communities, livestock holders, weavers, internally displaced, and other vulnerable communities.* Through training, *skill development, market connects, and other support mechanisms*, ALC India helps social enterprises become self-sustainable and profitable. From farmer producer companies to exploit cooperatives, most of those enterprises are reaping crores in revenue today.

8.6.2. UnLtd **India** has helped in creating quite 12,000 jobs and has touched the lives of around 1 million individuals through the initiatives they need supported. Their selection criteria includes the power of the entrepreneur to deliver results and therefore the potential social impact of the project. The organisation offers both *financial and non-financial support*, from inception to graduation of the social enterprise.

8.6.3. **Mirakle couriers**

Their back office is run by 20 hard working deaf women with learnt-by-doing knowledge in data entry and manipulation, tracking and scanning, sorting and other branch operations. On the field we have a team 44 talented male deaf courier agents that navigate the complex lanes of Mumbai. They travel on public transport, avoiding traffic and remaining conscious of the environment.Founded by DhruvLakraMirakle Couriers is a unique enterprise that hires only the hearing impaired to help them stand on their feet.

8.7. Social Start Ups: Ray of hope

Ideas in the impact or social space take time to be adopted by their end-users, who are usually the base of the pyramid (BoP) segments. Hence, time to scale is longer than an urban business-to-consumer business and consumers cannot be bought through discounts in this space, Paul Basil, Founder and CEO at Villgro — India's oldest and among the largest incubators for social startups — told Financial Express Online in an interview. "Investors are few in this space in India but they are growing their realization. More foreign investors are looking at India now. But crucially, all look primarily for solid unit economics and gross margins. The parameters to gauge this space is profitability and technology innovation, not paper valuations," Basil said. Social startups in India haven't been able to get the spotlight of investors to attract billions of dollars much like regular technology startups. Moreover, the number of social startups pales in comparison to the number of technology startups. Since past close to 20 years, when social entrepreneurship was still at a nascent stage in India, let alone incubation for it, the ecosystem has evolved with many stakeholders realising the need for social entrepreneurship.

Business models pave a useful path and are effective tools for corporate decision-makers to capture information, analyse situations and make decisions so as to make competitive advantages for enterprises. Nevertheless, with more competition and fewer market capacity, traditional businesses face many challenges. There are numerous opinions about the drivers of business model innovation like the push of technology and market demand, the pressure of competitors and therefore the influence of the inner decision-makers etc. but a sole driver cannot entirely describe the phenomenon. A varying model is that the essential rationale for an industry to stay profitable during a dynamic environment. Business model innovations can outspread and leverage core assets, capabilities and relationships.

In comparison to the normal ones, social entrepreneurships function during a fundamentally different way thanks to the primary mission of a social value. Subsequently, it is a Journey-Model-Innovation. The motives that social entrepreneurships use to pick a replacement business model depend upon the instinctive demands of the society. As the eventual purpose of business model innovation of social entrepreneurship is trying to find the balance between social value and keeping sustainable development. If we only target social value stupidly through the economic capability, it cannot uphold long-term growth. On the contrary, highlighting the economic profit maximization but disregarding social mission is that the traditional logic Boundaries of social entrepreneurship

8.8. Boundaries of Social entrepreneurship

In defining social entrepreneurship, it's also important to determine boundaries and supply samples of activities which will be highly admirable but don't slot in the definition. Failing to spot boundaries would go away the term social entrepreneurship so wide open on be essentially meaningless. There are two primary sorts of socially valuable activity that we believe got to be distinguished from social entrepreneurship. The first sort of social venture is welfare work Provision and therefore the other is Social Activism.

For India's youth to be able to fuel its great demographic dividend, there must be a simultaneous growth in professional skills to enable an efficient and fruitful social enterprise ecosystem. Social enterprises have started equipping children with skills that might sustain them within the workforce: 56% of the social enterprises were creating direct employment by employing disadvantaged groups in their workforce, 62% worked with the target of constructing employment, and 53% were providing skills training to vulnerable groups.

However, skills development must start at an earlier, academic level, with more educational institutions delivering courses to equip young professionals with the management skills necessary to steer social enterprises and thus the technical skills necessary to drive forward its activities.

Female social enterprise leaders face challenges in securing funding: Although social enterprises perform significantly better on gender ratios than the mainstream businesses in India (24% women leaders in social enterprises versus 8.9% in mainstream enterprises) the disparity between male and female leaders remains high. Female entrepreneurs and leaders of social enterprises interviewed for the study identified challenges around gender biases when trying to source funding and investments. They claimed that they are often asked questions around family, maternity leave, and work-life balance as how to guage their performance and capability. Assets and businesses, moreover, are generally inherited by men, which suggests that girls often face constraints with respect to a scarcity of collateral.

Enabling access to finance for proof of concept and reducing regulations to receive foreign capital: 33% of the social enterprises reported that access to investors was low due to limited networks and 21% reported that their limited performance record was a heavy constraint to securing finance, Social enterprises find it difficult to attract funding without having shown an effect on the underside first.

However, social enterprises are usually constrained for resources that enable them to hold out pilot work, thereby trapping them during a vicious circle . A pilot investment fund could be discovered to enable social enterprises to prove their impact and assess whether or not they must receive further funding. Moreover, opening up NGOs to capital investments would further encourage social enterprises operating under the legal structure of an NGO.

8.9. Future Research

Social entrepreneurship has evolved tons during a little or no span of your time and is accompanied in government institutions, organizations and NPOs. This paper has tried to supply a framework to suit a venture into social entrepreneurship which in fact can't be limited but ideally there's a requirement to research on forming a theoretical system. For social entrepreneurship, recognizing the chance is that the basic foundation which starts the entrepreneurial behaviour and further broadens social, cultural, and environmental goals. Non-profits and non-governmental organizations, foundations, and individuals play the role to market, fund, and advise them. A growing number of schools and universities are establishing programs focused on educating and training social entrepreneurs. Future research are often helpful in simplifying the structure of opportunity recognition in social entrepreneurship and implementation of the various theoretical suggestions. There is a requirement to propose precise measurement indicators which may benefit in inquiry. Moreover, other aspects affecting the method of recognition of opportunity need to be researched. Entrepreneurial activities with exclusive social missions have been on the rise in recent decades, leading to the emergence of the term "social entrepreneurship" to identify them. People in transient and emerging economies may find it very natural to create businesses with social missions. There in need to understand Indian social enterprises with in-depth case studies from different regions of the country because, as an expert said rightly, "no two communities or regions are same, which makes the context quite different for various social enterprises". Detailed qualitative research would be needed, involving ethnographic observation of the practices of social enterprises and case specific interviews/focus groups with multiple stakeholders, to identify conceptually strong dimensions of market orientation and social value creation. This research sets that stage. Future research would also need to build a scale for measuring the impact of market orientation activities, social value creation activities, and entrepreneurial qualities, on the scalability and sustainability of social enterprises in India.

REFERENCES

Asian Development Bank (2012) Indian Social Enterprise Landscape Report.

British Council (2014) UK-India University Dialogue on Social Enterprises: Report and Recommendation. London: British Council.

CIA website. The World Factbook. www.cia.gov/library/ publications/resources/the-world-factbook/geos/in.html

Darko, E. et al. (2015) Social Enterprise – Overview of the Policy Framework in India. British Council, Social Enterprise UK, Overseas Development Institute.

GIZ (2014), Compass due North-East: Mapping the Regional Social Enterprise Landscape. Deutsche GesellschaftfürInternationaleZusammenarbeit (GIZ) GmbH.

Government of India (2011a) 12th Five Year Plan. Planning Commission. http:// planningcommission.gov.in/ plans/planrel/12thplan/ welcome.html.

Government of India (2011b) Population Census 2011. http:// censusindia.gov.in/2011-prov-results/indiaatglance.html.

Government of India (2015a) Economic Survey 2014-15, Vol. II. Ministry of Finance. http:// indiabudget.nic.in/es2014-15/ echapter vol2.pdf).

Government of India (2015b) Economic Survey 2014-15, Statistical Appendix. Ministry of Finance. http:// indiabudget.nic. in/es2014 15/estat1.pdf).

Intellecap (2012) On the Path to Sustainability and Scale; A study on India's Social Enterprise Landscape. Hyderabad and Mumbai: Intellecap.

Intellecap (2012a) Pathways to Progress: A sectoral study of Indian social enterprises. Hyderabad and Mumbai: Intellecap.

Intellecap (2012b) Understanding Human Resource Challenges in Indian Social Enterprise Sector. Hyderabad and Mumbai: Intellecap.

Intellecap (2014) Invest. Catalyze. Mainstream: The Indian Impact Investing Story. Hyderabad and Mumbai: Intellecap.

Labour Bureau, Government of India (2015), Labour Bureau Report 2014-15.

Ministry of Finance, Government of India (2016) Economic Survey 2015–16.

MoSPI (2016) Annual Report 2015-16. New Delhi: Government of India, Ministry of Statistics and Programme Implementation. http://mospi.nic.in/Mospi_New/ upload/mospi_annual_ report_2015-1

CHAPTER NINE

Crisis & Innovation in Indian Banking Sector

Kamlesh Chawda

Centurion University of Technology and Management, Odisha

&

Sisir Ranjan Dash

Centurion University of Technology and Management, Odisha

Introduction.

The banking system considered as the financial backbone of a nation. It plays a pivotal role in building a nation. It acts as a facilitator for various kinds of economic activities.

Firstly, it creates a sense of savings attitude among general public. They save their surplus money in the banks. The banks on the other hand acts as a liaison between the investors and the borrowers. In the process it kicks off the income cycle. The valuable savings of public is mobilized to accelerate economic activities in a country.

Secondly, it provides credits to different segments of the society such as students, senior citizens, corporate, farmers, startups etc. Thirdly, it helps in financial inclusion and brings different sections of the society under banking ambit.

Further, it helps in capital formation as the credit is used for infrastructural development. Banks also provides various financial services to business. They encourage the usage of digital currency by means of Debit cards, Internet banking, e-wallets etc.

They finance different durable goods such as motor bikes, refrigerators, Air conditioners etc as a result of which people find it convenient to make a purchasing decision. This ultimately revives production activities which boosts GDP of a nation.

Hence, we can easily come to a conclusion that, banking system plays a major role in the economy of a country.

Accordingly, Indian banking system is no exception. But, in recent times this sector has weathered many storms in the forms of financial irregularities, rising NPAs (Non performing assets), siphoning of funds etc.

Following is a short journey about some of the major banks of India, their crisis and how they successfully implemented the concept of Innovation in Brand management and averted a certain financial death.

1.   The ICICI bank Fiasco:-

It all started in 2016, with a letter by Arvind Gupta, an investor in the bank and VIL (Videocon India Ltd.) group. It highlighted the fact that Chanda Kochhar,the head of ICICI bank, had shown undue favor and forwarded a loan of Rs. 3250 crore rupees to Venugopal Dhoot's VIL. This, according to Mr. Arvind Gupta was a conflict of interest. He alleged that Mrs. Kochhar granted the loan just because her husband, Mr.Deepak Kochhar had good relations with Venugopal dhoot.

The Reserve bank of India took a note of it and conducted an investigation but didn't find any merit in the allegations and sent the matter to the Finance ministry.

In 2018, the matter resurfaced and this time the name of Mrs. Kochhar was in question. ICICI bank's board submitted a report to the SEBI (Securities and exchange board of India) the regulator of stock market in India, and cited no irregularities from the side of the then MD&CEO of ICICI Bank,Mrs. Chanda Kochhar while granting loan to VIL.

Later, the matter was taken over by CBI (Central bureau of investigation) and it ultimately filed an FIR against Mrs. Chanda Kochhar, her husband Mr. Deepak Kochhar and Venugopal Dhoot the head of VIL group.

2.The Yes Bank Debacle:-

Yes bank started banking operations in India in 2003 and right from its inception, the founder Rana kapoor took an aggressive strategy by lending to corporate. That was not a problem in any way but what went wrong was the fact that the bank granted loans to even stressed companies. As a result the outcomes were not very difficult to predict. Though, very soon the company rose to become the fifth largest bank in India but with inherent flaws. The financial accounts of Yes Bank turned out to be stressed assets. There were grave governance issues with the bank as well. The problem was ballooned when SEBI (securities and exchange board of India) started investigations about alleged Insider trading in the bank.

3.The PMC Bank Issue:-

The PMC Bank (Punjab and Maharashtra bank) was the next in line which fell into the traps of rising NPAs (Non-performing assets) and misgovernance.

This bank was founded in 1984 as a cooperative bank. It had its operations mainly in Maharashtra focused around Mumbai .

The problem started when the promoters of HDIL(Housing development & Infrastructure Limited) were shown undue favour and were granted huge sum of loans amounting to Rupees 6500 crores which were nearly 73 percent of the bank's total loans. The problem was fuelled when the management of the bank didn't classify the loan amount as NPA even after the HDIL had repeated non-payment of instalments.

Further, the bank created several fake accounts through which the HDIL drained the hard earned savings of common people. It further went on to publish false financial reports to hide the irregularities of the HDIL loans.

The Economic offences wing of Mumbai police registered a case against the top management of the bank and the promoters of HDIL.

They have been levelled with charges of forgery, cheating and criminal conspiracy.

How Innovation in Brand Management Saved the Day:-

Banks are institutions where common people save their hard earned money with a sense of security that their money is safe. But when some people in the management, due to their vested interests mould the rules to their advantage and put the hard earned money of the depositors in unsafe hands, it erodes the integrity of the bank. As a result, the faith of the common investors over banks dwindles. This ultimately has an adverse effect not only on the particular bank but on the entire banking industry as a whole.

In order to counter this problem, many banks have started promoting innovation in Brand Management to regain the lost confidence over the banking system.

For example, in the case of ICICI bank, soon after the issue of Mrs. Chanda kochhar emerged, the bank replaced her with Sandeep Bakshi as the new MD & CEO. This was done to boost the level of confidence of investors on the bank.

It further roped in superstar SRK (Shahrukh Khan) as the new brand ambassador. According to the principles of Brand Management, People are inspired when they see their favourite celebrities endorsing products.

In a similar event, the PMC management sacked their director Joy Thomas to boost investor confidence.

On the other hand, Yes Bank appointed Ravneet Gill, the former head of Deutsche Bank India, as the new CEO. Further, two most trusted public sector undertakings such as SBI and LIC came forward with a bailout plan to revive the fortunes of this bank.

But the question arises, is this enough to sack the heads of banks in order to regain the lost confidence of the investors? The clear answer is perhaps NO.

As a result, many bankers have started adopting various innovative Brand Management strategies to regain the lost ground.

What is a brand after all? Something which is projected by the marketer in the minds of the consumers so strongly that when somebody talks of a product or a particular service, immediately a brand comes in mind. For an example, when someone thinks of a cold drink, Immediately Coca cola comes in mind.

In the same way, when someone thinks of a reliable bank, no doubt , immediately, SBI (The State bank Of India) comes in mind.

The traditional banks seldom invested in branding , because they had a notion that the banking industry more or less offers similar products and investing in advertisements will least affect the revenue.

But over the period of time, there is a change in the banking environment and the bankers of the day are not letting any stones unturned to earn a larger market share.

Some of the innovation in Brand Management strategies are as follows.

Firstly, banks are bringing in young and dynamic celebrities to attract the young investors. For an example, Axis bank roped in energetic Deepika Padukone, Bank of Baroda had P V Sindhu, ICICI bank roped in Shahrukh Khan and so on.

Secondly, offering new financial services such as cashback offers on the use of debit card payments, savings bank accounts for kids, dedicated services for senior citizens, mobile recharge through phones, paying utility bills, mutual funds etc.

Thirdly, advertising on new platforms such as social media sites like Facebook,Instagram and the conventional internet sites.

Fourthly, Sponsoring events like marathon, cricket matches, reality shows etc.

Further, spreading social awareness about important issues such as online frauds, fake calls for prizes, pandemics such as COVID 19 etc.

The latest one being the Kotak Mahindra bank introducing the dynamic Ranveer singh to promote it's 811 digital savings bank accounts during lockdown. This campaign was a big hit as this bank aggressively utilized the digital platforms like Twitter to promote its product.

Conclusion:-

By this time we have come a long way from the traditional form of banking to the modern era and we can say that the banking industry has got a reincarnation. On the one hand we have the debt ridden banks waiting for someone else like government to come like a crusader and inject fresh liquidity into the ailing banks. On the other hand we have the new generation banks such as the Bandhan bank, IDFC bank, kotak Mahindra bank to name a few, who have broken the glass ceiling and converted the threats into opportunities.

In any case, crisis comes with a set of opportunities. It upon individuals how they take it. For banks such as Kotak Mahindra , it turned the lockdown into an opportunity with its Innovative Brand management strategy by introducing Ranveer singh and crafting the media campaign which suited all sections of the society. For example,in its ad campaign "811 is for everyone", It projected Tibetan spiritual guru, rappers, house wives, rural farmers etc.

From the above it is quite clear that Innovative Brand management strategy is an ever-changing process but with infinite possibilities. There are banks which have perished by the passage of time but a few are shining in the sky of the banking world just because of their practical application of Innovative Brand management strategy.

Someone rightly said " Every dark cloud has a silver lining."

Bibliography

1.   https://commerceatease.com/bank-meaning-importance-and-types/#:~:text=Role%2FImportance%20of%20Banking,the%20development%20of%20a%20nation.&text=It%20acts%20as%20an%20intermediary,money%20for%20various%20business%20activities.

2.   https://blog.ipswitch.com/branding-in-banking-5-reasons-strong-brands-win

3.   https://www.oliverwyman.com/our-expertise/insights/2017/dec/risk-journal-vol-7/emerging-risks/the-public-sector-banking-crisis-in-india.html

4.   https://www.crifhighmark.com/news-events/news/2019/july/indian-bank-crisis-a-major-crisis-may-be-brewing-for-indian-banks-crif-insights

5.   https://www.business-standard.com/about/what-is-pmc-bank-crisis#:~:text=Loans%20given%20to%20financially%20stressed,based%20bank%20for%20six%20months.

6.   https://www.livemint.com/industry/banking/patterns-behind-the-pmc-bank-meltdown-11570449287851.html

7.

        https://www.google.com/search?q=banks+advertisement+in+india&source=lnms&tbm=i

sch&sa=X&ved=2ahUKEwj20aOfmsruAhVPGaYKHT_rDAYQ_AUoAnoECAcQBA&biw=13
66&bih=625#imgrc=EKR2vimn3vyQQM&imgdii=FifIG7VBmmPwHM

8.   https://www.exchange4media.com/marketing-news/how-kotak-mahindra-is-banking-on-its-advertising-to-attract-customers-102025.html

9.   https://www.mediainfoline.com/advertising/811-indiainvited-campaign-champions-banking-ranveer-singh

CHAPTER TEN

Innovative Integrated Marketing Communication Strategies Adopted by Byju's-The Learning App

Kamlesh Chawda

Centurion University of Technology and Management, Odisha

Sisir Ranjan Dash

Centurion University of Technology and Management, Odisha

Introduction: In a rapidly changing world, the technology is changing swiftly. Something which used to be a dream earlier has become a reality today and at the same time which appears difficult today may become a reality tomorrow. This has all become possible because of technology. For example, at one time people believed that only birds can fly and human beings can never fly. But this perception was changed by the invention of airplanes. Similarly many children died at early ages and people thought it as their fate. But the present day vaccines have proved it wrong and the infant mortality rate has declined significantly.

Hence, it is quite evident that technology has that power to transform many things including education. And when we talk about education by using technology, we mostly indicate towards online education. One interesting fact about education in India is that the government of India has not recognized education as an Industry. But several startups have entered in to this segment looking at the size of this market and the economic opportunities hidden in it. Education in India has a wider scope because of the fact that we as a country are the second most populous country in the world and even more importantly we are a green country in terms of demography.

By that I mean, we have a large proportion of young population as compared to the total population. This young mass is ready to go that extra mile to realize their dreams. They are dynamic and never satisfied with the orthodox ways of doing things. Not surprisingly, more and more young students are finding it easier to learn through online platforms. And to tap this ever growing market, many new and innovative entrepreneurs have come up with customized learning packages that suits the requirements of the students. In this article we will try to get an insight into the various innovative integrated marketing communication tools adopted by various online educational platforms and how they have able to realize their organizational goals.

Company Overview:

Founded in 2011 by Byju Raveendran, this company has over the years become one of the most valued EdTech (Education Technology) companies in the world. They have achieved this feat by applying a very fundamental principle of marketing, i.e; understanding the target audience. And for companies like Byju's , the challenge was multiple. That means , in this segment the customers are the students along with their parents. Simply speaking, the students must be captured by innovative ways of learning at the same time the parents must be motivated to go for a purchasing decision. And , Byju's has undoubtedly achieved this twin objective. But let's understand how they have done it.

First upon all, they have developed their marketing strategy in such a way which allows them to interact with the students and the parents simultaneously. Further, they have realized the demands of the students. For an example, students are scared of certain subjects such as maths. Hence, Byju's has hired expert faculties who have innovative ways of making fun with learning. On the other hand the types of subscription charges they have priced are affordable. And after all, parents throughout the world have a common tendency that is, they will be ready to pay anything for the educational improvement of their kids. Byju's has a psychological advantage in this segment.

A closer analysis of the innovative marketing communication tools adopted by Byju's will reveal the following facts.

Student's centric Approach:

For motivating the students Byju's have developed their products in such a lucrative way, that a student perceives it to be the ultimate learning app. The students, particularly , the kids find these videos very attractive. And once the perception has been developed, it's very difficult to change it. For this they have developed Interactive videos which gives them a better feel of the subject, educational games and quizzes, innovative worksheets etc.

Further,to completely capture this segment of kindergarten kids, they have tied up with the Disney. They have developed a product called, Early learning app which provides them original stories of Disney. And kids are naturally fond of animated videos.

There is still lot more to be talked about. On Independence day occasion, Byju's ran an ad campaign with a tag line "The freedom to learn". In it a small girl is narrating her experiences of getting low marks in her class,how her teacher scolds her, how she was pressurized by her parents to read in a traditional way i.e; the black and white books. And to rescue her Byju's providing innovative products. This ad campaign was a big hit as it portrayed a common sentiment of students. Again Byju's played an emotional appeal to parents to give freedom to their kids to live their dreams.

There was another ad campaign titled "Byju's – Every child's best friend". In this, a group of kids are shown talking inside a classroom about their best friend. In this campaign, Byju's has beautifully projected itself as the best friend of the school kids as it does everything a best friend does, like helping in difficult subjects, playing for hours and so on.

In yet another marvelous ad campaign on children's day, Byju's played a master card. The ad campaign showed asking the parents a simple question, i.e; What they want their kids to become when they grow? This ad campaign was so beautifully choreographed that it connected with the parents and the students at the same time.

Parent centric Approach:

On the other hand, persuading the parents to go for a purchasing decision in no less challenging job. The products that Byju's has developed are actually very carefully crafted. The biggest concern about the parents now a days is the over involvement of their kids in smart phones.

It's very natural that the parents can't change this habit, and here Byju's has come up with a solution. They have literally played an emotional card. The parents feel relaxed when they see their kids engaged in constant learning even though they are using the smart phones. They see it as a constructive use of technology. And this feel of relief is enough to encourage the parents to pay that extra amount even though expensive.

In one of the ad campaigns, a father and daughter are shown playing table tennis and daughter asks ,"why are you not worried about my studies anymore?" The father replies, after joining Byju's there no need for parents to take that extra headache of their children's progress. This psychological ad portrayed a message called "Parents se Partner tak ka faasla" which means"With Byju's app, the parents becomes partners". Again a masterstroke by Byju's.

In yet another ad campaign, in a classroom, Shahrukh khan is shown asking some basic questions to a group of parents about the progress of their kids. Questions such as "How many of you feel the progress of study has slowed down this year?"

"How many of you feel that your kids needs more personal attention?"

"How many of you feel you don't find good tuitions in your areas?"

And the ad ends up with a tag line "Toh ab school ke baad sirf Byju's classes" which means "So from now only Byju's classes after school"

Branding Strategy:

The most important factor of success of Byju's did was by roping in superstar Shahrukh Khan as the brand ambassador. This was one of the brilliant moves by Byju's. Because in Indian market conditions, in order to convince some prospective customer, you need to have a big name behind your company. And SRK (Shahrukh Khan) itself is a brand.

Further, to strengthen the customer base and improve the visibility, Byju's started sponsoring many significant events. Firstly it became the chief sponsor of the Indian cricket team. It meant a lot when the logo of Byju's was placed at the front side of the jersey of Indian cricket team. This particular move gave Byu's that extra popularity.Further, it beame the title sponsor of India's biggest cricket cum entertainment event, i.e; The IPL(Indian premiere league).

Conclusion:

In a digital world, when we are increasingly dependent on technology, it becomes very important that we use it in a productive way. Here comes a few startups who, through their deep understanding of their potential markets blended with cunning marketing strategies are able to become market leaders. The success story of Byju's is a glaring example of how a small company ultimately turned out into a brand in itself.

And after all, the digital world is open to everyone. But what is required is an understanding about the basics of marketing tools and the right selection and their careful application.

Byju's is a perfect fit into this category. It has put all the practices of marketing communication in right places. It has carefully planned for the needs of the students both through content as well as dynamic presentation. On the other hand it has dual strategies for parents. They first scare the parents about the loopholes of their kids and their long term repercussions and then promoting their products.

For marketing, byju's followed different approaches. They included everything right from sponsoring sports events to emotional advertisements for parents and teachers.

In any case, Byju's has emerged as a market leader and will remain a milestone in the field of online education.

Bibliography

1.   https://www.webfx.com/industries/education/online-education/

2.   https://ieltsonlinetests.com/writing-correction/advantages-and-disadvantages-studying-online-course-corrected-essay

3.   https://en.wikipedia.org/wiki/Byju's

4.   https://grocurv.com/blog/2019/11/24/deconstructing-byjus-marketing-strategy/

5.   https://www.quora.com/How-did-BYJU-grow-so-quickly

6.   https://www.youtube.com/watch?v=tjfzwPNfSGc

7. https://www.youtube.com/watch?v=_W7UP7O7qAA

8. https://www.youtube.com/watch?v=xOEWLeRHq6k

CHAPTER ELEVEN

Innovative way towards Sustainable Business development through Corporate Social Responsibility in India

Brij Lal Mallik,Utkal University, Odisha

Sisir Ranjan Dash,Centurion University of Technology and Management, Odisha

Introduction:

Corporate Social Responsibility initiatives are not only about charity but decoding these ideas into functional business approaches. Corporate Social Responsibility decisive efforts does not only relate to contributing funds but it talks about assimilating social and ethical performs into business strategies that help the consumer in generating a positive brand image. With the upsurge in Corporate Social Responsibility consciousness some companies endorse a very basic sympathetic of corporate governance and ethical standards.

What is CSR?

- **The global context**

There may be no single collectively accepted definition of CSR, every definition that currently are in use underpins the influence that businesses have on society at large and the societal expectations of them. Although the heredity of CSR lie in humanitarian activities (such as donations, charity, relief work, etc.) of corporations, globally, the concept of CSR has evolved and now encompasses all similar concepts such as **triple bottom line, corporate citizenship, philanthropy, strategic philanthropy, shared value, corporate sustainability and business responsibility.**

- The CSR approach is holistic and integrated with the central part of business strategy for addressing social and environmental impacts of businesses.

- CSR needs to address the welfare of all stakeholders and not just the company's shareholders.

- Performing humanitarian activities are only a part of CSR, which otherwise encompas a much larger set of activities entailing strategic business benefits.

The Pyramid of Corporate Social Responsibility model by Carroll, 1991

CSR in India

CSR in India has traditionally been seen as a charitable activity. And in keeping with the Indian practice, it was an activity that was performed but not deliberated. As a result, there is limited record on specific activities related to this concept. However, what was undoubtedly evident that much of this had a national character encapsulated within it, whether it was endowing institutions to actively participating in India's freedom movement, and embedded in the idea of trusteeship.

As some observers have pointed out, the carry out of CSR in India still remains within the philanthropic space, but has moved from institutional building (educational, research and cultural) to community improvement through various projects. Also, with global pressure and with communities becoming more vigorous and demanding, there appears to be a perceptible trend, that while CSR remains largely constrained to community development, it is getting more strategic in nature (that is, getting linked with business) than philanthropic, and a large number of companies are reporting the activities they are commission in this space in their official websites, annual reports, sustainability reports and even publishing CSR reports.

The Companies Act, 2013 has mandated the idea of CSR to the vanguard and through its disclose-or-explain mandate, is promoting greater intelligibility and disclosure. Schedule VII of the Act, which lists out the CSR activities, suggests communities to be the central point. On the other hand, by discussing a company's relationship to its stakeholders and integrating CSR into its core operations, the draft rules suggest that CSR needs to go beyond communities and beyond the concept of philanthropy. It will be interesting to observe the ways in which this will translate into action at the ground level, and how the understanding of CSR is set to undergo a change.

CSR and sustainability:

Sustainability (corporate sustainability) is derived from the concept of sustainable development which is defined by the Brundtland Commission as "development that meets the needs of the present without compromising the ability of future generations to meet their own needs" 4. Corporate sustainability essentially refers to the role that companies can play in meeting the agenda of sustainable development and entails a balanced approach to economic progress, social progress and environmental stewardship.

CSR in India tends to focus on what is done with profits after they are made. On the other hand, sustainability is about factoring the social and environmental impacts of conducting business, that is, how profits are made. Hence, much of the Indian practice of CSR is an important component of sustainability or responsible business, which is a larger idea, a fact that is evident from various sustainability frameworks. An interesting case in point is the NVGs for social, environmental and economic responsibilities of business issued by the Ministry of Corporate Affairs in June 2011. Principle eight relating to inclusive development encompasses most of the aspects covered by the CSR clause of the Companies Act, 2013. However, the remaining eight principles relate to other aspects of the business. The UN Global Compact, a widely used sustainability framework has 10 principles covering social, environmental, human rights and governance issues, and what is described as CSR is implicit rather than explicit in these principles. Globally, the notion of CSR and sustainability seems to be converging, as is evident from the various definitions of CSR put forth by global organizations. The genesis of this convergence can be observed from the preamble to the recently released draft rules relating to the CSR clause within the Companies Act, 2013 which talks about stakeholders and integrating it with the social, environmental and economic objectives, all of which constitute the idea of a triple bottom line approach. It is also acknowledged in the Guidelines on Corporate Social Responsibility and Sustainability for Central Public Sector Enterprises issued by the DPE in April 20135. The new guidelines, which have replaced two existing separate guidelines on CSR and sustainable development, issued in 2010 and 2011 respectively, mentions the following:

"Since corporate social responsibility and sustainability are so closely entwined, it can be said that corporate social responsibility and sustainability is a company's commitment to its stakeholders to conduct business in an economically, socially and environmentally sustainable manner that is transparent and ethical."

Benefits of a robust CSR programme

As the business environment gets increasingly complex and stakeholders become vocal about their expectations, good CSR practices can only bring in greater benefits, some of which are as follows:

Communities provide the licence to operate: Apart from internal drivers such as values and ethos, some of the key stakeholders that influence corporate behaviour include governments (through laws and regulations), investors and customers. In India, a fourth and increasingly important stakeholder is the community, and many companies have started realising that the 'licence to operate' is no longer given by governments alone, but communities that are impacted by a company's business operations. Thus, a robust CSR programme that meets the aspirations of these communities not only provides them with the licence to operate, but also to maintain the licence, thereby precluding the 'trust deficit'.

Attracting and retaining employees: Several human resource studies have linked a company's ability to attract, retain and motivate employees with their CSR commitments. Interventions that encourage and enable employees to participate are shown to increase employee morale and a sense of belonging to the company.

Communities as suppliers: There are certain innovative CSR initiatives emerging, wherein companies have invested in enhancing community livelihood by incorporating them into their supply chain. This has benefitted communities and increased their income levels, while providing these companies with an additional and secure supply chain.

Enhancing corporate reputation: The traditional benefit of generating goodwill, creating a positive image and branding benefits continue to exist for companies that operate effective CSR programmes. This allows companies to position themselves as responsible corporate citizens.

Conclusion

India's development needs are immense. The country is host to some of the world's most striking social problems, often at massive scale. Yet the country is also on a clear path of economic growth that is quickly expanding prosperity to new sections of society. Focusing policymaking efforts on economic growth will ensure this age of prosperity continues, yet, at least initially, its benefits are likely to be most immediately felt by those in the regions of the country that are poised for quick growth.

With India's federal system, central policymaking will also have uneven application across states. Haryana, for instance, enjoys a per capita income level that is four times higher than the state of Bihar. This inequality will likely balance out over time, but will persist in the near term.

The new corporate social responsibility provisions included in the Companies Act will increase the level of CSR giving in India. However, limiting the use of these funds to areas where companies have operations could limit the impact of this spending to the states that already have relatively high levels of development. The Indian government should instead clarify that using CSR funds in areas outside of the companies' operational footprint is acceptable and will not result in discriminatory action.

There is also ambiguity in terms of what the Indian government considers the "areas around which it [a company] operates." Limiting this definition could preclude the widespread use of important new pools of CSR funds to the areas that have the greatest need.

The potential changes to the rules requested in this paper should be considered for immediate action. Companies are already considering how best to comply with the rules, and setting plans in motion that may be difficult to amend shortly after. At the very least, if the Modi administration plans to keep the CSR requirement, the Ministry of Corporate Affairs should conduct a rigorous review of the results of this new requirement to ensure compliance, and also that it contributes evenly to alleviating the health, educational, and other development goals enumerated in the Companies Act. And if the intended results are not met, the Indian government should look at ways to strengthen the Act's provisions and implementation.

The CSR concept has encompassed a wide range of economic, legal, ethical and philanthropic (discretionary) activities of business performance at a given point in time, without any hierarchic order (Carroll, 1979; Carroll, 1991). Carroll (1979) was one of the first researchers who debated and had a big influence on the CSR concept. He claimed that the economic category was the most important within social responsibility, and the other three were ranked in the following decreasing order of importance: legal, ethical and philanthropic. Carroll (1991) developed the most known and a leading paradigm of CSR in the in the management field: The Pyramid of Corporate Social Responsibility (Carroll & Schwartz 2003). To this day, Carroll's paradigm remains the most known within business.

CHAPTER TWELVE

Digital Age Pedagogy for English Language Teachers

Ajit Kumar Pradhan
Associate Professor, Department of English
Centurion University of Technology and Management, Odisha

Amit Kumar Singh
Research Scholar
Centurion University of Technology and Management, Odisha

Introduction

There is a need to use digital technology tools to ensure that the teaching and learning process continues in distance mode when there is a complete closure of educational institutions due to the outbreak of the COVID-19 pandemic. The use of digital tools also is recommended in a face-to-face mode of class, especially language classes. The present paper makes a descriptive study of some of the digital technology tools, which can be handy for the language teachers, especially those of them deal with the English language in higher education. A detailed on each tool has been attempted and some suggestions have been offered how language teachers can use the tools to make their classes more interactive and effective.

The effect of COVID-19

The pandemic COVID-19 has brought the world into a complete halt especially to the educational sphere worldwide. According to a recent survey by The United Nations Educational, Scientific and Cultural Organization (UNESCO), many schools were completely closed for more than 14 weeks since the rise of the pandemic. The duration of the closure of schools varies according to regions which are up to 5 months also. The following figure (Figure 1) from the UNESCO highlights how the details of the closure from different regions of the world.

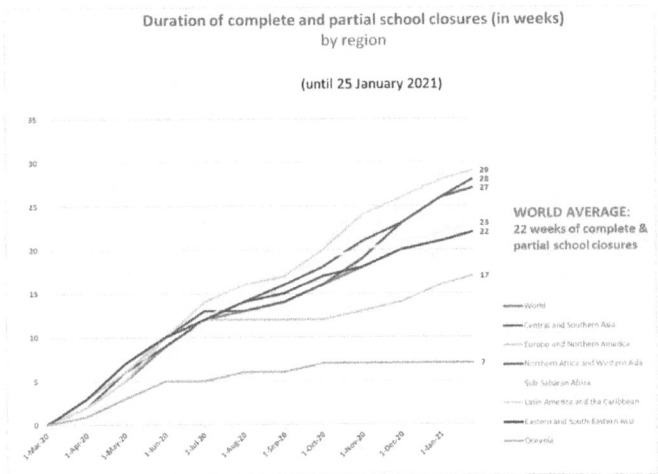

(Figure 1: Duration of school closure due to COVID-19 Source UNESCO Website)

Issues with Language Teachers

Many teachers were not ready to cope with the situation of addressing to the sudden change due to COVID-19. Interacting with the students was suddenly changed to online mode in digital platforms, where there were enormous issues in the part of the teachers to deal with. Unlike the face-to-face mode, where the students were more receptive, at least teachers were able to find out from the faces of their students, in the digital platform it was hardly possible to find out whether students were paying attention to the teachers or not.

Integrating technology in the language classroom: TPACK Model

There have been many studies which highlight the significant positive effect of integrating Information and Communication Technology (ICT) in the language classroom. One of the major reasons for integrating technology in the classroom to ensure learners' motivation level. (Chapelle, 2005). Furthermore, many scholars are of the views that using ICT in language teaching makes learning 'more fun and interactive'. The teaching process with the assistance of technology can be a challenging task if teachers are not familiar with social and contextual issues (Koehler et al., 2011). Teachers need to possess technological skills along with pedagogical and content knowledge. The following model (TPACK) has been adopted for analysis in this paper.

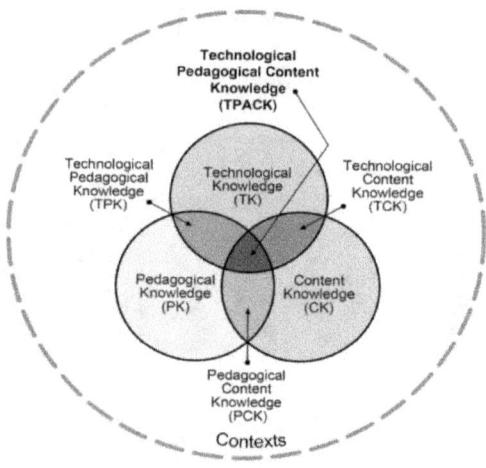

(Figure 2: **TPACK Model Source: http://tpack.org/**)

As it is evident from the Figure 2, the TPACK model, a teacher needs to familiar and upskill in the three areas; technological knowledge (TK), Pedagogical knowledge (PK) and Content knowledge (CK). Technological skills mean the use of ICT in the classroom for effective teaching. The flipped classroom model is another example of using digital tools for learning. Further, content knowledge means knowledge about the subject-matter and pedagogical knowledge how to deliver the subject knowledge by using technological skills.

In this paper, a few tools for the language teachers have been discussed which can be used readily in the language classroom. The software resources are free to use and user-friendly.

Free educational websites

A few software resources which are in open sources and free to use and user-friendly are discussed below. The software resources include padlet.com, Flipgrip.com, Kahoot.com, vocabulary.com, and Visuwords.com

1. Padlet.com

Padlet is an online open-source which can be used for remote teaching. It provides an infinitive digital space where students can share their ideas. The students can upload not only text messages, but also upload files, audios videos, images and many other files. Teachers can create padlet and manage it by sharing the link with the students. There are various formats in the padlet which teachers can directly use. Students can communicate with each other in this platform also and thus learning becoming more interactive and interesting.

A language teacher can ask a probing question in language based on their topic, for example, write a formal letter on a topic. Teachers can also upload a link or video to give students some inputs on the assignment. Students can share their assignments by uploading a file or writing in the space provided. The assignment can be very interesting as each student can find out what others have written and provide their feedback. Teachers, as moderators, can control the interaction. Group and pair work can be assigned in this platform where students in groups can upload their projects or assignments. There are various ways where a language teacher can use padlet to develop language skills i.e., listening, speaking, reading and writing.

2. Flipgrip.com

It is a free platform which can be used for various uses including videos. There is a Flipgrid app which can be loaded in any smartphones or personal computers. The teacher can be a moderator, who can control the class by making the grid either private or public. There are so many options in the grid, videos can be recorded or edited very easily, which can range 30 seconds to five minutes. Flipgrid can be best suitable for speaking assignments, where students can record or upload their videos and obtain feedback. Flipgrid also assists for remote teaching.

3. Kahoot.com

Kahoot is a wonderful platform for teachers for effective remote teaching. It is a free and open platform. One can join through Google or Microsoft account. The platform is user friendly and easy to share it with students. It is a tool where a teacher can use games or materials. A teacher can add music and make the quiz more interesting. Collaborative games or tasks can also be used using the platform in live activity. It is mostly used as a free assessment tool which can be very interesting and interactive. A teacher can also create polls, puzzles or any online games.

4. Vocabulary.com

Vocabulary.com is a free open online tool for enhancing one's vocabulary or crosschecking one's vocabulary skills. The site has many game-based interactive platforms where one can progressively go to the levels which are graded. Morphology and syntax can also be learned using this platform. User can also learn different aspects of vocabulary by using vocabulary lists available on the platform. A teacher can easily create a vocabulary class and invite students to join the class by sending an email or the generated URL. A teacher can give vocabulary assignments in the class and evaluate the assignments. In a nutshell, Vocabulary.com is a handy tool for vocabulary lessons.

5. Visuwords. Com

It is a free tool for vocabulary skills building. This site used mind map techniques which are called spiderweb to ensure that learners learn and memorise the words which they come across in the platform. Students get changes to create a web-based on a word. Effective lessons can be designed to teach prefix or suffix, antonyms or synonyms or any other categories. As the name of the site represents, it provides an opportunity for the students to perceive colourful dictionary, which can be interactive.

Concluding Remarks

The Chapter attempts to discuss a few free web sources to be used in remote teaching and learning process. The websites and tools mentioned in the paper are very limited and not exhaustive. However, there are plenty of sources which can be explored based on individual teachers' needs. There are discussions, whether technology can replace language teachers. There is no doubt that the role of technology is very significant at present. A teacher with adequate TPACK skills has a better future.

References

1. Chapelle, C. (2005). "Computer-assisted language learning," in *Handbook of Research in Second Language Teaching and Learning*, ed. E. Hinkel (Mahwah, NJ: Lawrence Erlbaum Associates), 743–755.

2. Koehler, M. J., Shin, T. S., and Mishra, P. (2011). "How do we measure TPACK? Let me count the ways," in *Educational Technology, Teacher Knowledge, and Classroom Impact: A Research Handbook on Frameworks and Approaches*, eds R. N. Ronau, C. R. Takes, and M. L. Ness (Hershey, PA: IGI Global), 16–31. doi: 10.4018/978-1-60960-750-0.ch002

3. Nunan, D., and Richards, J. C. (2015). *Language Learning Beyond the Classroom*. New York, NY: Routledge.

4. TPACK Retrieved from https://en.unesco.org/news/unesco-figures-show-two-thirds-academic-year-lost-average-worldwide-due-covid-19-school

CHAPTER THIRTEEN

Need of Listening Skills in the Second Language Acquisition Process: An Innovation

Pradeep Kumar Sahoo (PhD)

Centurion University of Technology & Management, Odisha

Introduction

Learners of English from non-western former British colonies are termed as second language (ESL) users irrespective of the fact that it is possible that the learner may not speak the first language usually associated with the mother tongue or ethnic identity. Despite linguistic diversity in Odisha, English has been chosen as the medium of instruction for college students at degree level continuing their studies under all the Government as well as private universities except Sanskrit University present in the state. But, in real classroom practice, it has been observed that Hindi and Odia are being used in the classroom along with English. The teachers themselves, as Tickoo (2004) pointed out, are not well-equipped to teach neither correct English pronunciation nor speaking or reading skills to students. Except for reading and writing skills, no other skills are being practiced. It may be because the teachers might have been brought up in a similar educational system, with little expertise in ELT and phonetics as there is no provision in the state universities to teach phonetics or spoken English in the undergraduate courses. Moreover, there are scopes (like on-line courses) for the teachers engaged for undergraduate courses to master the language skills but there are various reasons why teachers do not subscribe to these courses inducting lack of motivation. The complete teaching-learning system, Tickoo (2004) pointed out, could be at fault due to lack of English proficiency in our students, as they have been taught by teachers those who are not highly proficient in its use. Gokak (1964) points out that "The foundational years for the teaching of English in schools are in the hands of teachers who neither know enough English nor are familiar with the latest and far-reaching developments in the pedagogy of English" (p.65).

Observing the rapid change in the place of English in IndiaScrase (1989) remarked:

"English is recognized as an important global or international language, essential for professional employment and significantly, a key component of the cultural capital of middle-class Indians."

Lax English language proficiency restricts the ESL students in Odisha for their academic and professional growth. It cannot be denied that better English language proficiency has been considered to be an important parameter in the selection process for getting well- paid jobs or better institutions for higher studies. It has been treated as the most significant language in India. So, to compete with the students of other states and countries, the students of Odisha at degree level have to be proficient in English language skills. In this regard, the assessment of their language competence becomes essential. It will help them not only in acquiring the English language but also all other subjects that they go through. To make them well equipped to face the academic and professional career in life the assessment of English language skills and finally, the recommendation for improvement is to be made.

Listening as a Skill

Listening has often played second fiddle to its counterpart, speaking. Speaking a language is not possible without listening to it. So, listening skill may be treated as a component of speaking skill. One's speaking ability is well connected to one's listening ability. If we analyze a day's activity, we find people do more listening activity than speaking. Aural comprehensions outstrip oral production in terms of effort, number of words, time and attention.

"Listening is a bridge to learn a language", as stated by Nation and Jonathen (2009). So, good ability in listening is essential in language learning. Hammer (2007) agrees to this and opines that listening can be helpful for students in running successful communication. Bulley-Allen (1995) and Flowdew (2010) state that listening is a dominant activity in daily communication covering almost 40% of the total communication process.

Listening for comprehending the aural information involves both linguistic and non-linguistic knowledge. Linguistic knowledge deals in the learner's abilities in understanding phonology, semantics and syntax of the language whereas; non-linguistic knowledge discusses the topic and overall context.

Ghaderpanahi (2012) concerns about the barriers like native speaker's pronunciation, pace, intonation etc. create barriers in the effective language listening process. Moreover, background information also affects the comprehension process during listening. Hsueh-Jui (2008) in his study states the significant relationship among students' listening strategy, style, and proficiency levels.

Proficiency Tests

As per Oxford Advanced Learners' Dictionary (2015), A skill is "an ability to do something better". The general ambience or in other words, the environmental stimuli stand responsible for the easy and quick acquisition of any language.

Proficiency tests have been designed to assess the learner's language proficiency. These tests are highly required for academic and other reasons like travel and a short stay in native English-speaking countries. There are many standardized proficiency tests and among them tests like TOEFL, IELTS, SAT are very popular among test-takers. In these tests related to listening skill,the test takers are being evaluated on their ability to synthesize and convey information for the integrated questions. The spontaneity, clarity and coherence in the speaking abilities of the test takers are tested.

Methodology

The mixed-method approach has been followed for the current study. Both qualitative data and quantitative data have been taken through participant observation, literature review, semi-structured interview, questionnaire and a standardized language proficiency test. Random sampling technique has been adopted to achieve accuracy in the result.

The samples for the present study have been carefully chosen among the ESL college students of Odisha using random sampling techniques. For this purpose, students from five different technical and non-technical degree colleges have been taken into account. In total 300 numbers of students, equally from each college, form the sample size for the current study.

Instruments used

A semi-structured questionnaire, standardized language proficiency test with reference to listening skill and an interview protocol were the instruments used to carry out the present research work. A statistical tool like SPSS 21.0 has been used for data interpretation. Before administering the questionnaire and the test for listening skill a pilot study was conducted in order to check the level of difficulty of the test questions designed for the study. It helped to adopt and standardize the test questions. The participants were well informed about the purpose of the test and ethical practices as prescribed by American Psychological Association (1982) was followed which deals with human samples.

Results and Discussion

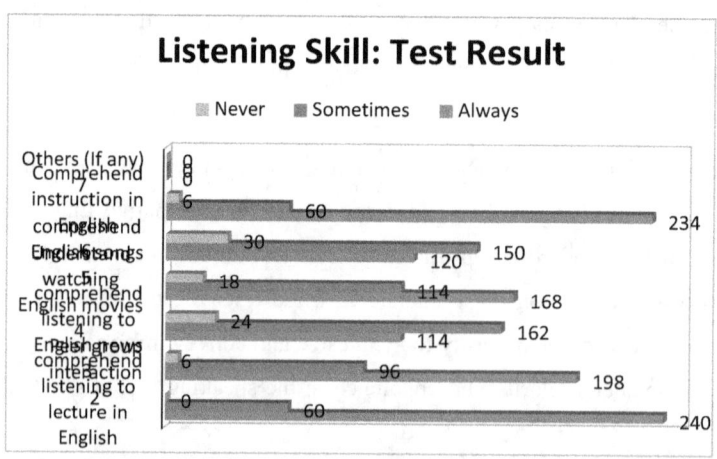

(Figure 1: Listening Skill: Students' perceptions)

The diagram (Diagram No.-1) highlights learners' perceptions about their proficiency in listening skill. There are seven specific statements posed to the students to encapsulate this information. A three-point Likert scale (i.e. always, sometimes and never) is used to find learners' perception on this statement. The first statement is whether learners can comprehend while listening to lectures in English inside the classroom. As per the diagram (Diagram No.-1), it is evident that 240 students out of 300 responded that 'always' theycan comprehend lectures in English inside the classroom. Only 60 students responded that they 'sometimes' comprehend English inside the classroom. However, there are no such responses for 'never'. During peer-group interaction 198 students, as diagram(Diagram No.-1) shows, are able to comprehend in English 'always' and there is a response from 96 students in favour of 'sometimes' and 6 students only responded 'never'. Likewise, data reveal 114 students can comprehend English news 'always';162 students, 'sometimes' and 24 students 'never'. Further, 168 students are 'always' able to comprehend while watching English movies; 114 students, 'sometimes' and 18 students 'never' comprehend English movies. Similarly, diagram (Diagram No.-1) shows that 120 students are 'always' able to comprehend English songs; 150 samples, 'sometimes' and 30 students 'never' understand English songs. In the same manner, 234 students out of 300 are 'always' able to understand instructions in English; 60 students only 'sometimes' and 6 students only 'never' understand instructions even in English. The last question in this section, as shown in the diagram (Diagram No.-1) gives a scope to the respondents to opine about their personal interest (if any). There is no response to this question.

Conclusion

After the reality check by administering the standardized language proficiency test focusing on listening skill and the interview protocol, it has been observed that the average standard of the language proficiency level of ESL college students is far below than the global standard. Hence, it may be suggested that proper infrastructure may be provided in different institutions to enable a healthy environment to enhance language proficiency and to boost up academic growth of the students. Moreover, not only the language teachers but also the teachers of all other subjects and peer-group interaction must contribute towards the creation of the general ambience to enhance ESL students' language proficiency.

References:

Gokak, V.K. (1964) English in India—It's Present and Future. London, Asia Publishing House

Lado, R. (1957) Linguistics across cultures. Applied linguistics for language teachers. University of Michigan Press.

Scrase J. Timothy (1989) Place of English in India, The Hegemony of English, Asia Pacific

Tickoo, M.L. (2004). ELT in India. New Delhi: Orient Longman

CHAPTER FOURTEEN

Impact of Management of Service Product Innovation on Business Success Through Organizational Culture

Satyaprakash Naik[1], Dr Sabyasachi Dey[2*] and Dr Sisir Ranjan Dash[3]

Research Scholar[1] and Assistant Professor[2,3], School of Management, Centurion University of Technology and Management, Odisha, India

1. Introduction

The practice of innovation management and its effect on growth and performance is achieved through the domain of organizational culture. Higher output is created by organizations with a culture of positive measures towards change. In order to effectively promote the implication of creativity, organizations should change their internal actions by creating external relationships, which actually demonstrate the organizational culture, according to Naranjo-Valencia et. al (2011). However, it is important to research to what degree the practice of service product innovation management increases the level of market efficiency. This chapter provides a brief conceptualization of the service product and its industry at the beginning. The proposed conceptual model of service product innovation management follows this section. Afterwards, the following sections will address the management of service product innovation and organizational culture to help the proposed model. The paper's suggestions, the debate, and the possible course of the study will be observed consecutively.

2. Service product and its industries:

In terms of "product," many companies have specifically redefined their service businesses. The service-oriented company's products have now become the composition of a tangible and intangible commodity, which in turn poses a dilemma. The product creation method in service industries has been elaborated and critically clarified by Hull (2003) and Hull and Tidd (2003). The scholars used the service product extensively, thus explaining the method. It very well may be finished up from the translation of the academic works that the center contribution is an assistance in help item. These administrations are well fitting, alluded to as a result of activity. Any of the unmistakable arrangements that accompany the assistance, then again, can likewise allude to it as a help item. Truth be told, their contribution is viewed as a product by the quantity of businesses, for example, banking, broadcast communications, lodging, the travel industry. An examination by Hull and Tidd (2003), in any case, alludes to the utilization as an assistance result of administrations from monetary foundations (for example banks, protection, and venture), schooling, medical services, travel/inn, and media transmission. It can likewise be proposed based on the arrangement that these areas can be alluded to as administration creating enterprises. Hence, this paper will accept the wording of administration item, which is really the unmistakable and immaterial contribution of administration businesses.

3. Organizational culture:

Analysts accept that organizational culture assumes an essential part in the results of advancement regarding development and hierarchical culture. The hierarchical culture is seen by Barney (1986) as a powerful assortment of standards, convictions, and presumptions that an organization should found in its organization. It depicts the connection between applicable laborers, customers, providers and adversaries as central participants (Louis, 1983; as refered to in Barney, 1986). As per Naranjo-Valencia et al. (2011), associations should meet inward activities and outer relationship norms that line up with the corporate culture to successfully advance the presentation of development. Development, truth be told, is an entering power in administration methodology and acquaints a calibrating with the way of life of the organization that permits principal changes to the hierarchical construction.

Organizational culture impacts the organization's imaginative activities twoly: through the cycle of socialization and through essential standards, major qualities, assessments, and suppositions that mirror the construction, technique, the executive's idea, and strategies of the association (Martins and Terblanche, 2003). Accordingly, if an organization's corporate culture accepts imaginative thoughts, underpins and executes them, the difficulties and limitations can be set up and settled. Hierarchical culture may, in all actuality, be a wellspring of groundbreaking thoughts inside the association (Uzkurt, Kumar, Kimzan, and Eminoglu, 2013). The organizational culture, however, is divided into four viewpoints, namely Chang and Lin, cooperativeness, creativity, continuity, and effectiveness (2007). Cooperativeness focuses mostly on coordination, exchange of knowledge, trust, empowerment, and teamwork. Innovativeness has taken external and flexible orientations into account, with an emphasis on innovation and adaptability. Consistency stresses order, laws and regulations, and effectiveness. Effectiveness emphasizes focusing on competition, achievement of goals, and performance.

Various investigations have zeroed in on the impacts of authoritative culture on business accomplishment in different settings (Chang and Lin, 2007; Uzkurt et al., 2013). Authoritative culture decidedly affects the connection between's lean six sigma basic achievement factors with hierarchical execution (Jayaraman, Kee, and Soh, 2012) and execution administration conduct (Yiing and Ahmad, 2009). Distinctive hierarchical societies affect organization proficiency, as per Itakura (2011).

Organizational culture ponders advancements in the worldwide economy, extraordinary rivalry, and rethinking conventional administration rehearses. It supports imaginative activities among hierarchical members that can lead them to acknowledge advancement as a key estimation of the association (Hartmann, 2006). The authoritative culture regularly advances innovativeness by utilizing a characterized set of standards to deal with staff, customers, providers and others (Barney, 1986). Hence apparently, associations the individuals who have solid societies should have incredible administration in the end bringing about improved market execution.

4. Discussion:

Organizational culture can likewise assume a significant part in overseeing advancement. The arrangement of authoritative culture is relied upon to cultivate development the board significantly in the help item industry, while they need to think worldwide and act locally. The organization which expands its territory for information sharing and learning even across the boundary will have critical upper hands over the rivals on the lookout. Such hierarchical culture really eliminates the obstructions to effective advancement the executives. While having the effect of dimensions of innovation management to market performance, it is justifiably expected that organizational culture would influence the relationship. Organizational culture cultivates the practices within the organization which shape up the innovation management. Having the values, norms, attitude in light of consistency, innovativeness, cooperativeness, and effectiveness, company can pursue for better market performance. The organization and its employees who have such culture embedded expected to have enhanced market performance.

5. Conclusion:

Innovation needs expected changes in the vast majority of the business in the present economy since it has been called attention to be the fundamental impetus to the company's development. Advancement is the stage which can totally and vigorously pivot any association. Indeed, advancement is an unpredictable issue for all nations. To make the development fruitful and have better market execution, it is surely essential to zero in on certain worries which are generally overlooked by the business associations. Persistent disregarding these issues lead to frame obstructions for development. For example, keeping the speed up with innovative progression is fundamental for the organization. Nonetheless, it has been seen that numerous organizations discovered to be very much coordinated as far as devices/innovation. It has additionally been distinguished that authoritative culture separation is unmistakable hindrances that influence the development the board and accordingly brings down the market execution. From a complete view, generally speaking authoritative culture would be resolved for the fruitful development the executives. The hierarchical culture inside the organization would encourage the administrators to be more proactive in assistance item the executives and improved market execution. Nonetheless, to accomplish long haul vital objectives and make a serious edge in the business field, firms ought to see how to construct a way with the assistance of advancement as catalysis. Despite the fact that it is hard to dissect the full ramifications of development in business, the current study proposes associations to oversee advancement in such a manner, which is wanted by purchasers and subsequently financially carry an incentive to the firm.

References:

➤ Barney. (1991). Firm resources and sustained competitive advantage. *Journal of Management, 17*(1), 99-120.

➤ Chang, Shuchih Ernest, & Lin, Chin-Shien. (2007). Exploring organizational culture for information security management. *Industrial Management & Data Systems, 107*(3), 438-458.

➤ Hull. (2003). Product development in service enterprises: Case studies of good practice. *Service innovation: organizational responses to technological opportunities & market imperatives*(9), 371.

➤ Hull. (2004). Innovation strategy and the impact of a composite model of service product development on performance. *Journal of Service Research, 7*(2), 167-180.

➤ Hull, & Tidd, Joe. (2003). A Composite Framework of Product Development and Delivery Effectiveness in Services. In J. Tidd & F. M. Hull (Eds.), *Service Innovation; Organization Responses to Technological Opportunities & Market Imperatives* (Vol. 9, pp. 343-370): Imperial College Press.

➤ Itakura, H. (2011). Business Management of Japanese Corporations in China: Focusing on the China-Japan Comparative Study of Leadership and Organizational Culture. *Journal of Transnational Management, 16*(4), 221-238.

➤ Jayaraman, K., Kee, T.L., & Soh, K.L. (2012). The perceptions and perspectives of Lean Six Sigma (LSS) practitioners: An empirical study in Malaysia. *The TQM Journal, 24*(5), 433-446.

➤ Martins, EC, & Terblanche, F. (2003). Building organisational culture that stimulates creativity and innovation. *European Journal of Innovation Management, 6*(1), 64-74.

➤ Naranjo-Valencia, J.C., Jiménez-Jiménez, D., & Sanz-Valle, R. (2011). Innovation or imitation? The role of organizational culture. *Management Decision, 49*(1), 55-72.

➤ Uzkurt, Cevahir, Kumar, Rachna, Kimzan, Halil Semih, & Eminoglu, Gözde. (2013). Role of innovation in the relationship between organizational culture and firm performance: A study of the banking sector in Turkey. *European Journal of Innovation Management, 16*(1), 92-117.

➤ Yiing, L.H., & Ahmad, K.Z.B. (2009). The moderating effects of organizational culture on the relationships between leadership behavior and organizational commitment and between organizational commitment and job satisfaction and performance. *Leadership & Organization Development Journal, 30*(1), 53-86.

CHAPTER FIFTEEN

Entrepreneurship Development Leading to Growth of MSME

Dr Sabyasachi Dey, Assistant Professor
Centurion University of Technology and Management, Odisha

1. Introduction:

The nation's economic development is depends on its industrial development. The industrial development is based on the entrepreneurial competencies of the people. Hence, the concept of building entrepreneurship Promotion is need of the hour. The term "entrepreneurship" comes from the French verb "entreprendre" and the German word "unternehmen", both means to "undertake". Bygrave and Hofer in 1891 defined the entrepreneurial process as involving all the functions, activities, and actions associated with perceiving of opportunities and creation of organizations to pursue them". In simple, entrepreneurship is the act of being an entrepreneur, which can be defined as "one who undertakes innovations, finance and business acumen in an effort to transform innovations into economic goods".

A new business venture is a key for the success of a country. Specialists concur that business venture is perhaps the most impressive motors for financial development (Gedeon, 2014). This is on the grounds that business people open enormous number of new organizations that give occupations to more works, which thus lessen the degree of joblessness. Business people likewise will in general be creative in their business activity. For example, they regularly use innovation that can upgrade creation measure productivity, so that expansion the upper hand of their nations. By and large, it very well may be said that business information is a basic factor to accomplish achievement (Welsh and Dragusin, 2013).

The North East Region of India, comprising of the seven sisters for example conditions of Assam, Manipur, Meghalaya, Nagaland, Tripura, Arunachal Pradesh, Mizoram and Sikkim have so far been not able to stay up with the development occurring in rest of the country. Indeed, even with the Government apportioning explicit supports each year for its improvement in framework and different zones, the advancement has not been according to assumption. The assorted geology, climatic conditions, language and identity of the locale bring along formative difficulties. The difficulties like framework shortage especially network in all structures is regular to the area. Henceforth tending to issues of nearby foundation, interest in human asset and ability advancement has been a focal point of improvement endeavours the area.

2. Review of Literature:

Bala Subrahmanya (2004) highlighted the impact of globalization and domestic reforms on small-scale industries sector. The study stated that small industry had suffered in terms of growth of units, employment, output and exports. The Researcher highlighted that the policy changes had also thrown open new opportunities and markets for the small scale industries sector. He suggested that the focus must be turned to technology development and strengthening of financial infrastructure in order to make Indian small industry internationally competitive and contribute to national income and employment.

Bargal et al. (2009) examined the causal relationship among the three variables GDP, SSI output and SSI exports and also have compared the performance parameters of SSIs in the pre and post liberalization era. The study found that the annual average growth rate of different parameters of SSIs have declined in the period of nineties vis-à-vis the pre-reform years. There is an absence of any lead-lag causal relationship between exports and production in small-scale sector and GDP of Indian economy.

Singh et al. (2012) analyzed the performance of Small scale industry in India and focused on policy changes which have opened new opportunities for this sector. Their study concluded that SSI sector has made good progress in terms of number of SSI units, production & employment levels. The study recommended the emergence of technology development and strengthening of financial infrastructure to boost SSI and to achieve growth target. Venkatesh and Muthiah (2012) found that the role of small & medium enterprises (SMEs) in the industrial sector is growing rapidly and they have become a thrust area for future growth. They emphasized that nurturing

SME sector is essential for the economic well-being of the nation. The above literature highlights the various aspects viz. performance, growth & problems of MSMEs in Indian economy and induces for continuous research in this field.

Mohanty (2018) analyzed the performance of the MSME sector in India. He suggested that in India MSMEs has achieved steady growth over the last couple of years. The role of MSMEs sector is growing rapidly and they have become a thrust area for future growth. India should promote the growth of SMEs in order to avoid monopolistic and oligopolistic markets with the right kind of policies and regulatory framework. The Indian market is growing and the Indian industry is making rapid progress in various Industries like manufacturing, food processing, textile and garments, retail, precision engineering, information technology, pharmaceuticals, agro and service sectors. Under the changing economic scenario the SMEs have both the opportunities and challenges before them. The support given by the national and the state governments to the SMEs is not adequate enough to solve their problems. However for the sector to fully utilize its potential, it is essential that the entrepreneurs along with the government support take necessary steps for further development. It is quite evident that, nurturing this sector is essential for the economic wellbeing of the nation. It is essential to take care of the sector to enable it to take care of the Indian economy.

3. MSME Developments in India:

The primary duty of advancement and improvement of the miniature, little and medium ventures area lies with the State Governments. Notwithstanding, Government of India perceived the significance and capability of the Micro, Small and Medium Enterprises area for the development and advancement of the public economy and for age of business. It likewise saw the requirement for all-India structure for approaches and measures for the turn of events and advancement of Micro, Small and Medium Enterprises and has looked into enhancing the endeavors of State Governments in an unexpected way. The Micro, Small and Medium Enterprises Development (MSMED) Act, 2006 is a consequence of the equivalent. After the institution of this Act a different Ministry of Micro, Small and Medium Enterprises (MSME) was shaped on 9.5.2007 by the consolidation of past Ministry of Small Scale Industry (SSI) and Ministry of Agro and Rural Industries (ARI). The area includes 633.88 lakh units according to National Sample Survey 73rd Round (2015-16) and has made 11.10 crore occupations.

The Ministry of MSME is additionally seen with the advancement of Khadi, Coir and Village Industries. Khadi and Village Industries Commission (KVIC) not just serves the fundamental requirements of the handled merchandise of the huge rustic area of the country yet in addition gives practical work to around 152 lakh people in provincial regions. Khadi and Village Industries Sector address a flawless legacy item, which is ethnic just as moral. The area has a possibly solid customers among the center and more elite classes of the general public. The coir business has stretched out its base from Kerala to different States including Tamil Nadu, Andhra Pradesh, Karnataka, Goa, Odisha, Maharashtra and Gujarat. This industry gives work to more than 7.30 lakh people and has contributed essentially in expanding trades throughout the long term. Utilization of coir has seen upsurge because of its current circumstance benevolent nature. There is an extraordinary potential for esteem expansion in coir items through mechanical mediations and broadening into items like coir geo-material.

MSME is become the achievement of reinforcing the work to the jobless in different areas, for example, coir, craftsmanship, bamboo creating and furthermore made open doors in little ventures. The public authority is taking the commencement to elevate a few plans to construct pioneering exercises among the metropolitan and provincial youth. Monetary help through different nationalized and co-employable banks are likewise given to inspire the general public. The leader's expertise improvement program is likewise one of the pieces of specialized help towards the youthful and growing business visionaries. There are a portion of the accomplishments rattled off to make mindfulness among the residents.

4. Status of MSME in North-East:

As per the latest Census (Fourth Census) as well as data extracted from Economic Census 2005 conducted by Central Statistics Office (CSO), Ministry of Statistics and Programme Implementation (MoSPI) for activities excluded from Fourth Census, namely wholesale/retail trade, legal, educational & social services, hotel & restaurants, transports and storage & warehousing (except cold storage), the number of Micro, Small and Medium Enterprises (MSMEs) in the North-Eastern Region, including Assam are as under:

Sl.	State	Number of MSMEs (in lakh)

No.		
1.	SIKKIM	0.17
2.	ARUNACHAL PRADESH	0.41
3.	NAGALAND	0.39
4.	MANIPUR	0.91
5.	MIZORAM	0.29
6.	TRIPURA	0.98
7.	MEGHALAYA	0.88
8.	ASSAM	6.62
Total		**10.64**

The Government encourages the advancement and improvement of MSMEs in the nation including North-Eastern Region by improving admittance to fund through execution of Credit Guarantee Scheme, Performance and Credit Rating Scheme, and so forth and supporting innovation advancement through usage of different plans/programmes like Credit Linked Capital Subsidy Scheme, National Manufacturing Competitiveness Programme and so on

The Government is executing Prime Minister's Employment Generation Program (PMEGP) in the nation including North-Eastern Region to encourage age of business. The Margin Money Subsidy delivered during the current year (as on 16.07.2015), for North-Eastern Region under the PMEGP is Rs. 108.01 Crores. There are four MSME-Development Institutes (DIs) situated at Guwahati, Agartala, Gangtok, and Imphal with their Branch organizations in the locale.

Miniature, little and medium endeavors (MSMEs) in Arunachal Pradesh, Assam, Manipur, Meghalaya, Mizoram, Nagaland, and Tripura - the 'seven sisters' that make up the North Eastern Region (NER) - remain to profit by focal government activities to empower business, advancement and supported improvement in the area.

CRISIL's examination of more than 500 MSMEs in these states shows they face significant difficulties to development as absence of admittance to innovation, concentrated tasks and powerless framework. Around 47 percent have concentrated activities (either in item, geology or clients), and around 30% have frail framework. The units face difficulties in getting to gifted work, as just 45 percent of the complete representatives are perpetual. Around 48 percent of these are working in the assembling area, of which 95 percent have semi-robotized or manual innovation.

CRISIL accepts that different activities dispatched by the focal government in the NE area for expertise advancement, business improvement, innovation and hatching, and adventure assets for new companies will quicken business and lift the accessibility of talented specialists and improvement of MSMEs in this locale to make them serious.

5. Conclusion:

Business is a motor for public economy. In such manner, MSME could be the various hands of work age and development of Indian economy. According to the accessible information, there are 10.64 lakhs of MSME spread across the north east piece of the country. The North Eastern Region (NER) of India including eight states-Assam, Arunachal Pradesh, Meghalaya, Mizoram, Nagaland, Tripura, Manipur and Sikkim is right around ten years behind the remainder of India. The district is honored with a lot of normal assets like backwoods and oil, tea, water (which is extremely scant in many pieces of India) and so forth, yet there exists an asset slack.   It   is frequently said that the north east offers enormous potential for development on Micro Small and Medium Enterprises (MSMEs). The geological area which has so far been viewed as the worst thing about upper east has gotten an aid for the district with the changing strategies of the public authority and accentuation on look east approach. The market is probably going to encounter impressive extension when this emerges and along these lines it is vital that the district gears itself up to confront the test and snatch the chance .There is thusly need to recognize territories where the locale has the potential for development. As of late, the Central Government has reserved around Rs 1,000 crore for usage of different plans for Micro, Small, and Medium Enterprise (MSMEs) in the Northeast locale during the current monetary year to improve the states of business person.

The Ministry of Micro, Small and Medium Enterprises (MSME) coordinated Udyam Samvad Workshop as of late where eleven meetings were held with various services and monetary associations like Ministry of Development of North Eastern Region (DoNER), SIDBI, ASSOCHAM, CII, FICCI, FISME, PHD Chamber of Commerce and MSME Foundation. Different issues confronting business people and Start-ups in North East States of India like getting to credit, handholding for setting up organizations, getting to business sectors in India and abroad and R&D for refinement of craftsmanship-based items fabricated in the North East were examined. Clergyman in his location said that there is earnest requirement for setting up MSMEs in cultivating and non-cultivating areas in the north East locale and the Ministry will assume the part of facilitator to give R&D, market access and better plans for MSME items. The Minister additionally added that Micro businesses will be given more help in this district. For this innovation habitats are being set up in Imphal, Dimapur, Tinsukia and Agartala.

References:

1. Gedeon, S.A., 2014, Application of Best Practices in University Entrepreneurship Education: Designing a New MBA Program, *European Journal of Training and Development*, Vol. 38, No. 3, pp. 231-253.
2. Welsh, D.H.B. & Dragusin, M., 2013, The New Generation of Massive Open Online Course (MOOCS) and Entrepreneurship Education, *Small Business Institute Journal*, Vol. 9, No. 1, pp. 51-65.
3. Jha, A.K., 2014, Promoting Entrepreneurship In North East India, Employment News, Vol. 38, No. 39, p. 56, December, 2013-January, 2014.
4. Desai,V., 2003, Small Scale Industries and entrepreneurship, Himalaya Publishing House, Mumbai.
5. Khanka, S. S., 1999, Entrepreneurial Development, S.Chand & Co., New Delhi.
6. Rinalini P. K., 2003, New Lesson from the Successful Entrepreneurial Firm, Entrepreneurship Development, Sunmarg Publication and Distributors, New Delhi.
7. Barthwal, R. R., 1996, Industrial Economics, New Age International (P) Limited Publisher, New Delhi.
8. Mali, D.D. (1998), Development of Micro, Small and Medium Enterprises of India: Current Scenario, Vol. 12. Pp.62-64.
9. Bala Subrahmanya, M. H. (2004), Small Industry and Globalization: Implications, Performance and Prospects, Economic and Political Weekly, Vol. 34, No.18, pp 1826-1834.
10. Bargal, H., Dashmishra, M., and Sharma, A. (2009), Performance Analysis of Small Scale Industries - A Study of Pre-liberalization and Post-liberalization period", International Journal of Business and Management, Vol. 1, No. 2.
11. Dixit, A. and Pandey, A.K. (2011), SMEs and Economic Growth in India: Co integration Analysis, The IUP Journal of Financial Economics, Vol. 9, No. 2, pp. 41-59.
12. Singh, R., Verma, O.P., and Anjum, B. (2012), Small Scale Industry: An Engine of Growth", Zenith International Journal of Business Economics & Management Research, Vol.2 Issue 5 UNIDO (1969), Small Scale Industry in Latin America, Publication no. 11B. p.37.
13. Mohanty, J. J., 2018, A Study on Micro, Small and Medium Enterprises (MSMEs) in India: Status and its Performance, International Journal of Research and Scientific Innovation, Vol. 5, No. 5, pp. 105-114.

CHAPTER SIXTEEN

The Growth and Performance of MSME Segment: A study on Odisha's Perspective

Dr.Pramod Kumar Patjoshi, Associate Professor,
Centurion University of Technology and Management, Odisha, India

Dr.Girija Nandini, Assistant Professor,
Centurion University of Technology and Management, Odisha, India

1. INTRODUCTION

Odisha is a state of dreamland for natural resources. Despite being rich in resources; it is still one of the backward States and has huge potential for further industrialization, especially for the MSME segment. The ratio of gross capital outlay to GSDP has not been encouraging over the years. Odisha has observed that the credit which flows to the MSME segment is quite unproductive due to the lack of credit immersion capacity of this sector. MSME segment is facing many challenges in related to different areas of production and operation process, marketing of their products, an arrangement of funds, shortages of skilled manpower, and many other outside challenges. In other words, the MSME segment is finding difficulties connecting to availability credit from banks and financial institutions, obtainability of appropriate technology, problems in marketing of products, accessibility of resources, the nonexistence of skilled human resources etc. Consequently, this study is related to analyse the growth and performance of MSME in Odisha.

As per "Odisha MSME Development Policy, 2016", "Odisha located in the eastern region of India, has a traditional past, a vibrant present then an enormous possibility for MSME segment. Odisha is correspondingly a treasure trove for natural resources. Odisha is finely associated through superficial transport, air as well as water. Odisha has a widespread rail in addition to the road system connecting numerous development epicenters. The State admittance to wide-reaching markets, existence of accomplished human resources, superior logistics, and well infrastructure in addition to an optimistic commercial atmosphere creates Odisha a preferred station designed for the corporate sector. Odisha's Gross State Domestic Production (GSDP) has improved at a Compound Annual Growth Rate (CAGR) of 10.23% from Rs.281450 crore to Rs.330200 crore between 2011-12 and 2015-16. Cumulative FDI inflows in Odisha from April 2010 to March 2016 stood at Rs.1027 crore. State Government has proclaimed strategies to smooth development in the manufacturing segment by means of year on year growth of 15% till 2020. Rendering to the Ministry of Commerce and Industry, total exports from Odisha in 2015-16 were valued at Rs.19746 crore. The value of exports from the state improved at a CAGR of 2.5% between 2006-07 and 2014-15. Odisha ranks high in the country in terms of the total value of mineral output. Throughout 2015-16, the total production of minerals in the state noted down at 239.45 million tonnes. The mineral resources of Odisha establish an arduous share in national deposits of Chromite 98%, Nickel 93%, Graphite 71%, Pyrophyllite 65%, Manganese 67%, Bauxite 59%, China Clay 31%, Fire Clay 25%, Dolomite 18%. Odisha is the fourth biggest producer of Coal as well as the fifth biggest producer of Iron ore in India".

Therefore it can find from the above that the MSME segment in Odisha has made considerable effort to the economic growth in overall further creation of job opportunities in the state as well. This sector also contributes to the exports in precise over and above this segment also placed it merely following to the agricultural segment in Odisha in positions of employment creation. The MSME segment in Odisha has perceived a growing inclination with regard to the amount of MSME units' establishment, significant improvement in investment in addition to job creation during the past few decades. Although the MSME segment has made remarkable contributions, simultaneously it has faced numerous challenges for its development in Odisha. The MSME segment suffers from the shortage of finance as well as the timely arrangement of funds. MSMEs are facing many challenges related to different areas of production and operation process, marketing of their products, an arrangement of funds, shortages of skilled manpower, and many other outside challenges. In other words, the MSME segment used to face difficulties in the area of bank credit conveniences, accessibility of appropriate equipment and technology, difficulties in the marketing of their products, obtainability of incomplete possessions, unavailability of proper human resources, etc. Though, the depiction is less blushing in the eastern part of India. To discourse, the different type of arrangements as well as for the growth of the MSME segment has been started by the central government's as well as state government's agencies. Different central as well as state organizations deliver wide-ranging assistance aimed at the progress of the MSME segment in eastern India. Therefore this research is related towards analysing the development and performance of the MSME segment in Odisha.

The objectives framed for the Study are: to study of growth and performance of the MSME segment in Odisha. And to examine the effect of the growth of the MSME segment, the investment made then employment generation in Odisha. This research is related to convinced shreds of evidence than the secondary information, which has composed from the different bases for a span of five years from 2012-13 to 2016-17. The data collected from the secondary sources comprise "Annual Report of MSME", "Economic Survey of Odisha", "MSME Department, Govt. of Odisha" and "RBI Website" and related articles. The regression analysis has been used for examining the effect of the growth of the MSME segment, the investment made then employment generation in Odisha.

2. Progress of MSME Segment in Odisha
The Progress of MSME Segments in Odisha have discussed below

2.1 MSME Segment in Odisha from the Year 2012-13 to 2016-17
The table 1 has explained the MSME segment in Odisha from 2012-13 to 2016-17.

Table 7.1: MSME Segment in Odisha from "2012-13 to 2016-17".

Year	Numbers of MSME	MSME Established	Investment (Rs.in Crore)	Employment (persons)
2012-13	123292	5931	432.9	27104
2013-14	130301	7009	669.41	32136
2014-15	160167	29866	2267.24	107011
2015-16	214087	53920	2679.64	166731
2016-17	271870	57783	3034.64	175221
Total	271870	154509	9083.83	508203

Source: Odisha Economic Survey 2017-18

MSME segment displays a collective trend over the years by increasing the number of MSME enterprises established, the investment made over the years as well as the creation of employment opportunities. It can depict from table 1 that the MSME segment in Odisha has accomplished the greatest development by setting up 57783 numbers of units. MSME segment in

Odisha has recorded an investment made of Rs.3034.64 crore then created employment opportunities of 1.75 lakh persons in the financial year 2016-17.

2.2 Numbers of MSME and their Growth Rate in Odisha from 2012-13 to 2016-17
The table 2 displays the numbers of MSME and their growth rate in Odisha from 2012-13 to 2016-17.

Table .2: Numbers of MSME and their Growth Rate in Odisha from 2012-13 to 2016-17

Year	Numbers of MSME	Growth Rate in Number of MSME
2012-13	123292	
2013-14	130301	5.68%
2014-15	160167	22.92%
2015-16	214087	33.66%
2016-17	271870	26.99%

Source: Odisha Economic Survey 2017-18

Graph .1: Numbers of MSME and their Growth Rate \ in Odisha from 2012-13 to 2016-17

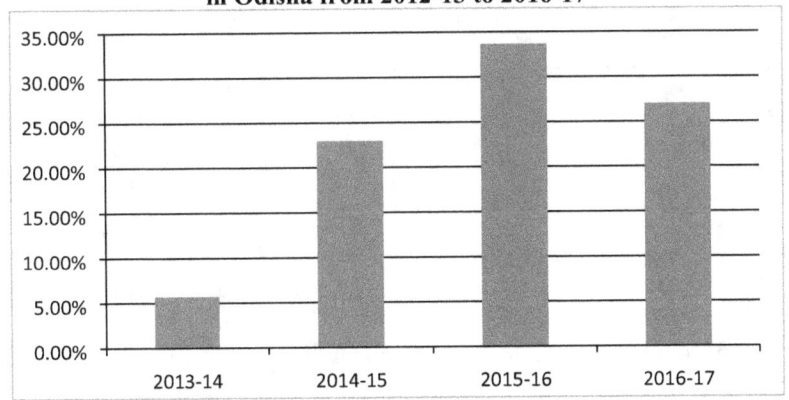

This one is clear from the above table that the numbers of MSME have gone up cumulatively from 123292 units to 271870 units over a span of 5 years from "2012-13 to 2016-17".

It can observe from the above table and graph that the numbers of MSME growth have shown an increasing trend over a span of 4 years from 2012-13 to 2015-16 and have shown a declining trend during the last year of study 2016-17. The numbers of MSME have documented the growth rate of 5.68%, 22.92%, 33.66%, and 26.99% respectively for the four years 2013-14, 2014-15, 2015-16, and 2016-17.

2.3 MSME units Established and their Growth Rate in Odisha from 2012-13 to 2016-17

The table 3 shows the MSME units established and their growth rate in Odisha from 2012-13 to 2016-17.

**Table.3: MSME units Established and their Growth Rate
in Odisha from 2012-13 to 2016-17**

Year	MSME Established	Growth Rate of MSME Established
2012-13	5931	
2013-14	7009	18.18%
2014-15	29866	326.11%
2015-16	53920	80.54%
2016-17	57783	7.16%

Source: Odisha Economic Survey 2017-18

**Graph .2: MSME units Established and their Growth Rate
in Odisha from 2012-13 to 2016-17**

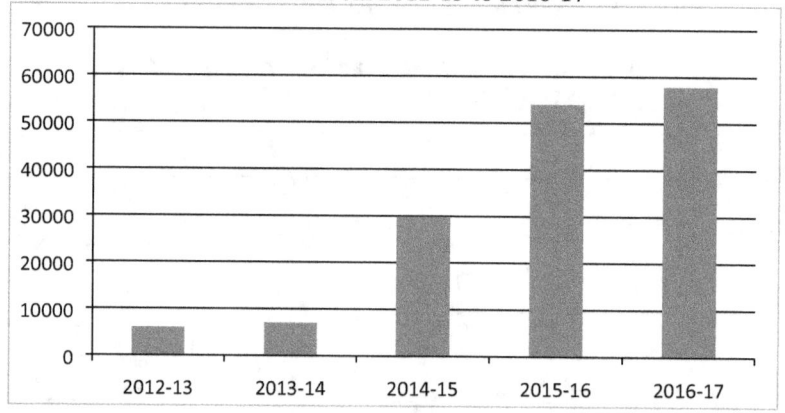

It can clearly find from the above table and graph that the numbers of MSME units established have shown a growing trend for the study period from 2012-13 to 2016-17. The numbers of MSME units established were 5931 units, 7009 units. 29866 units, 53920 units, and 57783 units respectively for the five years 2012-13, 2013-14, 2014-15, 2015-16, and 2016-17. Whereas it has observed from the above table and graph that the numbers of MSME units established a logged growth rate of 18.18%, 326.11%, 80.54%, and 7.16% respectively for the four years 2013-14, 2014-15, 2015-16 and 2016-17.

5.4 MSME units Established, Investment Made and Employment Generated in Odisha from 2012-13 to 2016-17

The table 4 appearances the details of established the numbers of MSME units, investment made and employment generated in Odisha from 2012-13 to 2016-17.

Table.4: MSME Established, Investment Made and Employment Generated in Odisha from 2012-13 to 2016-17

Year	MSME Established	Investment (Rs.in Crore)	Employment (persons)
2012-13	5931	432.90	27104
2013-14	7009	669.41	32136
2014-15	29866	2267.24	107011
2015-16	53920	2679.64	166731
2016-17	57783	3034.64	175221

Source: Odisha Economic Survey 2017-18

For the period of five years from 2012-13 to 2016-17, the numbers of MSME units established were 154509 then logged Rs.9083.83 crores of investment by means of creation of employment opportunities of 5.08 lakh persons in Odisha. It also can be observed that at the end of 2016-17, total numbers of 2.72 lakh MSME units were operating in Odisha. In the same time, it has made an investment of Rs.13726.40 crore in addition to creating 11.87 lakh employment opportunities.

It is also clarified from the above table that the number of MSME units established has shown an increasing trend for the study period 2012-13 to 2016-17. The number of MSME units established was 5931 units, 7009 units. 29866 units, 53920 units and 57783 units respectively for the five years 2012-13, 2013-14, 2014-15, 2015-16, and 2016-17. Similarly, the investment made has also shown a growing trend from 2012-13 to 2015-16. The investment made was 432.90 crores, 669.41 crores. 2267.24 crores, 2679.64 crores, and 3034.64 crores respectively for the five years 2012-13, 2013-14, 2014-15, 2015-16, and 2016-17. As a result of the above, this one also can clarify from the above table that the numbers of employment generated in persons have shown a mounting trend for the study period 2012-13 to 2015-16. The numbers of employment generated in persons were 27104, 32136. 107011, 166731, and 175221 respectively for the five years 2012-13, 2013-14, 2014-15, 2015-16 and 2016-17.

2.5 Regression Analysis for Investment as Dependent Variable and MSME units Established as Predictors

The table 5 displays regression analysis for investment as dependent variable and MSME units established as predictors.

Table .5: Regression Analysis for Investment as Dependent Variable and MSME units Established as Predictors

Particulars	Coefficients	t Stat	P-value
Intercept	376.3632	1.4477	0.2435
SSI/MSME units Established	0.0466	6.8144	0.0065

Table.5 reflects the regression analysis among for investment as dependent variable and numbers of MSME units established as independent variables. The above table stated that MSME units established has a positive coefficient of 0.0466 and is a statistically significant association among investment made and numbers of MSME units established with a p-value of 0.0065 (Sig. < 0.01). 0.01).

2.6 Regression Analysis for Employment as Dependent Variable and MSME units established as Predictors

The table 6 shows regression Analysis for employment as dependent variable and MSME units established as predictors.

Table .6: Regression Analysis for Employment as dependent variable and MSME units Established as Predictors

Particulars	Coefficients	t Stat	P-value
Intercept	13368.8961	3.1435	0.0515
SSI/MSME units Established	2.8565	25.5280	0.0001

Table.6 reproduces the regression analysis between for employment created as dependent variable and numbers of MSME units established as independent variables. The above table specified that MSME units established have a positive coefficient of 2.8565 and is a statistically significant association among employment created and numbers of MSME units established with a p-value of 0.0001 (Sig. < 0.01). 0.01).

2.7 MSME units established, investment and employment created in Odisha of different Segments at the ended of 2016-17

The table 7 displays the MSME units established, investment and employment created in Odisha of different Segments at the ended of 2016-17.

Table .7: MSME units established, investment and employment created in Odisha of different Segments at the end of 2016-17

Category	MSME Established	Category	Investment (Rs. in crore)	Category	Employment (persons)
Livestock & Leather	619	Livestock & Leather	14.58	Livestock & Leather	3060
Electrical & Electronics	1945	Electrical & Electronics	109.94	Electrical & Electronics	9917
Rubber & Plastics	2066	Paper & Paper Products	177.18	Rubber & Plastics	12558
Chemical & Allied	3854	Forest and Wood based	200.48	Paper & Paper Products	19962
Paper & Paper Products	3940	Rubber & Plastics	285.99	Chemical & Allied	26980
Glass & Ceramics	10326	Chemical & Allied	317.00	Forest & Wood based	61748
Forest & Wood based	13124	Textiles	351.84	Misc. Manufacturing	69544
Textiles	15109	Glass & Ceramics	752.48	Textiles	73247
Misc. Manufacturing	16450	Misc. Manufacturing	753.87	Engineering &Metal Based	111972
Engineering & Metal Based	16603	Engineering & Metal Based	1219.68	Glass & Ceramics	148312
Food & Allied	35246	Food & Allied	2018.45	Food &Allied	179115
Repairing & Services	152588	Repairing & Services	7524.91	Repairing &Services	471026

Source: Odisha Economic Survey 2017-18

It can observe from the above table that Repairing & Services segment has contributed maximum numbers of MSME whereas the Livestock & Leather segment has contributed lesser numbers of MSME as compare to other segments. It can be observed that the top three better performer categories which have established maximum numbers of MSME are Engineering & Metal Based (16603), Food & Allied (35246), and Repairing & Services (152588). On the contrary, the bottom three categories that have established minimum numbers of MSME are Livestock & Leather (619), Electrical & Electronics (1945), and Rubber & Plastics (2066).

Similarly, in the case of investment made in different categories, it can see from the above table that investment made is higher in Repairing & Services segment but the investment made is lower in the Livestock & Leather segment as compared to other segments. It can be witnessed that the top three categories where maximum investment made are Engineering & Metal Based (1219.68 corers), Food & Allied (2018.45 corers), and Repairing & Services (7524.91 corers). On other hand, the bottom three categories where minimum investment made are Livestock & Leather (14.58 corers), Electrical & Electronics (109.94 corers), and Paper & Paper Products (177.18 corers).

As a result of the above, it can find from the above table that Repairing & Services segment has generated maximum numbers of employments whereas the Livestock & Leather segment has generated lesser numbers of employments as compare to other segments. It can be observed that the top three better employment generation categories which have generated maximum numbers of employments are Glass & Ceramics (148312), Food & Allied (179115), and Repairing & Services (471026). On the contrary, the bottom three categories that have generated minimum numbers of employments are Livestock & Leather (3060), Electrical & Electronics (9917) and Rubber & Plastics (12558).

3 Conclusion:
This study displays that there is constant progress in the area of the number of MSME units established. The development section of these segments improves employment opportunities in addition to the investment of Odisha also for India. By way of the primary objective of this study is to analyse the growth and performance of the MSME segment in Odisha. It is found that the MSME segment displays a collective trend over the years by increasing the number of MSME enterprises established, the investment made over the years as well as the creation of employment opportunities. From the regression analysis, it is established that MSME units established has a positive coefficient and is a statistically significant association among investment made as well as employment created. It has observed from the different Segments that the top better performer categories are Engineering & Metal Based, Food & Allied, Repairing & Services and Glass & Ceramics in establishing of MSME, investment and creating employment. On the contrary, the bottom three segments in establishing of MSME, investment and creating employment are Livestock & Leather, Electrical & Electronics and Rubber & Plastics and Paper & Paper Products.

References:

1. Annual Report, Government of India, Ministry of Micro, Small and Medium Enterprises, www.msme.gov.in; 2017-18
2. Das, K. (2008), ‗SMEs in India: Issues and Possibilities in Times of Globalisation', in Lim, H. (ed.), SME in Asia and Globalization, ERIA Research Project Report 2007-5, pp.69-97.
3. Financing for MSMEs The eastside story- CII Report, 2013, https://www.pwc.in/assets/pdfs/publications/2013/msme.pdf
4. Fridah Muriungi Mwobobia (2012) ―The Challenges Facing Small-Scale Women Entrepreneurs: A Case of Kenya‖, International journal of business administration, Vol 3, issue 2, PP 112-121.
5. Gisha.P.Mathai (2015) ―Challenges and Issues in Micro, Small and Medium Enterprises (MSMEs) in India: A Current Scenario of Economic Growth‖, Vol 4, Issue 7, PP 162-163 in Malaysia‖, Asia pacific business review, vol.12, no.4, PP 465-485.
6. https://investodisha.gov.in/odisha-MSME-policy/
7. Ishu Garg & Suraj Walia (2012) ―Micro, Small & Medium Enterprises (Msmes) in Post Reform India: Status & Performance‖, Vol 1, No 3, PP 134-141.
8. Mishu Tripathi, Mr. Saurabh Tripathi, Mr. RikinDedhia (2016) ―Challenges faced by Micro, Small and Medium Enterprise (Msme) Sector In India‖, International Journal of Science technology and management, Vol 5, Issue 3, PP 69-77
9. MSME AT A GLANCE 2016, http://msme.gov.in/sites/default/files /MSME at a GLANCE 2016 Final.pdf
10. Mukund Chandra Mehta (2013) ―Challenges and Opportunities in Micro, Small and Medium Enterprises in India‖, 2nd International Conference on Management, Humanity and Economics (ICMHE'2013) May 6-7, 2013 Kuala Lumpur (Malaysia), PP 134-136
11. N. Aruna (2015) ―Problems Faced By Micro, Small and Medium Enterprises – A Special Reference to Small Entrepreneurs in Visakhapatnam‖, IOSR Journal of business and management, Vol 14, issue 4, PP 43-49
12. Neeru Garg (2014) ―Micro, Small and Medium Enterprises in India: Current Scenario and Challenges‖, Paripex - Indian Journal of Research, Vol 3, Issue 9, PP 11-13.
13. Odisha Economic Planning and Convergence Department, Survey, Directorate of Economics and Statistics, Government of Odisha, March 2018
14. Odisha MSME Development Policy – 2016, http://www.msmeodisha.gov.in/PDF /FINALbyDI(O)-Odisha_MSME_Dev._Policy.pdf
15. Odisha MSME Development Policy 2015 – Draft for Discussion, http://www.osicltd.in /Content/images/PDF/Draft%20-%20Odisha%20MSME%20Dev%20Policy%202015.pdf
16. Odisha MSME Development Policy, Micro, Small & Medium Enterprises Department Government of Odisha, 2016
17. Sangita G.Patil & P.T.Chaudhari (2014) ―Problems of Small Scale Industries in India‖, International Journal of Engineering and Management Research, vol 4, Issue 2, PP 19-21

CHAPTER SEVENTEEN

A significant role of innovative entrepreneurs in Animation and Visual Effects industry

Saban Kumar Maharana
Asst. Professor

Centurion University of Technology and Management, Odisha, India

1. Introduction

Animation and visual effects marketing is invariably the latest phenomenon which is very indispensable in the era of science and technology. The animation and visual effects has been associated in the films, cartoon pictures, advertising agencies, TV programmers and online publicity media's besides applying android mobile devices. Animation is the process and methods of making the motion pictures or images by changing the sequence and texture of static images rapidly. The type of animated movies can be classified into two types based on the production technology.

    (a) Traditional animation or classical animation, cel animation, hand-drawn animation, is an animation technique in which each frame is drawn by hand using the light box.

    (b) Computer Graphic animation is created by computer graphic in the whole process, such as using Adobe Flash for 2D animation, and using Maya for 3D animation.

The current study and research focusing on the entrepreneurial skill, kind of human resources and expertise in production of 2d and 3d animated cartoons, movies and short animated documents in the advertisement which is now the need of the hour in the world trade and industry.Animation and visual effects have become key to the making of feature films while cutting-edge work carried out by Indian production houses has catapulted the country on to the global animation and visual effects seen and the Bollywood space is witnessing certain projects that are pushing animation and visual effects to the spearhead of movie making. However, piracy, lack of uniform media policy for foreign investment, content regulation, price regulation, cross-media ownership rules and lack of empowered regulators are hampering the progress of India entertainment and media industry. Newborn players in expanding media marketplaces tend to have a notable advantage over mature entrants due to network effects, whereby the value of the marketplace increases as the number of participants increase. Many states like Maharashtra, Karnataka, Telangana and Tamil Nadu have announced, or are coming up with, policies in support of the animation and visual effects industry and enable the Indian animation and visual effects industry to successfully participate in the battle of well-constructed markets such as the US, Canada and developing centers like Australia, South Korea, France, Japan, China and India. Broadcasters are collaborating with animation studios for original content, with channels like Cartoon Network, Sonic, Pogo and Nick for animated cartoons. In addition, the digital space also saw a shot in demand for kids content with the introduction of channels such as Amazon Prime and Netflix signing exclusive content licensing deals with various studios in India. The animation and visual effects industry continues to acquire acceptance with Indian talent controlled to compete with global counterparts and registering the CAGR of 15.5 per cent in 2017 to reach a size of USD 0.91 billion, driven majorly by a 31 per cent growth in visual effects, with animation remaining steady at a growth rate of 9 per cent. Animation and visual effects market with the substantial value of market share in 2017. However, animation and visual effects tend to cover the larger portion of the market in the forecast period at CAGR of 11.3 per cent. The report covers the present ground scenario and the future growth prospects of the facility management market for 2017-2030 along with the market players' analysis. We calculated the market size and revenue share on the basis of revenue generated from major players worldwide. India's animation and visual effects industry Outlook is forecasted on the basis of revenue analysis, product benchmarking and strategic developments of key market players. India animation and visual effects industry Outlook 2017-2030, has been prepared based on an in-depth market analysis from industry experts. "India animation and visual effects industry Outlook Report" also recognizes value chain analysis to understand the cost differentiation, pricing models to provide competitive advantage to the existing and new entry players. Animation and visual effects growth to develop motion graphics artists, 3D modelers, Texture artists, Animator, Rigger artists, Lighting artists, Storyboard artist, and compositing other in demand skills. If you have aspiration to set out your career in this challenging animation and visual effects industry, the best animation training institute in India will mentor you with all the right attributes to get your career soaring high.

The Indian media and entertainment Industry reached 1,50,000 cores in 2017, which is almost to 13 per cent growth when comparing to 2016. Based on these report by 2020 it will reach to 2,00,000 cores. For this vast growth animation and visual effects industry is one of the main reason. Why because animation and visual effects industry growth percentage is almost 25. Animation and visual effects industry is on boom and witnessing a surge in its growth like never before. With the increased digitization, the animation industry is expected to be one of the driving sectors of the world's economy. The question that arises what is this animation and visual effects all about? The mixing of the actual shootings by the film industry with images and slides. This is the role of animation and visual effects industry. The special effects which you see in any of the animated films is the visual effects.

The most exciting part about animation and visual effects is that it is even available the masses. To learn more about these animations and visual effects industry. In fact, you will also find immense YouTube videos about animation and visual effects industry, but you would be large about practical knowledge. So join in animation courses to gain good knowledge in animation and visual effects industry and get job in any animation studio. In India more than 148 studios are there. Because of Indian studios only Indian media and entertainment industry report is growing.

According to the latest report by research and market, the industry is pegged at US$ 254 Billion. According to the industry report, the games market is projected to increase US$ 270 billion by 2020. The scenario of animation and visual effects industry in India is analogous to that of world. According to KPMG India-FICCI report, Indian animation and visual effects industry achieved a growth rate of 25 per cent in 2019 to reach INR 49.5 billion. It will continue to maintain that rate in coming years.

The main drivers behind the sector's growth include deep internet penetration and mobile devices. There was an increasing demand for high visual movies from movie watchers. Therefore, nearly 20-25 per cent of production cost on a movie is spent on visual effects. The industry is not limited to few online video streaming sites like Netflix, Amazon Prime, Hot star etc. Even websites like YouTube and Facebook had adapted to the new user demands.

The next segment of animation and visual effects industry is video gaming across all digital platforms. The global video gaming industry is currently estimated to be US$ 92 Billion. This industry too had major stakes in animation and visual effects industry development. This is because it requires more graphical content for virtual reality and cloud based games in the coming decade.

There was a paradigm shift in the working of this industry with regard to Indian context. Indian animation and visual effects industry had switched from traditional outsourcing model to own intellectual property and co-productions model. This will give further boost to the sector in the future. Mainly 3D Max, Maya, After Effects, Nuke software programs are used in the animation and visual effects industry.

2. Research Objectives:

i. To study and analyze the practical aspect and process of animation and visual effects productions in India and its software process being implemented by the dynamic and innovative driven entrepreneurs to promote this industry rapidly across the globe.

ii. To study and analyze the various dynamic and scientific factors for 3d animated designs and development in India, and its technical qualifications, skills and experience invariably required for this field besides the potentially of human resources management.

3. Review of Literature:

The emerging literature review has been focusing on methods of understanding the technical skill and qualifications of human resources based on the suitability of media organizations. To indicate and derive the capacity of animation production in India. For this the researcher has to prepare and built questionnaires based on the results of thematic analysis of interview data and getting qualitative and quantitative information from the 3d animation and visual effects industry as there was lacking of any specific research in India. At the outset the researcher has to explore this topic by using qualitative and structural aspect of animation production industry in India. The researcher intend to ask the key and indispensable information of software production and visual effect creation besides choosing the expertise based human resources to augment this industry by showing the acumen ship and dexterity of innovative entrepreneurs.

4. Scope of Future Study:

The creative and innovative driven entrepreneurs has to emphasize the qualitative and quantitative aspect of the project as the emerging animation and visual effects is a growing concept in order to create an own copyright project to enhance and heighten the reputation and image in a long run to sustain and survive in the international arena of market and industry. The entrepreneur has a tremendous and significant role and responsibly of adopting the latest skills, ideas, strategies and techniques to promote this industry rapidly to retain and survive in international market gaining long term profit. The dynamic entrepreneurs have to develop and explore innovative and divergent strategy to capture the foreign projects by inducting qualified and experienced manpower to augment and accelerate this industry in the global economy. Owing to tremendously growing industry especially in the metropolitan cities like Bangalore, Chennai, Delhi, Mumbai and Hyderabad the employees should improve their skill, personality, responsibly, enthusiasm and communication skills to keep abreast with the changing scenario in India in particular and abroad in general. Apart from these the researcher has to explore and find out the attitude and potentially of the employees in the animation industry besides collecting the demographic data. Most of the animation companies are using Maya and Adobe tools for designing the movies and animated TV programs by means of sophisticated and advanced software technology. The current studies also explores the practical problems and its constraints, needs and tendency of animation industry besides to understand the policy of the government as most of the projects and industries are supported by government. The entreprenuer has to analyze and realize the genuine problems and obstacles in the animation field which can enable the animation school to prepare their students by designing suitable curriculum and course for future scholars. It also formulates strategies and plans for ascertaining the education, salary and work culture and character of the employees.

The researcher has to implement and adopt the thematic approach and analysis to analyse in-depth and profound data. In this study it is imperative to say that the modern creative entrepreneurs have tremendous and enormous role and responsibility to procure and manage funds and competent professional power for viable management of script writing, animating and advertising in special effects for movies and cartoon pictures. Even most of the foreign projects and companies from Denmark, Germany and Japan hiring professional manpower in the field of animation and visual effects productions. For example Little Krishna, Chhota Bheem, Roll No.., Little Krishna, Motu Patlu and Oggy etc. are the outcome from the animated designs which has been broadcasting in Cartoon Network channels in India.

REFERENCES

[1] https://www.goldsteinresearch.com/report/india-animation-vfx-market.

[2] https://www.fxanimation.in/about-animation-and-vfx-industry.html

[3] https://onelightvfx.com/studio-list/complete-list-of-2d-3d-animation-post-production-and-vfx-studios-in-india

[4] https://www.animationxpress.com/latest-news/ficci-ey-report-vfx-grew-25-per-cent-in-2019-to-reach-inr-49-5-billion

CHAPTER EIGHTEEN

Constraints in Cashew nut Entrepreneurship in India and Suggestive Measures

Kalee Prasanna Pattanayak[1] and Chitrasena Padhy[2]

[1]Assistant Professor, Centurion University of Technology and Management, Odisha
[2]Assistant Professor, Centurion University of Technology and Management, Odisha

1. Introduction

Over the past decade the new entrepreneurial endeavours have grown rapidly in India. The government has extended a helping hand in this effort through some of the most effective programmes like Stand up India, Start-up India, Make in India and Mudra scheme etc. The India entrepreneurial sector, with the active support from the government is capable of grooming the youth to be successful entrepreneurs.

Development of agribusiness sector is vital for uplifting the economic situation of the rural people. Rural entrepreneurship has been identified as areas of new research to bring out the development of the agribusiness sector (Vijay, S. 2016). The task of developing entrepreneurship in the cashew processing sector quickly, seems encouraging as this sector falls under the category of agro-based industry, which attracts a preferential treatment from the government. This industry has a huge potential to provide employment to large masses of rural workforce in the form of employment as workers in the cashew factories. This is a labour intensive industry, employing approximately three lakh persons (Binu Kumar, 2018), majority among them being women from socially disadvantaged and weaker section of society. Therefore, there is a need for the government, authorities and general public to understand this potential of cashew processing sector and make all possible effort to encourage it.

2. Constraints

Although cashew processing industry holds a huge potential to impact the livelihood of rural people positively, it has been observed that new entrepreneurs are reluctant to enter this industry. This may be due to an array of reasons which are making the industry unattractive to the new entrepreneurs. One of the major reasons is the difficulty faced by the entrepreneurs in sourcing labour for working in their factories throughout the year (Sampat, P. 2015). It has been noted that many micro and small cashew nut entrepreneurs have faced the issue of shortage of labour during their processing process (Shinde-Desai et. al, 2012). The deteriorating and unhealthy working conditions maintained in the factories is the reason for many of the workers to shift to other industries. The main stages in the cashew processing are shelling, peeling and grading. These processes are primarily performed by women. Women usually sit for seven to eight hours a day in a squatting position to perform these processes. Squatting for such long hours on a daily basis causes them to develop pain in backbone, knee and stomach. During the shelling process a caustic liquid which is highly acidic is released. Upon coming into constant contact with this liquid, the workers develop a skin condition called dermatitis and blistering of skin, causing severe discolouration of skin (Eagleton, M.H. 2007). Therefore due importance should be given by the authorities to the safety of these workers for attracting new workers and retaining old workers in this industry. Another challenge for entrepreneurs is the irregularity of the women workers in reporting for work. This may be due to their varied responsibility as home makers. Moreover, during the agricultural seasons a majority of them do not go for processing work as they join their family members in agricultural activities. So steps should be taken by the authorities as well as the processors to improve their working condition, increase their wages and provide a safe working environment.

Apart from the issue of shrinking workforce, the entrepreneurs face the challenge of inadequate working capital. Working capital is the money required to keep the factory functioning at any point of time. Maintaining adequate working capital is also considered a sign of good financial health and operational efficiency of the enterprise. Bhosale, V.R (2016) mentions that agro based industries like cashew processing require less fixed capital and more working capital. Kamath, V.R (2016) opines that at least 50 per cent of the total funds of an enterprise should be in the form of working capital. Hence, the provision of quick credit for working capital requirements should be made easily available to the entrepreneurs. Many entrepreneurs often choose to shut down their units for lack of adequate facilities to avail quick credit to meet their working capital requirements. All the input costs for processing, including that of raw materials, have increased dramatically and this when combined with the highly volatile nature of cashew prices in the market, throw a great deal of challenges for the entrepreneurs. Insufficient and poor quality of raw nuts has been identified as the major constraints faced by cashew nut entrepreneurs (Shinde-Desai et. al, 2012).

If these bottlenecks can be removed and quick credit facilities are provided, many new entrepreneurs could be prevented from leaving the industry due to lack of financial support. It is a well-accepted practice by the banks, not to offer credit to ventures started by new entrepreneurs. Sotunde,O.(2017) mentions that banks always find it risky to offer credit to ventures started by new entreprenuers. Few new entreprenuers are successful in opeing their enterprises at a micro- level by the support of their friends, relatives and family members.new entreprenuers would be attracted to this industry if credit facilities are made available quickly with simpler banking formalities.

A set of events happening simultaneously in the year 2016, had given a severe setback to the efforts of cashew processing entrepreneurs across the country. There was a general consensus among entrepreneurs on the demand for simplification of banking procedures for making the credit disbursal system efficient and effective. In 2016, the entrepreneurs faced a real difficulty when the union government decided to impose a 9.4 per cent import duty on raw cashew nuts (Ameerudheen, T. 2018). Around the same time, the international prices of raw cashew nuts increased from $800 per tonne to $ 1,800 per tonne, maiking the import of raw cashew nuts very costly for the processors. During that time this was seen as an attempt by the government to suffocate the growth of MSMEs (Micro, Small and Medium Enterprises) in the country. Many entrepreneurs thereafter started shutting down their units due to non-availability of fresh credit, after defaulting on their previous loans. The banks took recourse to the provision under the Sarfaesi Act to recover their unpaid loans. Under the Sarfaesi Act provisions, the banks are authorised to recover their loan dues after selling the hypothecated assets of the defaulters (Jose, T. 2017). The banks cited that it would not be appropriate to extend further credit to units which were already incurring losses. On the contrary, entrepreneurs were of the opinion that government should have intervened and instructed the banks to offer fresh credit to them instead of selling their hypothecated assets to recover the due amounts of loans.

It is important for the government to take steps to recover the loss making units by injecting fresh credits into this industry. It is also important for the government to protect the entrepreneurs from price risk resulting from the volatility of cashew nut prices in the international market. The entrepreneurs who are engaged in the processing of raw nuts into processed kernels face a big price risk (Sampat, P. 2015). The entrepreneurs operating in this sector equate this business to high risk, so much so that, they compare it with gambling. The entrepreneurs normally start purchasing the raw material by seeing the current prices of finished product (cashew kernels) in the market. But, it may so happen that in later stages when their product is ready for sale, the price of kernels either drops or increases. So they incur profit or loss from their production, actually depends on the movement of cashew nut prices in the market. Therefore, the government should take an initiative and build a strong risk management system for cashew nut trade, where entrepreneurs have access to technical information relating to international prices, domestic prices, product forecasts and trends etc.

3. Suggestive Measures

India's climatic conditions and soil type is very much suitable for cashew cultivation. So the country possesses a comparative advantage in the production of cashew nuts when compared to other countries. India also has the highest area dedicated to cashew production than any other country (Karthic Kumar, 2014). Among India's most important export items cashew finds a fourth place after basmati rice, spices and tea (Ameerudheen, T. 2018). India has overtaken U.S.A to be the leading consumer of cashew kernels in the world (Nair, H. 2015). The above facts point at the scope that exists within this industry to nurture innovation and entrepreneurship in the country.

One more reason why this sector has the potential to support innovation and entrepreneurship in the country is that cashew is a sector falling under the agro-based industry category (Ambidattu, P. 2015). Industries that are directly or indirectly linked to agriculture are called agro based industries. Agro based industries act as a bridge between the agriculture and industry. Different types of agro-based industries exist in the country, but the cashew cultivation and processing industry has the greatest potential to employ excess rural labour (Bhosale, V.R., 2016). The government from time to time has floated many skill enhancement programs for the aspiring as well as current entrepreneurs. But, greater emphasis is given to skill enhancement in the agro-based industries sector as agriculture still remains the backbone of India's economy. As mentioned earlier, the import duty on raw cashew nuts which was escalated to 9.4 per cent in 2016 has now been brought down to 2.5 per cent (Ameerudheen, T. 2018), thereby creating an opportunity for domestic processors to import the required quantities of raw nuts at competitive prices. Bhoodes, R.K. (2019) mentions that government should consider waiving off the import duty completely, in order to facilitate easier import of raw nuts into the country. Bhoodes, R.K. (2019) also supports the notion that government should provide interest free loans to entrepreneurs in this sector in the first few years of their establishment.

Although it would not be practical to argue in support of waiving off the import duty completely and proving interest free loans to entrepreneurs, we should also look at the ever increasing demand for Indian cashew kernels in the international market. As per Aggarwal, P., 2019 the demand for cashews has increased considerably in the international market. The notion around cashews has shifted from being a luxurious product to that of a necessary and healthy product that should find a place in every body's plate. According to Sampat, P. (2015), there will always be a demand for cashew nuts in the market regardless of the quantities produced and consumed. If one person at least consumes on cashew per day, the whole world's production of cashew's can be consumed in sixty days (Sampat, P. 2015). So according to Sampat, P. (2015), there would not be any marketing and selling problems of cashews even if all the processing units operate at fullest of their capacities. The increased revenues so generated as a result of the successful marketing and selling strategies of cashew nuts could be used to impact the standard of living and wellbeing of numerous workers in this industry, especially the women workers belonging to rural areas. The opportunity to leverage the benefits of trading in internal markets should also be offered to small scale entrepreneurs through proper training and extension activities (Srinivasan, G., & Mehazabeen, A. 2018) .As per Bhoodes, R.K. (2019) there are more than one million workers, who are employed in the Indian cashew industry, and the majority of them are women. The operations involving cashew kernel production will always remain highly labour intensive (Srinivasan, G., & Mehazabeen, A. 2018), as the processes like peeling and grading will always require some human intervention. The major advantage to entrepreneurs in engaging women workers is that they are available in surplus in rural areas and also they are capable of handling tasks that are monotonous and demand acute concentration.

4. Conclusions

India has a leading position in the world in production and processing of cashews nuts. But, unfortunately the country is unable to tap the vast international export market as well as the domestic market. Therefore the government in consultation with the processors should scale up the efforts to tap these markets. Proper mechanisation of processing units needs to be done for improving their processing efficiency. Currently the processing units are operating mostly at 50 per cent or less capacity due to the lack of smooth supply of labour, raw material and technology. There is a need for promoting the cashew nuts in the similar fashion which is used by the

Almond Board of California for promoting the use of almonds throughout the world. The almond board of California has successfully marketed the product by highlighting the health and nutritional benefits of almonds. The government in consultation with different cashew boards of the country should make efforts to promote cashew nuts just like it has been done for almonds. Another area that needs attention is improvement of production and yield of raw cashew nuts for decreasing the dependence on imported raw nuts. Timely availability of credit at cheaper rates and transfer of technical know-how to the processors would be highly beneficial for them. Another important area which needs attention is framing of a robust risk management strategy for controlling the price volatility in the domestic as well as international market.

References

1. Aggarwal, P. (2019). 5th Edition of the World Cashew Convention & Exhibition. The 5th Edition of the World Cashew Convention & Exhibition 2019 was held in Abu Dhabi between 24 to 26 January 2019. (p. 2). Abu Dhabi: www.Cashewinfo.com.
2. Ambidattu, P. (2015). An analysis of the performance of agro-based industries in Kerala with special reference to cashew nut. Indian Journal of Economics and Development, 1-5.
3. Ameerudheen, T. (2018, March 27). Cashew crisis. Retrieved May 28, 2019, from scroll.in: https://scroll.in/article/873274/despair-in-kerala-as-banks-start-seizing-cashew-factories.
4. Bhoodes, R. K. (2019). World Cashew Convention & Exhibition. 5th Edition Of The World Cashew Convention & Exhibition 2019 (p. 2). Abu Dhabi: www.cashewinfo.com.
5. Bhosale, V. R. (2016). Agro-Based Processing Industries in Rural Development in India. KHOJ: Journal of Indian Management Research, 234-240.
6. Binu Kumar, B. J. (2018). Problems And Prospects Of Cashew Based Industry In Kerala. (pp. 74-84). Ghaziabad: National Research & Journal Publication.
7. Eagleton, M. H. (2007). Just Plain Nuts: Cashews from India. UK: Action Aid International.
8. Gray, C. (2002). Entrepreneurship, Resistance to Change and Growth in Small Firms. Journal of Small Business and Enterprise Development, 61-72.
9. Jose, T. (2017, July 14). Economy & Finance. Retrieved May 28, 2019, from https://www.indianeconomy.net: https://www.indianeconomy.net/splclassroom/what-is-sarfaesi-act-2002/

10. Kamath, B. R. (2016). Cashew Kernel Markets in 2016 - INDIA. Abu Dhabi: World Cashew Convention.

11. Karthic kumar P, S. V. (2014). Indian Cashew Processing Industry-An overview. Journal of Food Research and Technology, 60-66.

12. Nair, H. (2015). Cashew industry: Challenges and Opportunities. Kollam: Quilon Management Association.

13. Sampat, P. (2015). Global Cashew Kernel Markets- Sustaining the Growth Momentum. Dubai: World Cashew Convention.

14. Sarabu, Vijay. (2016). Rural Development in India through Entrepreneurship: An Overview of the Problems and Challenges.

15. Shinde-Desai, S. S., Kawale, R., Sawant, P., & Nirban, A. (2012). 13. Supply Chain And Constraint Faced By Cashewnut Processers Of Konkan By SS Shinde-Desai, RR Kawale, PA Sawant and AJ Nirban. *LIFE SCIENCES LEAFLETS, 25*, 112-116.

16. Sotunde, O. (2017, October 3). Tanzania: Entrepreneur overcomes financing challenges to launch cashew business. Retrieved May 28, 2019, from www.howwemadeitinafrica.com: https://www.howwemadeitinafrica.com/tanzania-entrepreneur-overcomes-financing-challenges-launch-cashew-business/59876/

17. Srinivasan, G., & Mehazabeen, A. (2018). A Constraint Analysis on Small Scale Cashew Nut Industiries In Tamilnadu.

CHAPTER NINETEEN
Digital skills, competencies and employment opportunities

Prajna Pani[1]

[1]Centurion University of Technology and Management, Odisha

1. Introduction

Youngsters are graduating into what could be one of the hardest employment markets in many years. Joblessness is rising, organizations are freezing enrolment. The ever-changing landscape of the COVID-19 issue leaves the grads questioning what about their future jobs. The job market is continually changing and technology-driven/ innovation driven careers are becoming more and more popular. Regardless of what field you pick, having hard skills and soft skills can increase success rate. This paper will review some of the most valuable modern skills to develop while looking for a job. It shares the insights that are intended to help job seekers understand the types of jobs and skills required for future jobs. It also intends to show pathways to educational organisations for integration of trending courses in their curriculum, help students to discover their skills and abilities, and identify areas to groom the students. The paper also highlights industry trends. The European Commission (see Punie & Cabrera, 2006) has defined digital competence as involving the confident and critical use of Information Society Technology for work, leisure and communication. COVID-19 impact on campus placement: 66% students without jobs, 33% awaiting response from employers (The Indian Express, 2020). Research by UK-based graduate jobs website Milkround shows just 18% of graduates are securing jobs this year compared to the typical 60% Jones, Jessica (2020). Technology reigns in the job market. According to McKinsey report, India is the second fastest digitising economy in the world. As per India Skills Report 2020, 53% of employers that that only some job seekers could satisfy their requirement.

Companies use various source channels such as job portals, professional networks and social media, and internal referrals to hire the right talents.

The high-tech landscape with automation replacing low-skilled jobs, it's the demand for human skills that is out stripping the supply (World Economic Forum report The Future of Job Skills, 2020). India's significant IT firms Infosys and Wipro also agree that while they are moving routine positions to atomisation, they are not firing their employees yet moving them to further advanced areas like machine learning and AI which require basic critical thinking, creative thinking and problem solving abilities. Deciphering this as far as curricular plan would mean a training that would teach students a mix of STEAM subjects for scientific research and innovation, humanities for understanding human practices alongside trade for making sense of businesses and financial markets. Nonetheless, the current generation who are concentrating in science, humanities and commerce streams would get themselves painfully deficient in satisfying such jobs roles

2. Career and job search sites

Majority of the jobs are tech-oriented. Students should be pursued in areas of popular courses, in-demand skills to expand their knowledge and enhance their skills to stand out different from other candidates. The paper outlines in-demand hard and soft skills

3. Promising Skills and Job Opportunities

While undergrads are searching for jobs on their own they are likewise turning towards online courses and affirmations to upskill themselves. Around 70% of undergrads have enrolled to online courses (The Indian Express, 2020). There has been a huge demand for customized courses following the changing social and financial aspects of the post-pandemic age. An age where achieved experts in portions, for example, health care, medicine, research, technology, and innovation will be particularly valued. As indicated by information shared through site Glassdoor, one of the top job searching sites, the best five roles for undergraduates with the most elevated Covid related business openings incorporate enrolled medical/healthcare services, communication, social work, project management, and technicians. There are different advantages of interning, not exclusively does the experience tally yet additionally the information gained helps in career enhancement. Setting off to a top college or graduating top of your batch probably won't be sufficient to find the dream job. An internship abroad can be a key competitive advantage for students, graduates and young professionals. As per a survey conducted by Institute for the International Education, students who interned abroad found that their experience abroad helped them acquire job skills, and they could find new jobs within six months of graduation (Sharma, 2020).

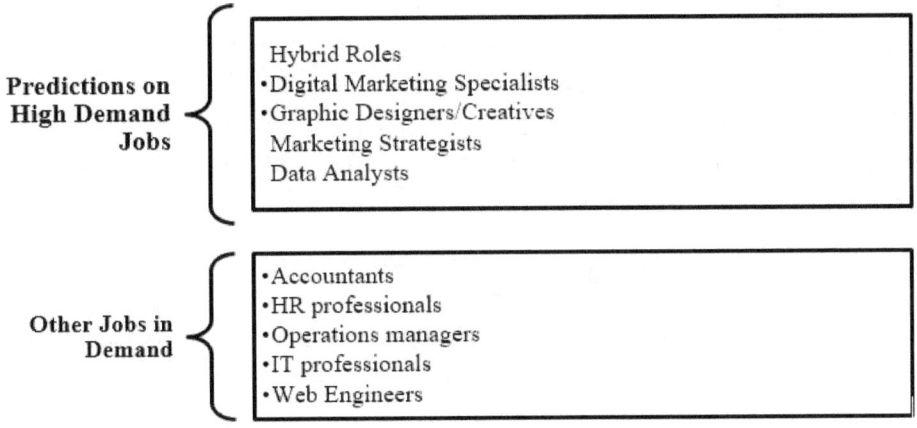

Predictions on High Demand Jobs

Hybrid Roles
•Digital Marketing Specialists
•Graphic Designers/Creatives
Marketing Strategists
Data Analysts

Other Jobs in Demand

•Accountants
•HR professionals
•Operations managers
•IT professionals
•Web Engineers

Figure 1. Career Group Companies, 2020

The economy might be recouping, however organizations are as yet attempting to recover their balance. This implies that they might not have a budget plan for different recruits and will require somebody who can play hybrid roles, i.e., somebody who can perform multiple jobs will be perhaps the best employment for 2021, however, one should be exceptionally unique and have both hard skills and technical skills. Companies have shifted to the digital market and eCommerce platforms. Because of this, they need more digital marketing professionals. A digital marketer's responsibilities will incorporate anything from SEO to online media to Google promotions. Graphic designer is one of the most demanding jobs in 2021. Companies are looking for dynamic candidates who can to run marketing campaigns and will need someone to actualize the marketing concepts. A job that allows you to express creativity is the right job for you. Part of the job description will include developing layouts for product illustrations, making new logos for new businesses and rebranding organizations, planning UI etc. Different positions sought after for 2021 that are identified with this job include creative directors, production artists, multimedia artists, and animators. In order to land these jobs, you will need experience with tools So as to get these positions, you will require skills Adobe Photoshop and Adobe InDesign, along with others.

4. Benefits of collaboration with career group companies

4.1. Collaboration with Career Group Companies can assist educational organisations for getting students ready for future jobs

4.2. Resume assistance helps in aligning the resume to the requirements of job position

4.3.Career advisors provide support and offer guidance on the jobs students should take and those students should give up. Students receive advise on what is practical and what they can anticipate from their pursuit of employment, given the current market and your range of abilities.

4.4.Interview Prep helps the students with pointers and unique selling points to crack job interviews.

4.5.Job Matching puts the students for jobs that they are sure will be the best fit for them.

4.6.Associations and Networking help with contacts with companies who do not publish /advertise some job positions. They are connected with those that are a perfect match.

5. Employability Training Framework

Employability training framework is designed in five blocks, namely, goal of the training, technical training, soft skills training, internships and certifications/projects.

Colleges and Universities should embed technical trainings in the trending areas such as blockchain, cloud computing, artificial intelligence, UX design, programming languages and operating systems, affiliate marketing, sales and video production.

The top important soft skills identified through the scoping review are integrated in the training framework. They are creativity, collaboration, adaptability, time management, persuasion, EI, project management, data analysis, complex problem solving, decision-making, negotiation and flexibility.

Communication skills are the most vital skills that are that are needed to continue oneself in the present market. Communicating the right message in the right manner make a huge difference at the workplace, and people who know how to do it always stay ahead in the game. Creativity empowers students to see concepts differently, which leads to innovation. Innovation is key to the adaptability and overall success of an organisation. It is seen as a method of transformation. Creativity is equally important as a means of adaptation. This skill empowers students to see concepts in a different light, which leads to innovation. Learning creativity as a skill requires someone to understand that "the way things have always been done" may have been best 10 years ago — but someday, that has to change. Collaboration means getting students to work in a team, accomplish goals, and get the positive outcomes from solving a problem. The key element of coordinated effort is willingness and readiness to achieve the team's goal. Companies are not only looking for the ability to recognise and manage one's emotions but also understand others emotions when working in a team.

Your way isn't always the right way
You need to realise your mistake and admit it
Your way isn't always the best way
You have to know and admit when you are wrong

Flexibility requires students to show humility. Realizing when to change, how to change, and how to respond to change is an expertise that will bring benefits to one's career. Time management, persuasion, data analysis skills, problem solving, decision making, negotiation are other top soft skills along with EI (emotional intelligence skills). The EI trainings will make the students sociable, amiable and improve their ability to handle complex situations with empathy and care. Flexibility is the ability to adapt to changing circumstances. This is one of the most moving characteristics to learn for students since it depends on two thoughts outside their comfort zones:

Certifications/projects can validate the skills and experience of students to prove that they have the mastery or expertise to get the job done. Certifications are the best way to strengthen the resume and set apart from different competitors in a pursuit of employment.

6. Conclusion

The study has explored the career and job search sites to find the recruitment trends. Based on the findings, a training framework is designed. A recommendation for further research is to implement the training module in colleges and universities. It is also suggested to determine impact of the training program.

References

Career Group Companies (2020), Jobs in Demand 2021: Top Careers for the New Decade. https://careergroupcompanies.com/top-careers-for-the-new-decade/

European Union. 2010 joint progress report of the Council and the Commission on the implementation of the 'Education and Training 2010 work programme', (2010). Official Journal of the European Union, (2010/C117/01) Retrieved August, 22, 2010 from http://eurlex.europa.eu/LexUriServ/LexUriServ.do?uri=OJ:C:2010:117:0001:0007:EN:PDF

Jones, Jessica The uncertain present and future for recent graduates, (2020). https://www.bbc.com/worklife/article/20200901-the-class-of-2020s-uncertain-present-and-future

Mckinsey Digital. Digital India: Technology to transform a connected nation (2019). Taken from https://www.mckinsey.com/business-functions/mckinsey-digital/our-insights/digital-india-technology-to-transform-a-connected-nation

Sharma, Som. The Tribune, An international internship is gateway for abroad Job Post Covid-19, (2020). Adapted from https://www.tribuneindia.com/news/jobs-careers

The New Indian Express Adapted from https://indianexpress.com/article/jobs/covid-19-impact-on-campus-placement (2020).

CHAPTER TWENTY

Entrepreneurship Development Cycle and Programmes in India

Dr. Girija Nandini, Associate Professor,
Centurion University of Technology and Management, Odisha, India

Dr. Pramod Kumar Patjoshi, Associate Professor,
Centurion University of Technology and Management, Odisha, India

I. Introduction

The entrepreneurship development cycle includes all the provision, support and help given to the entrepreneurs for their growth and sustainability. It generates and increases awareness of entrepreneurship among the people through proper planning. It supports people who want to be an entrepreneur. It helps the entrepreneur who finds some opportunity, can able to arrange resources, having a business plan, who can take a risk to achieve certain amount of profit within a specified time limit.

II. Stages of Entrepreneurship Development Cycle

Entrepreneurship development cycle has following stages:

Stage 1: New Project Growth Stage

This stage requires creativity and proper analysis of the resources which is required to start the venture. Vision, mission, plans, policies should be clear from the beginning.

Stage 2: Start-Up Stage

This stage requires a right business plan which should include different sources of finance, marketing strategy of the venture, identifying human resources, advantages and disadvantages of the project.

Stage 3: Stimulatory Stage

It requires creating entrepreneurship awareness among people. It includes identifying and train people for entrepreneurship and also to increase the technical skills and competencies of the entrepreneurs. Helping to solve their problems and issues related to entrepreneurship.

Stage 4: Support Stage

Support stage supports the entrepreneurs for starting and running their business. It helps in the registration of business, arrangement of the financial resources, purchase of plant and machinery, arranging land, water, selection of plant location and layout etc.

Stage 5: Growth Stage

Here knowing the competitors are important. Strategy and plans can be modified or changed according to the requirements. In this stage the entrepreneur has to belief and understands that only the fittest can survive in the long run.

Stage 6: Stabilization Stage

In this stage growth is at the highest stage and competition is very high and also the bargaining power of the customer is high. So the entrepreneur has to think about innovation and the future of the business. He has to think whether to continue the business by doing innovation or to exit.

Stage 7: Sustaining Stage

Sustaining activities helps entrepreneur to run their business in a profitable manner and modernization of equipment, products and finding substitution of the product. Guiding and helping if any problem is there.

Stage 8: Innovation or Decline Stage

In this stage the entrepreneur has to innovate or go for diversification or close the business. They can also go for merger and acquisition to survive.

III. Entrepreneurship Development programmes in India

Institutions for Entrepreneurship Development: NIESBUD, EDII, NAYE, ICC, TCOs, Commercial Banks and a Few Others. In India several organisations are engaged in entrepreneurship development programmes.

Some of these are given below:

1. The National Institute for Entrepreneurship and Small Business Development (NIESBUD), New Delhi

It is coordinating different organisations involved in Entrepreneurship Development.

Some of the important functions are:
i.   Developing and planning for training
ii.   Finding scientific selection methods
iii. Preparing training model, manuals for different target groups
iv.   Supporting the agencies involved in entrepreneurship development
v.   Increasing the benefits for entrepreneurs
vi.   Developing the culture of entrepreneurship

2. Entrepreneurship Development Institute of India (EDII), Ahmedabad

Its entrepreneurship development programme is quite comprehensive and successful consisting of the following steps:
i.   Choosing prospective entrepreneurs
ii.   Successful and practical training for entrepreneurs
iii. Preparation of project reports
iv.   Research and publication in entrepreneurship
v.   After training support to the entrepreneurs

3. National Alliance of Young Entrepreneurs (NAYE)

It has different schemes in alliance with public sector banks.

Some of the schemes are as follows:

(i) Bank of India-Naye – This scheme known as BINEDS was sponsored in August 1972. It is functioning in many Slates like Punjab, Rajasthan, Himachal Pradesh, J&K, Chandigarh and Delhi.

(ii) Dena Bank-Naye – It promotes supplementary units and small scale companies of Madras.

(iii) Punjab National Bank – This scheme started in March 1977 in West Bengal and Bihar

(iv) Central Bank of India-Naye –This programme is functioning in Maharashtra.

(v) Union Bank of India-Naye – This is operating in Tamilnadu.

All these schemes are helping young entrepreneurs for self-employment by giving them proper training and financial assistance.

4. Indian Investment Centre (IIC)

It is an independent non-profit organisation funded and sustained by the Government. It is helping in the collaboration of Indian and foreign entrepreneurs. It gives all the information to foreign entrepreneurs who want to invest in India. The IIC has set up an Entrepreneurial Guidance Bureau (EGB) for the development of entrepreneurs.

5. Technical Consultancy Organisations (TCOs)
Their main functions of TCOs are as follows:

(i)   Piloting studies on the prospective ventures

(ii)   Preparation of feasibility and pre-feasibility studies

(iii)   Making the technical and economic appraisal of the projects

(iv)   Making marketing research for the projects

(v)   Giving managerial support to the entrepreneurs

(vi)   Advising on setting up and organising laboratories, design centres and Machine shops and Workshops, standardisation units, etc.

6. Commercial Banks
Commercial banks are doing several activities to support and guide the entrepreneurs mostly in the rural and backward areas. Some of the banks have created entrepreneurship service cells or guidance bureaus, for this purpose. Commercial banks prepare several functions to assist and encourage small entrepreneurs.

Some of these are:

(i) Assistance in judging the technical and commercial viability of project proposals.

(ii) Assistance in preparing and evaluating project reports

(iii) Practical training in the selected industry

(iv) Assistance in obtaining Government clearances

(v) Assistance in procuring machinery and equipment

(vi) Assistance in raising the required funds

(vii)   Assistance and guidance in implementing the project, etc.

7.In addition to the above, the following institutes also offer facilities for training and developing entrepreneurs in India:
(i) National Institute for small Industry Extension Training (NISIET), Hyderabad

(ii) Indian Institute of Entrepreneurship (IIE), Guwahati

(iii) Centre for Entrepreneurship Development

(iv) Small Industry Service Institute (SISI) located in each of the states

(v) Entrepreneurship Development Cells in various IITs, Engineering Colleges, ITIs and Polytechnics

(vi) Science and Technology Entrepreneurship Development Park (STEP) sponsored by the Department of Science and Technology, Govt., of India

(vii) District Industry Centres (DICs) at district level

(viii) NGOs at district sub-division, block and village levels.

These institutions create awareness about entrepreneurship, provide necessary information and skills to aspiring entrepreneurs and provide support to them till they can stand on their own feet.

8. **Incubators:**

Indian Institutes of Technology (IITs) and Indian Institutes of Management (IIMs) have set up Incubation and Entrepreneurship Centres to foster student entrepreneurs. A large number of students start enterprises during or after studies. In case start-ups fail students can opt for placement afterwards. For example, IIT-Bombay has a Society of Innovation and Entrepreneurship (SINE) and IIM-Ahmedabad has a Centre for Innovation Incubation and Entrepreneurship (CIIE).

All these development programmes in India are supporting and helping the new and existing entrepreneurs for development and growth.

CHAPTER TWENTY ONE

A study on Locational Mobility of Entrepreneurs in India

Dr.Pramod Kumar Patjoshi, Associate Professor,
Centurion University of Technology and Management, Odisha, India

Dr.Girija Nandini, Assistant Professor,
Centurion University of Technology and Management, Odisha, India

Locational Mobility of Entrepreneurs in India

Mobility change has been happening for the past few decades plus will last in eternity then India has an occasion to be a global leader. Nevertheless, our country is recognized for hopping fast of the technology changes.

Nonetheless, mobility cannot proceed in a similar manner. India has to progress in a systematic manner and strong in it fundamentals. So that India can hold trends which will project its mobility services beyond other advanced nation. This will have a optimistic consequence on the Indian economy, on the reasonability of infrastructure development and the superiority of lifestyle of people of India. Mobility change is a continuous process and India has to change the art of mobility – from in an innovative way by adopting new technology as well as suitable location.

Moving and settlement is in social nature nonetheless different communities are different for each other some are additional mobile than others while few of the entrepreneurs are mobile. Their locational mobility depends upon availability of raw material and labour, experience, socio political information, etc.

Locational or geographical mobility of entrepreneurs signifies the drive as well as creativity to move to other places in search of healthier occasions. For example, Marwaris and Sindhis in our country have moved to almost every corner of India to carry on business activities. Such a spirit helps to reduce regional imbalances in economic growth.

Each entrepreneur has a 'spatial horizon' which depends upon resources, involvement as well as information-gathering capacity. In the preliminary stages of industrialisation, the spatial prospect is thin due to feeble communication scheme, poor info schemes, unavailability of capital resources in addition to absence of institutional provisions. As a result, most of the entrepreneurs establish businesses at or near their places.

For example, entrepreneurs from Bombay and Ahmedabad set up cotton textiles plants at these places. That is why there has been heavy regional concentration of industrial and commercial activity in India. New and small entrepreneurs generally have a limited spatial horizon and, therefore, form their businesses in the close proximity of their centres of activity.

This facilitates management of their enterprises. Location of new unit at a distance from the existing unit is likely to dilute effective control over the new unit. Moreover, the new enterprise may have backward or forward industry linkage and so will be set up near the existing unit. Language barriers, unfamiliarity with labour conditions, feeling of alienness at a strange place, political uncertainties and local property also inhibit entrepreneurial mobility.

Even after gaining some experience entrepreneurs mainly remain confined to a limited area. Some of them ambitious to build empires carve out their own political status and wield as much influence in the area as the political authority.

When resources enlarge, knowledge as well as information movements increase, entrepreneurs are probable to become mobile. In place of "local", he now becomes cosmopolitan entrepreneur. Instead of spatial horizon industry choice decides the location now. The entrepreneur is willing to move out over long distances from his usual place of working to exploit and seize opportunities. The entrepreneur may move to other States or even abroad.

Therefore, there are three phases of entrepreneurial mobility. In the initial phase entrepreneurs are secured to their normal places of working. By means of steady development, they are likely to become relatively mobile within a limited area. Once they become extremely inventive, larger degree of mobility happens. This suggests that in any nation only a handful of entrepreneurs will be mobile. If entrepreneurial class is limited then unequally dispersed, there will be robust regional inequities in industrial growth.

The key factors influencing the mobility of entrepreneurs are as follows:

1. Resources:

An individual with limited resources is willing to take limited risks. Therefore, he starts an enterprise within a zone he can easily manage. Setting up of a plant at a distance will require his staying away from his usual place of working or handing over management to others. But the entrepreneur with larger resources can assume greater risks and collect better information. He does not mind locating a plant at distant places. Thus, larger the resources at the entrepreneur's command the greater the degree of mobility.

2. Experience:

An experienced entrepreneur is more mobile than the new entrant. He has better perception or opportunities, greater access to sources of information and better analytical tools to judge the efficacy of an enterprise at a distant place. He better understands the problem of alienation, regional barriers, etc., at a new place. The experience may be technical, business, industry or any other.

The most mobile entrepreneur is one who is familiar with working of industry as he has acquired risk-taking attitude, knowledge of markets, rapport with Government officials, etc. The individual with business experience is less mobile as he is less prone to assume risks elsewhere. The entrepreneur with technical experience is likely to make a start at a place where he obtained practical experience or at his usual place of living.

3. Education:

An educated entrepreneur tends to be more mobile than an uneducated one. He is better able to comprehend the conditions at a distance and make his own studies of the area. He can better hold discussions with the authorities and better appraise the opportunities existing outside his area.

4. Language:

People speaking different languages see each other with suspicion as there often exists a communication gap among them. Labour having language affinity may combine against the outside entrepreneur or the local politicians may incite feelings against him. Local governments committed to regionalism may also pose threats. New and small entrepreneurs find it difficult to overcome these barriers. Only experienced and established entrepreneurs can assume such risks.

5. Culture:

The entrepreneurs uprooted from their traditional native places are more mobile than those who have not been, like a displaced person or a foreigner. They develop a more cosmopolitan outlook as they adjust themselves in new cultures and are free from the sanctions and bondages of their own culture.

6. Nature of Enterprise:

If the enterprise involves only expansion of the existing plant, the entrepreneur is likely to acquire additional land in the vicinity of the existing plant. Same will be the case when the enterprise has backward or forward linkages with the existing industry. But when the new unit cannot be started near the existing one, he will move out.

The above considerations are inter-related and influence simultaneously. However, the resources and experience of the entrepreneur play a decisive role and others may be considered as contributing factors.

CHAPTER TWENTY TWO

A study on Factors Affecting Growth of Entrepreneurs in India

Dr.Pramod Kumar Patjoshi, Associate Professor,
Centurion University of Technology and Management, Odisha, India

Factors in Favour of Entrepreneurship Development

Entrepreneurship is playing a vital role in the development of industrial culture. In developing economies the most required thing is balanced regional development, poverty alleviation, rural renovation, introduction to advance technology, innovation, human resource development and developed society.

In context to India, following facts are in favour to entrepreneurship development, these are:

(1) Enhancing the planned economic development.

(2) Providing opportunities of self-employment.

(3) Abolition of poverty.

(4) Removing regional imbalance.

(5) Proper use of natural and human resources.

(6) Helpful in capital formation.

(7) Maintaining conducive environment for industrial development.

(8) New research and product technology.

(9) Commercial use of scientific invention.

(10) Helpful in setup of socialist society and welfare society.

(11) Successful implementation of government's economic policies and programme.

(12) Scouting new domestic and international market.

(13) Scouting the feasibility of industrial development and their implementation.

(14) Enhancing social changes and living standard.

Entrepreneurship Development in India – Factors Affecting Entrepreneurship Growth: Economic, Social, Personality, Psychological, Sociological and Cultural Factors

In the under developed countries there are certain variables that influence the development of entrepreneurship.

Few of the major factors include-

1. Economic Factors.

2. Social Factors.

3. Psychological in addition to Sociological Factors.

4. Personality Factors.

5. Cultural Factors.

1. Economic Factors:

The economic factors effecting the growth of entrepreneurs in under developed countries are-

i. Unavailability of capital

ii. Unavailability of superiority raw materials and finished goods.

iii. Lack of adequate basic facilities.

iv. Higher risk involved in the corporate.

v. Unavailability of skilled manpower.

i. Unavailability of Capital:

To expand the business and grow in future research and development has to be conducted. To conduct a research either equipments have to be purchased or get exported from other developed countries, for this huge capital is required. Thus the non-availability of huge capital effects the growth of entrepreneurship in the country.

ii. Unavailability of Superiority Raw Materials as well as Finished Goods:

Since there is less availability of raw materials throughout the year, they have to be purchased in large quantity and stored during the period of its availability. To purchase heavy quality raw materials, capital have to be borrowed which involves heavy rate of interest. This effects the entrepreneurial growth.

iii. Lack of Adequate Basic Facilities:

Certain basic facilities such as power facilities, irrigational facilities, latest technology, transport and communication etc., are required for undertaking innovative activities which help in providing increased output and reduce the cost of production.

But in under developed country like ours there is in-adequate availability of these basic facilities. The entrepreneur have to get these facilities by themselves where heavy costs have to be beared. Thus again these factors causes hinderance in the growth of entrepreneurs.

iv. Greater risk involved in the business:

a. Due to seasonal fluctuations of demand there is instability in the market.

b. Instability in domestic and foreign economic policies.

c. An entrepreneur cannot make correct estimates for his proposed venture as there is lack of correct information, overhead facilities, market demand etc.,

Since lot of risks are involved the growth of entrepreneurship is affected.

v. Non-Availability of Skilled Labours:

As there are non-availability of skilled labours and no proper training facilities available, the entrepreneurs find it difficult to progress with these unskilled labours.

2. Social Factors:

Some of the social factors include-

i. Social system.

ii. Customs and traditions.

iii. Social set up

iv. Rationality of the society.

i. Social System:

The social system existing in the locality effect the growth of entrepreneurship in the country. If there is a joint family then one member of the family will not share his wealth with the other member of the family. Thus entrepreneurship cannot be developed.

ii. Customs and Traditions:

In few cases customs and traditions play a dominant role in the production decisions rather than critically assessing the facts.

iii. Social Set-Up:

In some societies very less importance in provided towards education, training, research etc., and more importance is given towards caste considerations. Thus no entrepreneurs can emerge from such societies who have great aptitude and skills.

iv. Rationality of the Society:

In under developed countries most of the societies are non-rational societies which is not suitable for the entrepreneurial growth.

3. Personality Factors:

In under developed countries, the entrepreneurs are looked up as a profit makers and exploiters of the resources and people. Thus causing a problem for the growth of entrepreneurs.

4. Psychological and Sociological Factors:

According to Mc Clelland, "need achievement motive induces entrepreneurship".

According to Paul Wilken, "entrepreneurship becomes the link between need achievement and economic growth".

Cole states that, "besides wealth, prestige, entrepreneurs seek power, security and serve the society".

Rostow had conducted research on inter-generation changes in the entrepreneurial families and found that, the first generation believes in seeking wealth, the second generation in prestige and third generation in art and beauty.

On the basis of motives, Even has distinguished three kinds of entrepreneurs:

i. Chief motive of managing entrepreneurs is security.

ii. Chief motive of innovating entrepreneurs is excitement,

iii. Chief motive of controlling entrepreneurs are power and authority.

Thus many psychological and sociological factors affect the growth of entrepreneurs.

5. Cultural Factors:

If the cultural factors prevailing in the country do not attach higher value to trade talents, industrial leadership etc., then entrepreneurs, people may not prefer to start up a new venture. Thus entrepreneurship is not developed.

Entrepreneurship Development in India – Entrepreneurial Performance in India

According to Dr. Sharma entrepreneurial performance is a function of the following factors:

(i) Socio-cultural Background of the Entrepreneur (SB) – This implies the environment in which the entrepreneur was born and brought up. It conditions the values and attitudes of the entrepreneur.

(ii) Motivational Force (MF) – It implies the motives which prompt a person to undertake entrepreneurship, e.g., wealth, status, self-employment, etc.

(iii) Knowledge and Ability of the Entrepreneur (KA) – It refers to the education, training and experience of the entrepreneur.

(iv) Financial Strength (FS) – It means the funds which an entrepreneur can mobilise from internal and external sources.

(v) Environmental Variables (EV) – These consist of Government policies market conditions, availability of technology and labour situation. Symbolically,

Where EP represents entrepreneurial performance.

Several studies have been conducted to judge the performance of Indian entrepreneurs.

The foremost standards used to evaluate performance of entrepreneurs are as follows:

(a) Gestation Period:

(b) Financial Results:

(c) Volume of Operation:

(d) Expansion as well as Diversification:

(e) Value Added by Manufacture:

(f) Growth of Offspring Enterprises:

(g) Others:

CHAPTER TWENTY THREE

A study on Reasons for Slow Growth and Remedies for Rapid Development of Entrepreneurship in India

Dr.Pramod Kumar Patjoshi, Associate Professor,

Centurion University of Technology and Management, Odisha, India

Reasons for Slow Growth of Entrepreneurship in India

There are numerous factors responsible for the development of entre-preneurship.

Following evidences prove that in India entrepreneurship develop-ment speed is very slow. These are:

1. Social Evils – Indian society is full of several social evils i.e., conser-vatism, superstitious, castism, family evils, dowery, show off tendency, and illiteracy etc. These factors are thoroughly responsible for the lack of entre-preneurship development in India.

2. Non-progressive Thinking – In India there is lack of trust towards creative thinking and lack of research tendency in society, so these factors are responsible for lack of creative ability in Indian society.

3. Lack of capital – In India per capita income is very less in comparison to foreign countries. In Indian society people do not invest their saving in industries while they invest in unproductive areas. This one is the main cause of less capital formation in India.

4. Lack of Technical and vocational education – Our education system only provides general knowledge about subject. It mostly affects the entrepreneurship tendency of youngsters and in India there is lack of technical and vocational educational institutes which is the main obstacle factor in the path of entrepreneurial development.

5. Lack of training and Motivation centres – There is lack of training and motivation centres in India. Most of training centres are located or situated in urban areas rather than rural and backward areas. So, it is also an important obstacle factor in path of entrepreneurship development.

6. Inadequate government facilities and Incentives – For encouraging entrepreneurial tendency among society, there is lack of proper government facilities and incentives. Government has not given full attention towards infrastructure facilities for industrial development along with lack of enthusiastic policy or programmes regarding raw material, techniques, market finance etc.

7. Fear of competition – There are numerous large industries situated in India and they have captured domestic and international market very effi-ciently. This is also an obstacle factor for entrepreneurship development in India.

8. Administrative lacunas – Inefficient Govt. department, bureaucracy, red tapism, corruption, delay and complexity of rules and norms are the cause of slow development of entrepreneurship.

9. Lack of entrepreneurial spirit – Today's younger generation believe in high salary or income so they are attracted towards service sector rather than industrial sector.

10. Competition by the public sector – Governments has been provid-ing incentives and preferences to public enterprise. Whereas small units lack of these facilities have not been compete to public units. So competition of PEs is an impeding factor to small units for creating their supremacy in market.

Other Obstacles:

(1) High taxes

(2) Complexity of legal formalities, i.e., Registration, project approval, license, other legal formalities.

(3) Technical backwardness.

(4) Limited to local market.

(5) Defective government policy

(6) Competition with Multinational Corporation.

(7) Lack of adaptable environment.

(8) Lack of external facilities.

Remedies for Rapid Development of Entrepreneurship in India

Development of entrepreneurship is a new concept in India. For rapid implementation of this concept, government, financial institutions, banks and other agencies should give proper attention towards it.

According to Udai Pareek and Monohar Nadkarni, "Entrepreneurship development would mean development of entrepreneurs and promotion of increased flow of individuals to entrepreneurial ranks."

In India, there are lots of potential in youngster but due to lack of proper motivation, incentives and training they cannot remark their identity at local and global.

Broadly Speaking "Think local, act global."

For rapid and faster development of entrepreneurship, government should take following steps. These are:

(1) Industrial feasibilities in each area should be searched and on the basis of received data and information, perspective Industrial maps should be prepared.

(2) Education system should be made employment and venture oriented.

(3) In backward area to identify the entrepreneurs, Identifying Mech-anism system should be developed.

(4) The number of technical and vocational education centres should be increased.

(5) Training and motivational facilities should be arranged for entre-preneurs.

(6) Self-employment plans should be diffused among peoples

(7) Expansion of consultancy services for entrepreneurs.

(8) All information about Government provide incentives and facilities should be generated amongst public.

(9) Research project regarding entrepreneurship should be encouraged.

(10) The working system of central co-ordinating agency should be made effective for entrepreneurship development.

(11) Bureaucracy tendency in government departments, financial institu-tions and other allied institution should be removed.

(12) Government should emphasise more on making of industrial estate and improving infrastructure facilities in backward areas.

(13) Government should be made tax-structure in accordance to entre-preneur relief.

(14) Government should make conducive business environment within India.

(15) Government should conduct specific development promotional plan for rural and small entrepreneurs.

(16) Some other suggestions –

(i) Strong capital market.

(ii) Economic stability

(iii) Co-ordination between public and Private sector.

(iv) Creative change in social structure.

(v) Sound legal and judiciary system.

CHAPTER TWENTY FOUR

A STUDY ON EVALUATION OF ENTREPRENEURIAL DEVELOPMENT IN INDIA

Dr.Pramod Kumar Patjoshi

Jasmeen Nisha

1. Introduction

Simply to say in India entrepreneurial development counts on generation wise doing family business, also exploring the technological progress. The skill of knowing how to do business has been passed through all the generation as the future generation is always ready to take place and follows the footsteps of their elders. As the time changes, it also changes the way of implying things from manually to technologically. But the societal needs are the same to will remain the same but there will be more modification into it.

2.Business Enterprises in The Past

As Indians people tends to follow the traditions which has become hindrance to perceive the modern ways to approach things. That is reason why western countries are way more advance and uncourageous than our country. Many research writers said that there had always been that thing called self- efficiency and external control over all things during computing it into act in business. The potential traders always follows the cast system their divisions and practices of following a family occupation rather than launching a new ventures. When the English rulers entered in our country everything began to change while some of the Bengali Nawab had come into the terms for doing business with the English people that is when British rulers takeover the Bengal in 1757. There had been many Jamindars or Seths who started to act as indigenous banks creating their own monopoly society. Then they also change the education system by reinforcing the occupational structure, signifying the cast system. And in India business was being held by low esteem during the past days.

And later in 19th centuries the Marwari business had taken the market in Eastern India before the independence, and then the typical political business history of Indians began to lose its connections with the new changes. It had become a tradition for bringing the occupational divisions which signifies the cast system more among the Hindus. As a result commercial activities became a monopoly of the Vishay sect. The other three Hindus Varnas, the Brahnmana, the Kshatriya and the Shudra never ware interested in trade and commerce even while India had extensive commercial relationship in outside the world.

3.Overview of Traditional Indian Society and Entrepreneurship Development:

Our country India has so many cultures and traditions. Likely saying that we are known in the society due to our traditions. Talking about traditions… Guajarati of Ahmedabad is known as one of the conservative society they have their own ways of doing business. While Bengalis were clever as well as sensitive while doing business using different tactics. Doing business in big cities (Bombay, Calcutta, and Mysore) always had provided more opportunities for the growth and helps with importing and exporting goods from outside the country. In the mid 19's the traditional method had starting to change the picture with the impact of urbanization and industrialization which are changing the rural consumption habits very much. Cities like Murshidabad and Navsari were very popular due to Parsi entrepreneurs affected the substitution of traditional products by new products which were cheaper as a result of large scale production. In later days marwari communities of Calcutta controlled the economic activity of east India they built their own merchant class of Rajputana, marwari mahajan. 'Decolonial motive' was the result of nationalism movement and entrepreneurs were carrying their activities demanded by the public. This movement has to be 'pre- colonial motive' of enriching both the enterprise and the society to take advantage of both opportunities created by the colonialists.

Todays' combined business had their origin in the 17th century; they achieved their growth by associating themselves with the Portuguese, Dutch and French business houses operating in important trading centers.

Then there comes Nehru legacy as the first prime minister of independent India he believed that entrepreneurs should focus their effort on nation building rather than selling products or competing with each other, because he felt that it did not directly contribute to this cause. He made sure that every entrepreneur should receive a certified nation building license from the relevant license officer.

CHAPTER TWENTY FIVE

Institutional Innovation in Promoting Access to Education for Children with Disabilities: A Case of Swabhiman

Bibhunandini Das[1]

1. Introduction

Inadequate healthcare, low income and poor nutrition are some of the major reasons for high exposure to disease and injuries (Solarsh and Hofman, 2006, Grech, 2009). Hence disability can be considered as cause as well as consequences of poverty because poor people always deprive off health, nutrition and education. Braithwaite and Mont (2008) in their paper found that out of world's poorest people, 20 per cent of poor are having some types of impairment. Hence, with the impairment it becomes difficult for them to earn enough to come out from the stage of poverty. In order to move out from poverty, education might play an important role. To facilitate education for differently abled children, institution innovation could play a major role. In this

[1] Associate Professor, Centurion University of Technology and Management, Odisha, India.

context, the present study is an attempt to understand the role of institution in facilitating education to disabled children.

The rest of the paper is organised as follows: following introduction section 2 discusses the data and methodology followed by narration of institutional architecture in section 3. Section 4 discusses how institution is playing a role in facilitating education to disabled children. Section 5 summarises the discussion with some concluding observations.

2. Data and Methodology

To address the issue at hand, the present study has adopted qualitative approach and taken Swabhiman as the institution. The data or information needed for the study was gathered through focus group discussions and interview with different stakeholders of Swabhiman. In the absence of any reliable secondary data, the issues, explored in the focus group discussion, were broadly related to the present and past.

The data needed for the study is gathered through focus group discussions with the coordinators of Inclusive Child Resource Centres (ICRC), team leader, project manager and project director.

The first focus group discussion was held with the project director and manager to understand the process and implementation strategies of 'Saksham'. Second focus group discussion included team leader and project manager. Third discussion was with ICRC facilitators. Members of the community, teachers, students, parents and some officials have been interviewed.

To understand the impact of the intervention, the study makes a comparative assessment on specified indicators with reference to the base line.

1. Swabhiman as an Institutional Innovation to facilitate Education for Disabled Children

Swabhiman is a registered non-profit organisation is established in the year 2001. It is a cross disability organisation, advocating for and serving persons with disabilities in Odisha, India and South Asia. It has been in the forefront of several policy changes that have positively impacted the lives of persons with disabilities. At international level it works with Disabled People's International. At national level, it collaborates with National Disability Network. In Odisha, it works with Odisha State Disability Network. Since the Foundation involves in the betterment of persons with disabilities, it took the lead in implementing project. Considering the fact that the education system of Odisha does not have enough support staff for disable students, the organisation took the initiative by setting of eight ICRC in the project area.

To facilitate education for disabled children, Swabhiman as an institution works with different stakeholders or actors like inclusive child resource centres (ICRCs), children with disabilities (CwD), facilitators, team leader, project manager, project director, parents of children, community, school and teacher and education department.

Swabhiman is facilitating holistic education through 8 ICRCs and to function different ICRCs sixteen facilitators were employed. These facilitators basically interact with CwDs for their overall development. Other than that, they take overall responsibilities of ICRCs. To supervise all the facilitators four team leaders were employed.

2. How Swabhiman as an institution Facilitate and Empower Disable through Education

a. Prevent School Dropouts

Swabhiman attempts to prevent school dropouts, it provided continuous support throughout the year. For instance, it provided remedial tuition classes that includes subject specific classes. Different tests were also conducted at the remedial tuition classes. These tuition classes include general tuition classes and special classes on language: Hindi, Sanskrit and English. Additionally, classes on effective communication were also conducted. Other than academic exercise, some co-curricular activities were also held that include hobby, extra-curricular activity and skill activities. Hobby classes include dance, music, fine art, yoga and sign language. Extra-curricular activity includes story-telling, craft work and sports.

b. Institutional Support

Providing infrastructural facilities to disable children is one of the major challenges. Based on the survey, intervention was done in strengthening infrastructural facilities such as construction of ramps, fitting of hand rails, white washing, electricity, putting up of Signage. Synthetic flooring has been completed in six ICRCs inaugurated till March 2016.

c. Skill Training

To ensure the livelihood of school dropout (YwD) through 'Saksham' project, various skill-based training programme was conducted. In February, 2016, 2 Employment Mobilization

Drives (EMD) were conducted for YwD. Training was mostly given in the field of hotel management, LED bulb making and retail sector. Other than that, self-employment training was given to YwDs on poultry farming, juice making and cooking. Some were also provided with employment kit like sewing machine and material for stationary shop.

3. Conclusion

Swabhiman as an institution is doing different innovations in providing better life to disabled children for bringing inclusive development. From the discussion with CwD and parents, it is found that CwDs are getting benefits from the intervention. It not only prevents school dropouts but also provides gainful employment.

References:

Braithwaite, J., & Mont, D. (2009). Disability and poverty: a survey of World Bank poverty assessments and implications. *Alter*, *3*(3), 219-232.

Grech, S. (2009). Disability, poverty and development: Critical reflections on the majority world debate. *Disability & Society*, *24*(6), 771-784.

Solarsh, G., Hofman, K.J., 2006. Developmental disabilities. In: Jamison, D.T., Feachem, R.G., Makgoba, M.W. (Eds.), Disease and Mortality in Sub-Saharan Africa. 2nd ed. World Bank, Washington, pp. 125–147.

CHAPTER TWENTY SIX

Insights on Modern Communication: An Allure for Entrepreneurs

Taneeva Das

1. Introduction:

The primary factors that regulate performance of new enterprises and their success rates are usually derived from the skills possessed by individual innovators and entrepreneurs. The technical and business skill is however still visible as the primary, yet the process of how one communicates being on the front seat of innovation does really describe the potential of being a successful communicator. It is fair to say that among the high technological works around us, the penetration of English language skills or Communication skills has been bringing a change in the way of our lives. It has made more of a critical entry than any other skill and is going to stay with us for the advantages it has. The fact remains that English not only welcomes advanced methods of communication but also is the most common language in the areas of science, innovation and business. As David Crystal quoted in his book *English as a Global Language* that historically, presently and in futuristically, English will remain as a leading international language.

The diversification and multilingualism of employees in work culture invites more bridges for business communication. The *Harvard Business Review* posted in one of their observations that English is used at a very general level by around 1.75 billion people across the globe and about 565 million people use English over the internet, which is why it is crucial to learn and maintain in order to run global business.

2. The Contrasts & Dichotomy:

To study the changing phenomena of language studies in various fields, the English for Specific Purpose (ESP) teaching plays a significant role in channelling the aims & objectives of mastering English at professional level. The main insights of such training and teaching reflects upon one's social media promotions, blogging, international client handlings, conventions & seminars, exhibitions & launches, etc. An ideal training acts like a double edged sword where professionals can deal with different aspects of communication ranging from cultural to business. However, there are huge lines of dichotomy between speaking and writing. It may not be about vocabulary or fluency but about 'saleability'. The ideas on pen and paper needs to eligible enough for credits and profits.

For speaking, the tangent of pronunciation and diction go side by side. Its again not about proficient vocabulary or accent, it's about the 'power of persuasion, negotiation and visibility'. The added cultural element is the soft accent and trust in the voice that adds to one's language. An off-beat pronunciation or tone is a big turn off for clients and potential business leads. In one of the *Forbes Insights* study it was found that more than 65 percent of senior executives believed the fact that language barriers and accent gaps can cause major problems in enterprises. So while we actively engage in broadening our proficiency skills, it is also the collective responsibility of all sorts of speakers (native and non-native) to keep communication channels open.

In case of writing one needs to be absolutely precise with spellings, punctuations and grammar. English native speakers appreciate the use of phrasal verbs, collocations and idioms that boost up the sense of content. Business people round the world like to believe and take this for granted that building strategies are more important that building communicative bridges. The quality of a good writing is that it leads to better credibility. It guarantees that a message that you wish send is presented and accepted properly. A good writing can possess vital information, questions, clarity of opinion, valuable feedback and filtered ideas. In some data it reflects that people spend 50 percent of their time in framing what they want to write whereas the rest 50 percent time could be spent for speaking, reading, etc. We currently live in the times of 140 characters where all that matters is good writing. For an instance; if one doesn't learn the difference between *they're, there* and *their,* they are likely to lose a potential employer/investor. A bad or wrong grammar sense may distract your audience from taking further steps.

3. Propositions:

It is often said, *"Write to be understood, speak to be heard, read to grow"*. The competitive pressure underlying in the globalization, tasks and resources stress on the attention on the importance of communication with a linguistically diverse range of people, customers, partners, etc. Using English is more of a vital skill for entrepreneurs as it helps to recognize professional opportunities, self esteem, skills and knowledge. Communication has the capability to paint the picture with words. It can initiate concepts, theories, resources and recognitions. Deborah Tannen in 1995 stated that, *"the people in positions of power and authority, such as investors and customers are more likely to reward those who have similar levels of linguistic ability, while anyone who seems uncomfortable or under-confident with their language skills is also seen as being insecure about their ideas"*. With writing, one can be disguise into someone else. One day you can be the employee and the other day you could be the employer. The written pattern in English is spread across many senses and hence, the accuracy matters the most as to whether the audience perceives the correct sense or not. The mistakes can be reread; they are visible completely which results in barriers. The mistakes distract attention as a result the reader can easily form an opinion of you based on your content and presentation. Unusual grammar sense makes people think twice about your ability, both professional and personal. It dilutes down your message and its impression.

4.Conclusions:

Investors, innovators, entrepreneurs and business people regularly need to upgrade themselves to various techniques of all round communication building; verbal and nonverbal, spoken or written, telephonic or face-to-face. An analysis of the professionals on these grounds provides both internal and external aspects of the team they are working with. While the internal components of a communicative team should be language diversity and strength, the external components could be misunderstandings and mismanagement of time. The larger the economy, the diverse is a market. Comparison and collection are two sides of the coin whose idea could be implemented here; comparison to peers and resources might not bring te result that collection of ideas and knowledge would do. As entrepreneurs and innovators of the modern world, an individual's idea of interaction & building relations need to be globalized too along with the globalization of power, time and infrastructure.

CHAPTER TWENTY SEVEN

Institutional Intervention to Tackle Socio-economic Problems: A case of Central India Initiative and Collectives for Integrated Livelihood Initiatives

Madhumita Das and Bibhunandini Das
School of Management
Centurion University of Technology and Management, Odisha

1. Introduction

Central India Initiative and Collectives for Integrated Livelihood Initiatives (CInI) aims to transform the lives of tribal communities in Central India by intervening in agriculture, water resources, energy, drinking water and sanitation. The aim of the intervention is to increase the quality of life and the livelihood of tribal communities. CInI introduced the "Lakhpati Kisan-Smart Villages" mission programmes in April 2015. The objective of the mission is to achieve measurable outcomes by 2020. For this intervention, selected blocks in districts of Jharkhand, Gujarat, Odisha and Maharashtra were identified.

2. Objectives of the study

As the aim of the project is to create 'Lakhpati Kisan', CInI intends to have base line information in selected blocks of different States. The baseline information is collected at household and village level on certain predefined indicators: economic and social and quality of life. Again sub-indicators are identified for these three broad indicators. Economic indicators include annual household income with source, asset base at household level. Social indicators include institutional platform, access to government services and role of women in decision making within and outside family. The quality of life indicators in this study basically includes education, health services, drinking water and sanitation. The broad objective of the study is to assess the overall socio-economic status in Bhagamunda Gram Panchayat of Harichandanpur Block, Keonjhar District and Chitri, Salijanga and Ranagundi Gam Panchayats of Dangadi Block, Jajpur District. The specific objectives of this study are:

- To assess the socio-economic status at the household and village level
- To develop a baseline document

3. Methodology

Qualitative data are collected to understand the socio-economic status at village level. For the purpose, Focus Group Discussions (FGD) and Personal Interviews (PI) are carried out. The data needed at the village level is gathered through focus group discussions with members of different households. An attempt is made to include at least one member from each household at hamlet level in the FGD.

4. Findings

This section discusses the socio-economic status of four gram panchayats.

4.1 Income Pattern

From our sample households, most of the households reported that their agricultural production is for their self-consumption. Only 3 % households are selling anything after their self-consumption during kharif season and 6 % households are selling rabi crops. None of the households reported any income from summer crop.

Comparing annual income across different panchayats, we found that, in Bhagamunda, 45.1 per cent of population have annual income of less than 5000, 19.7 per cent of having income ranges from 5000 to 10000 and 35.2 per cent of having annual income above 10000. Contrast to Bhagamunda, in Ranagundi gram panchayat, more than 60 per cent of households reported of having annual income less than 5000. 61.2 per cent of households reported of having income less than 5000, 16.4 per cent of households have reported of having income ranges from 5000 to 10000 and 22.4 per cent of households have reported of having annual income above 10000. In Salijanga, 73.3 per cent of households reported of having annual income less than 5000, 11.7 per cent of households have reported of having income ranges from 5000 to 10000 and 15 per cent of households have annual income more than 10000. In Chitri, 33.3 per cent of households have reported of having annual income less than 5000, 36.8 per cent of households of having income ranges from 5000 to 10000 and 29.8 per cent of households of having income more than 10000.

4.2 Analysis on Households' Assets

Out of total sample household, 50.2 % of households reside in kutcha house, 26.5 % of household live in pucca house and 17.1 % of households have both pucca and kutcha house. Comparing between gram panchayats, we found that in Bhagamunda, 50 % of sample households have kutcha house, around 17 % of households have pucca house and 29.6 % of households reside in both kutcha and pucca house. In Ranagudi, 60 % of households have kutcha house, 22.4 % of households stay in pucca house and 10.4 % of households have mix-kutcha and pucca house. In Salijanga, 58.3 % of households reported that they have kutcha house, 23.3 % of households reported that they have pucca house and 6.7 % of households reported that they have both kutchha and pucca house. In Chitri, 31.6 % of households have kutcha house, 47.4 % of households have pucca house and 21.1 % of households have both kutcha and pucca house. From this, it can be said that majority of households still reside in kutcha house. Comparing four gram panchayats, only in Chitri around 48 households out of 100 have pucca house while in other three gram panchayats, more than 50 households out of 100 reside in kutcha house.

4.3. Social and Quality of Life

Under social and quality of life, we have taken education, women's decision making power. In all the four gram panchayats, in most of the households, we found that male members are decision makers. They take all the financial as well as social decision of their house. If we will see educational background of the households, in all four gram panchayats, situations are more or less similar. The educational status of head of the households is either illiterate or primary level. They are mostly illiterate; however, all households reported that their children or grandchildren are going to the school.

5. Conclusion and Recommendations

The baseline study was an attempt to have a broad understanding on the socio-economic conditions of four gram panchayats of two blocks in Jajpur and Keonjhar districts. From Jajpur we have taken Dangadi blocks and include Chitri, Salijanga and Ranagundi gram panchayats whereas from Keonjhar, we have taken Bhagamunda gram panchayats of Harichandanpur blocks. The study aims to build up a base line report on the socio-economic conditions of people living in these four gram panchayats. Based on this report, possible intervention can be suggested.

From the limited study, we found that the socio-economic condition of households is not very encouraging. There is a need of intervention in many fields in an integrated manner, possibly through technology enabled, market linked sustainable manner. There is a need for local value addition and local market creation through entrepreneurship (individual and community based) development.

CHAPTER TWENTY EIGHT

Opportunities and Challenges of MSME Segment: A study on Odisha's Perspective

Dr.Pramod Kumar Patjoshi, Associate Professor,
Centurion University of Technology and Management, Odisha, India

1. Introduction:

Micro, Small, and Medium Enterprises (MSME) segment plays an important role in the economic growth of the country. MSMEs are apparent as extremely vibrant for sustained economic development and job creation. They provide to economic growth as well as decreasing poverty by creating jobs, invention, maximising the production capacity in addition to better communal parity. Over the past few decades, the MSME segment has developed as an extremely self-motivated segment in the Indian economy. The MSME segment not only plays a vital part in facilitating huge job creation at reasonably lesser capital cost besides assistance in the development of industries in rural as well as backward regions. The MSME segment is balancing to big scale manufacturing units as subsidiary units also provide tremendously in the area of socio-economic growth of the nation.

MSME Segment consisting of thirty-six million units as well as has provided employability of around eighty million persons in India. The MSME Segment with more than six thousand products provided around eight percent to GDP also fourty-five percent to the total manufacturing industry production in addition to the growth of fourty percent in exports. The MSME segment has the potential to boost the manufacturing unit's development around the nation then provides a vital supporting role as guide for comprehensive development.

On "9th May 2007", following towards a modification in the "Government of India (Allocation of Business) Rules, 1961", former "Ministry of Small Scale Industries" then the "Ministry of Agro and Rural Industries" had combined and come together to create the "Ministry of Micro, Small and Medium Enterprises (M/o MSME)". This Ministry is currently formulating strategies as well as encourages enables packages, schemes as well as arrangements in addition to televisions their application with an intention to supporting the MSME segment besides assistance them to grow in production capacity. The main accountability of up-gradation, as well as growth of the MSME segment, is the responsibility of the "State Governments". Nevertheless, the "Government of India" complements the contribution of the "State Governments" by means of numerous initiations. Therefore the MSME segment plays an important part and their administration is to contribute the States by its hard work to inspire entrepreneurship, job creation, and livelihood prospects as well as improve the attractiveness of the MSME segment in the transformed economic situation (Msme at a Glance, 2016).

As per "Odisha MSME Development Policy, 2016", "Odisha located in the eastern region of India, has a traditional past, a vibrant present then an enormous possibility for MSME segment.

Odisha is correspondingly a treasure trove for natural resources. Odisha is finely associated through superficial transport, air as well as water. Odisha has a widespread rail in addition to the road system connecting numerous development epicenters. The State admittance to wide-reaching markets, existence of accomplished human resources, superior logistics, and well infrastructure in addition to an optimistic commercial atmosphere creates Odisha a preferred station designed for the corporate sector. Odisha's Gross State Domestic Production (GSDP) has improved at a Compound Annual Growth Rate (CAGR) of 10.23% from Rs.281450 crore to Rs.330200 crore between 2011-12 and 2015-16. Cumulative FDI inflows in Odisha from April 2010 to March 2016 stood at Rs.1027 crore. State Government has proclaimed strategies to smooth development in the manufacturing segment by means of year on year growth of 15% till 2020. Rendering to the Ministry of Commerce and Industry, total exports from Odisha in 2015-16 were valued at Rs.19746 crore. The value of exports from the state improved at a CAGR of 2.5% between 2006-07 and 2014-15. Odisha ranks high in the country in terms of the total value of mineral output. Throughout 2015-16, the total production of minerals in the state noted down at 239.45 million tonnes. The mineral resources of Odisha establish an arduous share in national deposits of Chromite 98%, Nickel 93%, Graphite 71%, Pyrophyllite 65%, Manganese 67%, Bauxite 59%, China Clay 31%, Fire Clay 25%, Dolomite 18%. Odisha is the fourth biggest producer of Coal as well as the fifth biggest producer of Iron ore in India".

As per "Odisha MSME Development Policy, 2015, Draft for Discussion", "Odisha has large reserves of 45,000 MT power grade coal deposits in Mahanadi Coal Field and Talcher Coal Field area. Odisha is the home to some of the leading public sector enterprises like HAL, and private companies like Tata Steel, Vedanta Aluminum, Aditya Birla, Jindal Steel, etc. Odisha receives unprecedented investments in steel, aluminum, power, refineries, and port. This opportunity a perfect platform and presents a huge opportunity for downstream and ancillary industries and for the MSME sector."

As per "Odisha MSME Development Policy, 2015, Draft for Discussion", "The MSME sector in Odisha has made a substantial contribution to the economic development in general and generation of employment and contribution to the exports in particular and has positioned itself only next to the agricultural sector in the State in terms of employment generation. MSME in

Odisha has witnessed an increasing trend in respect of the number of MSME units set up, the quantum of investment made, and employment generation over a period of time".

As per "Odisha MSME Development Policy, 2016", "The State has notified Industrial Policy Resolution, 2015, which lays down policy framework and fiscal incentives for industries including MSMEs. However, the MSME sector suffers from intrinsic disadvantages in availing priority in infrastructure, credit linkages, and marketing and needs extra support especially in industrially backward districts. With a view to providing a conducive eco-system for promoting the growth of MSMEs in a focussed manner commensurate with the present scenario and anticipated future, the State is declaring."

It is identified from the review of literature that the MSME segment is finding numerous issues and difficulties. Then also different researchers observed that MSME segment is finding numerous issues and difficulties in connected to MSME segment used to face difficulties in the area of bank credit conveniences, accessibility of appropriate equipment and technology, difficulties in the marketing of their products, obtainability of incomplete possessions, unavailability of proper human resources, etc.. Apart from the above, the MSME segment is also finding great difficulties due to changing external environment erection. Das, (2008) revealed in his study that numerous difficulties are facing by the SME sector that are connected to funding availability, technology enhancement, insufficient infrastructure facilities, improper transportation conveniences, etc. While Fridah Muriungi Mwobobia (2012) expressed that the SME segment facing lots of issue and difficulties in Kenya in the part to financing and availability of funds, various tasks occupied by women, improper impartiality, absence of education, struggle, absence of a proper plan, absence of managerial skill, etc. And also Mukund Chandra Mehta (2013) indicates that the main problems faced by means of the availability of funding, lower on producing product unavailability of proper human resources, lack of infrastructure facilities, improper of manufacturing estate conveniences etc. Correspondingly Ishu Garg and Suraj Walia (2012) had also found in their research and highlighted that the "Small Scale Industries (SSI)" segment finds several difficulties connected towards the procurement of finance, recognizing upgrade technologies as well as skills, industrial exercise, excellence control etc. SSI segment is finding regular difficulties from large as well as medium subsidiaries in facets of producing product capacity besides marketing strategies of the products. Similarly, Garg (2014) exposed the various opportunities, issues as well as difficulties found by the MSME segment in India. His research revealed that numerous difficulties in outside factors, which are faced by the MSME segment, are mostly in funding their infrastructure and working capital besides subsidies granted by Government. Subsequently, after globalization, getting bank financing and credit facilities, upgradation in technological advancement, proper skill improvement, national industrial inexpensive databases, export elevation in addition to the growing infrastructure facilities, etc. Similarly, Sangita Patil and Chaudhari (2014) in their research found that the development of the MSME segment has improved over the year by means of an increase in the number of MSME establishments. They recognized small scale segment found various problems mostly in skilled human resources, unavailability of bank finance and support, well-developed marketing, insufficient infrastructural facilities, competitiveness, improper planning, management expert, transportation amenities, unavailability of power, unavailability of godown conveniences, unavailability of information as well as data, etc. Whereas Aruna (2015) revealed that the MSME segment is mostly finding difficulties in connecting to bank credit availability, obtainability of appropriate technology, difficulties in the selling of their products, improper skilled human resources, etc. The researcher recognized that bank finance as well as fund availability restrictions besides challenges connecting to power as well as unavailability of proper human resources, lack of proper raw material, etc. However, Mathai (2015) depicted the various difficulties found in the SME segment in India are mainly difficulties connected to unavailability of bank financing accommodations, infrastructure accommodations, lack of raw materials, unavailability of proper technology, unavailability of training, unavailability of skilled labour, and potential human resources, unavailability of rules relating to labour, competitiveness from large businesses, etc. Whereas Tripathi (2016) et.al designates main six difficulties as well as articulated obtainability of relaxed bank credit in addition to funding tools, complex monitoring strategies for establishing a commercial organisation, lack of upgrade as well as reasonable technology, unavailability of infrastructural conveniences, nonappearance of high-class marketing stands plus delivery channels, uncompromising labour laws then lack reasonably accomplished manpower.

Odisha is a state of dreamland for natural resources. Despite being rich in resources; it is still one of the backward States and has huge potential for further industrialization, especially for the MSME segment. The ratio of gross capital outlay to GSDP has not been encouraging over the years. Odisha has observed that the credit which flows to the MSME segment is quite unproductive due to the lack of credit immersion capacity of this sector. MSME segment is facing many challenges in related to different areas of production and operation process, marketing of their products, an arrangement of funds, shortages of skilled manpower, and many other outside challenges. In other words, the MSME segment is finding difficulties connecting to availability credit from banks and financial institutions, obtainability of appropriate technology, problems in marketing of products, accessibility of resources, the nonexistence of skilled human resources etc. Consequently, this study is related to analyse the growth and performance of MSME in Odisha.

Therefore it can find from the above that the MSME segment in Odisha has made considerable effort to the economic growth in overall further creation of job opportunities in the state as well. This sector also contributes to the exports in precise over and above this segment also placed it merely following to the agricultural segment in Odisha in positions of employment creation. The MSME segment in Odisha has perceived a growing inclination with regard to the amount of MSME units' establishment, significant improvement in investment in addition to job creation during the past few decades. Although the MSME segment has made remarkable contributions, simultaneously it has faced numerous challenges for its development in Odisha. The MSME segment suffers from the shortage of finance as well as the timely arrangement of funds. MSMEs are facing many challenges related to different areas of production and operation process, marketing of their products, an arrangement of funds, shortages of skilled manpower, and many other outside challenges. In other words, the MSME segment used to face difficulties in the area of bank credit conveniences, accessibility of appropriate equipment and technology, difficulties in the marketing of their products, obtainability of incomplete possessions, unavailability of proper human resources, etc. Though, the depiction is less blushing in the eastern part of India. To discourse, the different type of arrangements as well as for the growth of the MSME segment has been started by the central government's as well as state government's agencies. Different central as well as state organizations deliver wide-ranging assistance aimed at the progress of the

MSME segment in eastern India. Therefore this research is related towards analysing the development and performance of the MSME segment in Odisha.

2. Opportunities and Potentialities in MSME Segment in Odisha

The openings of development inside the MSME segment is massive by reason of the most important determinants alike are lesser amount Capital Intensive, Widespread reaching Promotion and Support by Government, Arrangement for High-class Production through small scale segment, Funding and Grants, Raw Material Locating, Human Resource Exercise, Cluster agenda meant aimed at growth in technical as well as entrepreneurial skills, Arrangement for fashionable purchase by Government, As a result of export growing, Increasing of demand inside the national market scope.

3. Challenges Faced by MSME Segment in Odisha

MSME Segment is finding problems in funding in addition to credit restraints then not getting the obligatory backing from the Government Subdivisions, Corporate sector, Financial Institutions and Banks. MSMEs find a number of difficulties as well as restraints in their track of development. They are as Absence of adequate as well as timely financing/Credit, Inadequate capital besides information, Non-availability of appropriate technology, Lower production, Nonexistence of marketing possibility, Globalization impression, competitiveness through large segments, Unavailability of extremely skilled manpower at a realistic cost, etc.

Even though many competitions by means of growth, the MSME segment has attained tremendously healthy in addition to allow our nation to accomplish an extensive range of industrial development. SSI segment has aided significant assistance to employment creation then correspondingly to rural industrialization. Thus MSME segment has backed to shape on by strengthening our outdated skills in addition to knowledge, through fermentation of technology supports, capital as well as advanced marketing strategies.

4. Odisha's MSME Development Policy – 2016

The major remarks of the Odisha MSME Development Policy – 2016 have elaborated below.

Objectives

The foremost purposes of the policy comprise

- Inspire new industrial volume related to better attractiveness.
- Deliver a favourable ecosystem aimed at promoting besides development of the MSME segment as a prospective segment.
- Deliver openings to indigenous entrepreneurship capacity.
- Make the most of the generation of employability opportunities for the younger generation.
- Enable MSME segment for retrieving national as well as international markets.
- Prepare concentrated efforts for revitalization of sick units.
- Formulate concentrating exertions for maintainable, comprehensive & composed development.

Ease of Doing Business

The major point's in ease of doing business of the policy includes

- The "District Industrial Centres (DIC)" intends to perform by means of a nodal intervention to upgrade of MSME segment inside the region.
- "Single Window Clearance & Online Combined Application Form (CAF)" towards enable time assured permissions for the investment.
- "District Level Single Window Clearance Authority" should evaluate and endorse the prerequisite of land.
- The "DICs" be about to strengthen as well as revitalize to remove the current blockages as well as simplify evenly make operation towards the requirements of the entrepreneurs.
- An online payment of incentives apparatus intends to be enforced in addition to the appropriate incentives mean to be granted within a time frame
- Online stage should likewise be introduced for the entrepreneurs to lodge complaints. and proper steps should be taken on the complaints

Infrastructure Development

The major points in infrastructure development of the policy includes

- MSME segment setup and frame in the Regions. "OSIC" as well as support for the implementation of the setup.

- Provision aimed at "Ancillary as well as Downstream" Initiatives Enable connections among entrepreneurs with big industries.
- Importance land portion for parklands/entrepreneurship.
- "Plant Level Consultative Committee" should frame aimed at great industries as well as "Plant Level Advisory Committee (PLAC) of CPSUs" in addition to "State PSUs".
- "Ancillary & Downstream Enterprise Cell" should frame inside of "Directorate of Industries".

Marketing Assistance

The major point's in marketing assistance of the policy includes
- "MSME e-Bazaar" intends to frame s deliver a stage near entrepreneurship development.
- MSME national fair means to remain prearranged by means of "OSIC".
- Obligatory procurement facilities as of Micro as well as Small entrepreneurs inside the Region.

Export Promotion

The major points in export promotion of the policy includes
- "Directorate of EP & M" to make in addition to inform a product country medium
- Provide support on Raw Material Provision.
- "OSIC/NSIC" towards starting "Raw Material Banks" straight or as "PPP" manner.
- "CPSUs, State PSUs, and large industries" towards source raw material towards "OSIC" through importance at the lowermost probable price.

Technology Upgradation

The major points in technology up-gradation of the policy includes
- Upsurge consciousness about the "Credit Linked Capital Subsidy Scheme (CLCSS)", "Quality Management Standards (QMS) and Quality Technology Tools (QTT)".
- Preferment of "Clusters".
- "Cluster Development Cell" means to frame in "Directorate of Industries" to meet resources besides merge finance aimed at cluster expansion
- Novel clusters of "Ancillary & Downstream" units intend to promote on main industrial centres

- Provide Financial Inducements

References:
18. Annual Report, Government of India, Ministry of Micro, Small and Medium Enterprises, www.msme.gov.in; 2017-18
19. Das, K. (2008), ˍSMEs in India: Issues and Possibilities in Times of Globalisation', in Lim, H. (ed.), SME in Asia and Globalization, ERIA Research Project Report 2007-5, pp.69-97.
20. Financing for MSMEs The eastside story- CII Report, 2013, https://www.pwc.in/assets/pdfs/publications/2013/msme.pdf
21. Fridah Muriungi Mwobobia (2012) ―The Challenges Facing Small-Scale Women Entrepreneurs: A Case of Kenyaǁ, International journal of business administration, Vol 3, issue 2, PP 112-121.
22. Gisha.P.Mathai (2015) ―Challenges and Issues in Micro, Small and Medium Enterprises (MSMEs) in India: A Current Scenario of Economic Growthǁ, Vol 4, Issue 7, PP 162-163 in Malaysiaǁ, Asia pacific business review, vol.12, no.4, PP 465-485.
23. https://investodisha.gov.in/odisha-MSME-policy/
24. Ishu Garg & Suraj Walia (2012) ―Micro, Small & Medium Enterprises (Msmes) in Post Reform India: Status & Performanceǁ, Vol 1, No 3, PP 134-141.
25. Mishu Tripathi, Mr. Saurabh Tripathi, Mr. RikinDedhia (2016) ―Challenges faced by Micro, Small and Medium Enterprise (Msme) Sector In Indiaǁ, International Journal of Science technology and management, Vol 5, Issue 3, PP 69-77
26. MSME AT A GLANCE 2016, http://msme.gov.in/sites/default/files /MSME at a GLANCE_2016_Final.pdf
27. Mukund Chandra Mehta (2013) ―Challenges and Opportunities in Micro, Small and Medium Enterprises in Indiaǁ, 2nd International Conference on Management, Humanity and Economics (ICMHE'2013) May 6-7, 2013 Kuala Lumpur (Malaysia), PP 134-136
28. N. Aruna (2015) ―Problems Faced By Micro, Small and Medium Enterprises – A Special Reference to Small Entrepreneurs in Visakhapatnamǁ, IOSR Journal of business and management, Vol 14, issue 4, PP 43-49
29. Neeru Garg (2014) ―Micro, Small and Medium Enterprises in India: Current Scenario and Challengesǁ, Paripex - Indian Journal of Research, Vol 3, Issue 9, PP 11-13.
30. Odisha Economic Planning and Convergence Department, Survey, Directorate of Economics and Statistics, Government of Odisha, March 2018
31. Odisha MSME Development Policy – 2016, http://www.msmeodisha.gov.in/PDF /FINALbyDI(O)-Odisha_MSME_Dev._Policy.pdf
32. Odisha MSME Development Policy 2015 – Draft for Discussion, http://www.osicltd.in /Content/images/PDF/Draft%20-%20Odisha%20MSME%20Dev%20Policy%202015.pdf
33. Odisha MSME Development Policy, Micro, Small & Medium Enterprises Department Government of Odisha, 2016
34. Sangita G.Patil & P.T.Chaudhari (2014) ―Problems of Small Scale Industries in Indiaǁ, International Journal of Engineering and Management Research, vol 4, Issue 2, PP 19-21

CHAPTER TWENTY NINE

Social Entrepreneurship

Dr. Girija Nandini, Associate Professor,
Centurion University of Technology and Management, Odisha, India

Anindita Bosu, Lecture in Commerce
Rajdhani College, Bhubaneswar, Odisha, India

1. Introduction

Entrepreneurship is a crucial factor in the development of economy and well-being of societies in a nation. Any country can be economically developed when there will be growth in entrepreneurship. In order to understand the term social entrepreneurship, one must start to understand the word of "entrepreneurship". Entrepreneurship is the ability and readiness to develop, organize the resources of land, labour, capital, natural and artificial resources and run a business enterprise in order to make profits. Social entrepreneurship is the preparation of mind-set after proper and continuous thinking and learning in both the business and non-profit worlds to innovate new ideas and to develop strategies that maximize their social impact by addressing social inequalities and social issues.

Social entrepreneur is a person who tries to solve some social issues and to make some social changes by utilizing the resources. They always want to make some social changes through social entrepreneurship. They try to do some innovations to solve the most critical problem of the society. They do business to create social values rather than to make profit. Their objective is not to make profit; they want the overall development of the society. They do entrepreneurship for the community.

Qualities of Social Entrepreneur

Some of the qualities of social entrepreneur are:

- **Creativity:** Social entrepreneurs must be creative. They should creative in solving problem and decision making.
- **Change Agent:** A social entrepreneur is playing a role of change agent in a community. He/she must have unwavering willingness to change others. It can be possible by engaged in a process of regular innovation, adaption and learning, adopting a mission to create and sustain social value, pursuing new opportunities to attain that mission.
- **Committed for Improvement of Social Welfare:** The first and foremost aim of Social entrepreneurs is improvement of community not to make money. Their ability fully devoted to make sure things actually progress in a way for the betterment of the society.
- **Philanthropic Bent & Social Value Creator:** Social entrepreneurs are not necessarily avid by fame, money, wealth or profit. They have a philanthropic bent. They distributed

whatever profits are earned to socially underprivileged and reinvest excess funds in the enterprise to their entity. This leads to positive effect on society and save more lives from different social issues. This helps for creation of social value.

- **Initiative Taker:** Social entrepreneurs take initiatives; organize social and economic activities towards the visionaries of their change which aims at the beginning.
- **Determination:** Determination is a pivotal quality of social entrepreneurs. Social entrepreneurs are about to take initiatives of their innovative ideas and take some risk. Sometimes they get failure also but they take it as a challenge to get success.
- **Innovator:** The minds of successful social entrepreneurs must have innovation. They encompassed technology in such way that improved things, products and services which increases the social wealth.
- **Risk Taker:** A social entrepreneur must take risk for the organization which works for the social welfare, to address social issues and hurdles faced by the society in their living life.
- **Entrepreneurial Quality:** They must have other entrepreneurial qualities along with above discussed qualities. A successful social entrepreneur must have the qualities of an entrepreneur such as a mission leader, dedicated, highly accountable, a good manager, organizes, strategic thinker, etc.

2.Functions of Social Entrepreneur

Social entrepreneurs are the individual or groups who are passionate and committed about what they do.

- Addressing Social issues and figure out a persisting solution to that problems.
- Providing Sustainable solutions to the most pressing hurdles in Social issues
- To create long term systems and frameworks for NGOs, Corporate Social Responsibility and Philanthropy, etc.
- Bring professionalism and innovation in social sector.
- Develop social ethics in Social service sectors.
- Create social value
- Engage in innovation, adaptation and learning to strategic thinking for betterment of the society.

3.Types of Social Entrepreneurs

Rashmi Bansal classifies Social Entrepreneurs in to three types:

- **Rainmakers:** They are revenue generating social entrepreneurs whose primary objective is not profit making.
- **Change makers:** They resolute in their belief for change.
- **Spiritual Capitalists:** They are completely devote themselves to the work for the development of society.

4.Role and Importance of Social Entrepreneurship

- It is focused on underprivileged section of the society.
- It creates major economic value by creation of employment and job opportunities to those individuals who have basic knowledge and skill.
- Social entrepreneurship develops new product and services by applying innovation, which is needed for the development of society as well as economy of the nation.
- It provides sustainable solutions to the most pressing hurdles in Social issues. It addresses the social issues and make solutions to tackle with that problems. Social entrepreneurship eradicate the social problems by applying entrepreneurial principles which includes, illiteracy, combat health issues like maternal health, HIV/AIDS, mental ill-health, malaria and other diseases, reduce child mortality etc.
- It solves different social problems by innovation.

5.Challenges Faced by Social Entrepreneurship

Social entrepreneurship has lot of challenges like any other entrepreneurship. These challenges can be controllable or uncontrollable but all are manageable.
Some of the important challenges are:

- It is always confused with social work.
- Creativity and innovation is less.
- Getting financial resources is difficult for social entrepreneurs.
- Shortage of talented people due to low incentive and personal gain.
- Shortage of an ethical framework in social entrepreneurship.
- It has some agenda in their business. As the primary motive of social entrepreneurship is welfare and betterment of society, to change the community in a positive direction. But it is difficult to track down the hidden agendas behind social entrepreneurship.
- Profit social enterprises cannot accept donations while non-profit social enterprises cannot accept investments even if both are working for social changes. As the primary motive of both the social enterprise is serving of the community but profit social enterprise is also aiming to earn profit, they are not getting any donation or government aids for their work. The non-profit social enterprise is not focused on making profits they are not getting any investments from different institutions.
- There is always a lack of proper planning in social entrepreneurship.

6.Methods to manage Challenges Efficiently

- Government should open development centers and training centers for social entrepreneurship.
- Courses should be included on social entrepreneurship in colleges.
- Starting awareness on this in different media and social network
- Government should provide basic infrastructure and facilities to the social entrepreneurs to attract more people into this area.
- Different training programs should be conducted to motivate social entrepreneurs.
- Funding should be given by private and public sources
- Government projects can be given to social entrepreneurs for various programs improvements of rural and semi urban areas.
- Awards and public felicitation programs should be organized to felicitate the social entrepreneurs for their work towards society.

7.Social Entrepreneurship in India

Social entrepreneurship can solve the issues and problems of society. Many of the startups and new ventures are working for social development through social entrepreneurship and innovation in India. Social entrepreneurship is very much essential in India because many of the products produced by the companies are for the reach people which deprive the poor people from getting the benefit. Social entrepreneurs can only give that benefit to the deprived section of our society.

Some of the social entrepreneurs in India are:
- Bindeshwar Pathak- Founder of 'Sulabh' Toilet
- Vineet Rai- Founder of Aavishkaar Social Venture Fund
- Harish Hande- Founder of SELCO, Solar Lighting Firm
- Arvind Kejriwala- Founder of NGO Parivartan, Citizen Empowerment via RTI Act
- Trilochan Sastry- Founder of Association for Democratic Reforms (ADR)
- Anshu Gupta- Founder of NGO Goonj
- Madhu Pandit Dasa- Founder of Akshaya Patra
- Baba Ramdev- Founder of Patanjali
- Vinayak Lohani- Founder of Parivar Ashram

CHAPTER THIRTY

The Other Voice: Revisiting Educational Radio during the pandemic

Dr. Chinu Bohidar
Assistant Professor
Centurion University of Technology and Management, Odisha, India

1. Introduction:

There are different media which are used by different people for the purpose of communication. Whether it is radio, television, newspaper, internet or any other forms of communication. Every medium has its own advantages and disadvantages in itself. Communication is a process of sharing ideas, feelings, knowledge and information among two persons or a group of persons. Sharing of ideas, knowledge and information is necessary for the smooth development of the society. The overall development of the society is possible only when communication will reach people of all segments and all location. The balanced flow of communication results in universal development of mankind. Every media has its own advantages and disadvantages. Television being the most powerful and immediate medium can't afford by all, whereas newspaper the oldest medium can't accepted and read by all, where as digital media which has now dominated all other forms of communication is still a dream for many. With the development of the society and adoption of different technologies the mainstream people of the society are equipped with all advance medium and technologies whereas the weaker, poor, illiterate and deprived are still inaccessible to all the forms of communication. There are people who are illiterate, can't afford television and do not understand digital media platform. They are still unaware of the happening of the world and major policies and provisions declared by the Government and bureaucrats for the needy. There are new laws, provisions, schemes and benefits which is meant for the below poverty line people, but still the message do not reach the needy.

Barriers in communication hinders the overall development of society. The participation of people from grassroots level to bureaucrats can help in overall development of the society. A media can called powerful only when it reaches and access by all segments of people.

Whether it is radio, television, newspaper or social media, their main motive and responsibility is to bridge the gap of communication. Their duties is to deliver the rights, thoughts, and ideas of one person to the other. That is why it is called media. It is the carrier of information, news and issues to the public. Every medium has its own features and characteristics. Every medium has its own strength and weakness.

Radio a Friend in Need:

Radio emerges when all other forms of medium fails. Radio is a medium which reaches the people when all other forms of communication breakdown. That's why the oldest medium is still the favorite of all. Whenever there is natural disasters, technical break down or connectivity issues, radio is the medium which carries the message to the people. Whether it is a tribal dominated area, hilly area or detach area radio is the only medium there, which connects its people to the rest of the world.

Radio which reaches to its listeners in the way of sounds wave usually creates no disturbance. It is one of the cheapest medium of communication. Radio is a medium which connects to the emotions of the people. It has the power to connect its listeners individually and personally. Listeners can use it personally and even can share with a group. One of the greatest disadvantages of radio is lack of feedback, lack of clarity and not rewind able.

Radio is the only medium which deliver education, information and entertainment. From the inception of radio, it was always used for developmental issues. Being a medium regulated by the Government of India, it has the potential to reach the maximum geographical location in the country. As it does not required electricity and monthly payment to run, it proved itself to be the poor man's medium. Now also in the 21st century, there are people who do not have access to any form of communication except radio. For them radio is the only source which makes them connected with the rest of the world. It is only the radio which brings the good news and progressive initiative of their government to their area. Radio is the medium which helps them to showcase their hidden talents and innovation to the rest of the world.

2. Radio in Delivering Education:

Radio when came to India in 1923, the purpose was to deliver the education to the people. All India Radio being operated and regulated by the Government of India, with all efforts it has reaches nearly 92% of the country's area and 99.19% of the total population (All India radio). From the inception of All India Radio, it has always focused on delivering formal and non-formal education. All the program format of AIR is based on social, educational and health awareness. It teaches people of all age. It broadcast program specifically for farmers, women, children and others. Education was first taken up by Radio in January, 1929 in Bombay then in

Madras. In November 1937 All India Radio, Calcutta broadcast education program in a systematic manner which become successful. After the success of the Calcutta station, AIR adopted broadcast of educational program in all other stations gradually. The main aim of AIR was to deliver free education to the school dropouts, illiterate and farmers.

As an audio medium radio is not accepted by all in the present scenario. But has failed to replace Television and social media. People in the urban India never prefer radio as they are well equipped with other media and latest technologies. But whenever the focus shifts to the deprived, neglected, rights to education for all radio proves to be the only alternatives. Imparting education through radio means supplement the work of the teachers. All India Radio airs school broadcast program in different language in 73 stations of India. There programs include the syllabus of school students in different regional language. The programs mainly include subjects like English, Sanskrit, Science, social Science, Mathematics etc. These programs are mainly broadcast for 15-20 minutes for 3 -5 days in a week.

Central Institute of Educational Technologies (CIET), National Council for Educational Research and Training (NCERT), National Council of Educational Research and Training (NCERT), State Institute of Educational Technologies (SIET) are the agencies created for quality educational program contents for radio. These institutions mainly focus on the interesting and informative contents of educational program that will be understood by all easily and clearly.

3. The Global Covid-19 Pandemic

Radio has always played an important role during natural calamity and natural disasters. It is a medium which emerges as an important carrier of information when all other forms of medium fails. All those people who never give priorities to this medium switch on to radio when their favorite medium fails to operate due to lack of electricity, subscription and cost. Like any other unpredictable situation, in the global Covid-19 pandemic, people have experienced the need of radio in bridging the gap of communication.

The outbreak of the novel coronavirus coming from Wuhan, China in December 2019 have been a worldwide issue. The pandemic commonly termed as COVID-19 is an infectious disease caused by Coronavirus. The human infectious disease usually causes pneumonia, severe acute respiratory syndrome, and kidney failure and ultimately leads to death. Mostly the virus infection can be symptomized if the person is suffering from dry cough, fever, shortness of breath, and breathing difficulties. Older and people with less immunity are mostly prone to this infectious virus. At this juncture, there is no specific vaccines, medicines or treatment process for this viral disease.

In India, lockdown was declared from 24 March 2020 in order to control the spread of coronavirus outbreak in the nationwide. Companies, educational institutes, restaurants, shops and malls, home deliveries, businesses and services all were held down due to the pandemic. Stepping out of the people from their homes were banned. All the commercial and private establishments were closed due to which work from home was opted. Social, political, sports, entertainment, academic, cultural and religious activities were forbidden. Social distancing was to be strictly followed.

Due to the lockdown, Students from all over the world were debarred from formal education. Schools, colleges, institutes and universities were lock downed for maintaining social distance. Educational Institutes started adopting online education to continue the process of delivering education and to keep student's interest intact in academic activities. Students also started adopting online education to continue their academic activities and process. The demand of net pack, high speed internet, smart mobile phone, audio visual devices started increasing. There is competition between different virtual apps and software companies to provide the cheapest and fastest services to both the teachers and students. The unpredictable lockdown has forced everyone to have personalize smart devices to keep them updated with syllabus and online digital class room. Recorded class room, flip classes, multiple screen sharing, numerous participants in one platform has given ample opportunity to the students to explore the new of learning during the lockdown.

But unfortunately, except the urban, literate and smart crowd, many of the student of the rural belt of India are unaware of online education. Internet, Wi-Fi, laptop and smart phones are still dreams for many. Many educational institutes have started delivering online teaching and online projects without even making a survey whether their students can access online teaching or not. Educational institutes have even completed their courses without introspecting the availability of smart phones and internet speed of the area from the place where the students belong. There are many debates on right to education for poor, tribal and rural during this pandemic as they are the worst sufferers of the new online education system.

4.Radio in Bridging the Gap of Online Communication:

As online education fails in most part of the India, Government of India has adopted many innovative ways to impart education to the students in every corner of the country. Radio is a medium which can guide students in education as another alternative to online teaching. This medium lacks visual communication and demonstration, which is possible through online teaching. But there where online learning is a dream. Radio has proved their as a friend in need. Many of the school and college students have happily adopted radio for learning purposes. Many state government have come forward to impart education to the students during global pandemic. Many interior part of Odisha and rural belt people have adopted radio to keep themselves up to date with their syllabus. The greatest advantages is that students learn their courses in their regional language.

5.Radio Pathashala in Odisha

Like any other state in India Odisha also suffered and affected by the corona virus and its. Being one of the poorest state of India many students were debarred from online education during the unpredictable shut down. The Government of Odisha introduced the Radio Pathashala to benefit students out of radio. The innovative way is adopted to deliver education to school student from standards 1 to 8 through radio program. The Radio Pathashala initiative was started from 28Th September 2020. The educational program comes on air from Monday to Friday from 10 am to 10.15 for 15 minutes. The radio programs are also uploaded in the DIKSHA platform for students' reference.

Odisha School Education Program Authority has issued an order all district education officers, all district project coordinators and all block education officers to broadcast "Radio Pathashala" from 28th September 2020. For the smooth functioning and better understanding of the students, five days of a week have been divided for specific class. Monday for class I and class V, Tuesday class II and class VI, Wednesday class III and class VII, Thursday IV and class VIII, Friday class VI, class VII and class VIII. The students are offered Science, English, Geography, History, Environmental Science, Sanskrit etc.

The students are offered 15 minutes of class per day. It was found that students can read a six page book in just 15 minutes that is why to put less burden on students Government of Odisha is offering 15 min radio lectures through radio.

All school headmasters and Cluster Resource Centre Coordinator (CRCC) have been asked to widely disseminate the information with the students and parents.

6. Role of Radio during Covid-19 Global Pandemic

Radio has always proved to be the only alternative medium that has helped people in disseminating information and news during emergencies. As per 2011 population of Odisha out of 52,73,194 child population in the age group 0-6 years recorded in the state 45,25,870 are concentrated in rural area whereas in urban area it is 7,47,324. The number of literates in Odisha is 2,67,42,595 out of which 2,13,77,915 are recorded in rural area whereas in urban areas the number of literates recorded is just 53, 64,680. The literacy rate of Odisha as per 2011 census is 72. 9 per cent. The above data shows that there is a huge difference between literacy rate of urban and rural area of Odisha.

Around 40 percent of Odisha's population lives below poverty line followed by Jharkhand 34.8 percent and Madhya Pradesh 32.4 percent.

There are many poor families in Odisha those who can't avail a smart mobile phone and can't have access to digital infrastructure. Those students have suffered a lot during this global pandemic.

With the effort of the Government of Odisha Radio Pathashala has got multiple slots in different community radio of Odisha. Many NGO and community radio volunteers have taken initiative for radio clubs and centres where students can listen radio in group.

7. Conclusion:

Radio though one of the oldest medium of communication, it has always played an important role in disseminating information to the voiceless. People equipped with smart infrastructure can never understand the importance and the role played by the radio during emergency and disasters situation. It is only the people who has availed the benefit of radio can say the importance of radio in shaping their life. All form of mass communication medium was developed with an aim of social change and overall development of the society. But eventually except radio all other forms of mass communication has been diverted from their actual aim and mission. But it is only the radio which has always given priorities to information, education and entertainment.

Whether it is digital advancement or technical up gradation, everything has failed to reach every corner of the society. But radio is the only medium which has almost 100 per cent reach. Lack of awareness and knowledge is the only barriers. Radio can make deep rooted changes only if it will be promoted and supported by both the government and accepted by the people.

Reference:

1. Myriad Global Media. 2020. Radio: One of the most powerful Communication Tools of the 21st Century- Myriad Global Media.

2. (n.d.). Retrieved November 25, 2020, from http://www.irrodl.org/index.php

3. Educational radio in India. (2002,July1). Research Fate.https://www.researchgate.net/publication/26339503_Educational_Radio_in_India

4. Radio as a medium of mass communication.(n.d.).UKEssays.com.https://www.ukessays.com/essays/media/radio-medium-mass-communication-1615.php

5. Odisha to achieve 100 per cent literacy rate by 2020. (2018, January 16). Odisha Breaking News/Odisha News/Latest Odisha News/ Odisha Diary.https://orissadiary.com/Odisha-acieve-100-per-cent-rate-2020

6. Odisha Govt to launch Radio Pathshala program for students upto class 8. (2020). Retrieved 5 December 2020, from http://newsonair.com/News?title=Odisha-Govt-to-launch-Radio-Pathshala-program-for-students-upto-class-8&id=400902

7. Radio Pathasala programme fpr school students in Odisha will be started from September 28.(2020). Retrived 5 December 2020, from https:// Orissadiary.com

8. Radio Pathasala programme for school students in Odisha will be started from September 28.(2002). Retrived 5 December 2020,from https://orissadiary.com/radiopathasala-programme-fpr-school-students-in -odisha-will-be -started -from -september-28/

CHAPTER THIRTY ONE

A Study on Gayatri Engineering Construction & Consultancy

Dr. Prasanta Kumar Mohanty

Centurion University of Technology and Management, Odisha

Unlike typical educated Odias who are job seekers, Mr. Pradipta Panigrahi, the first generation entrepreneur, is an exception. The 1973 born Physics graduate and a post-graduate in Business Administration treaded a different path. Immediately after his MBA in 1994, he started Gayatri Engineering Construction and Consultancy (P) Ltd, popularly known as Gayatri Solar. It earned the reputation of being the leading solar energy entity in the state of Odisha after two decades of hard work. Pradipta considers himself fortunate to get the unstinted inspiration of his wife and mentorship of his father and brother, the last two being the Chairman and Managing Director of the Company respectively.

Why Solar Energy Business?

As a student, Pradipta was fascinated by the Solar cooker in his home, way back in 1984. Considering his environmental sensitivity, understanding of the science and marketpotential of solar energy, and entrepreneurial ambition, it was logical for him to enter into solar thermal and photovoltaic business. Thus, Gayatri Solar was born. Now the "organisation is pan-Indian with leading position in Odisha" says Pradipta proudly.

Challenges faced

For Pradipta, the key challenge wasacquiring finance for the enterprise and creating an enabling environment for his business. From the beginning he worked hard to increase customer base and market share. Within two decades of work in green energy &environmental sector, he has built competence in technical, organisational and human issues affecting the business, i.e.Energy Conservation, Solar Energy and Climate Change.

Taking advantage of his competence and opportunities in the market, in 2007 he started a new entity, G-ON Energy Controls to work on green energy system and energy efficiency. The organisation is actively working in the broad area of energy efficiency, clean energy and new generation of energy technologies for domestic, commercial, agricultural and industrial applications. With the company's vision; "to combat global warming" through energy efficiency & Clean Development Mechanism (CDM), it is involved in creating awareness and promotion of green technology to reduce carbon dioxide emission to the environment. It is associated with Bureau of Energy Efficiency (BEE), Govt. of India; Dept. of Energy, Govt. of Odisha and Orissa Small Industry Corporation Ltd (OSIC), Govt. of Odisha. The company deals with diversified products and services.

Products

- LED lighting system(indoor & outdoor)
- LED traffic signal
- LED street light
- Green building material
- Water free urinals
- Day light harvesting system

Services

- Energy management
- Energy audit
- Lighting study
- Green building design consultancy & turnkey projects
- Promoting the concept of re-location of trees.

With an initial personal investment of Rs. 40 lakhs, the company got financial assistance from Oriental Bank of Commerce and Bank of Baroda. G-ON's close working with prominent players in the industry such as BEL, BHEL, Goldwyn, Bajaj, Wipro, VIN, Honeywell, etc. has resulted in its present turnover of about Rs. 20 crore with annual growth of 20-30%.

Learnings

Since 1994, the organisation's motto has been "to be genuine in what we do". "This approach has given us the rewards to be big, to be visible & to be stable which are the three important ingredients to be successful" says Mr. Panigrahi. Support from IREDA, BHEL, BEL, OREDA, CII, NSIC, OSIC, IDCO, SDA, GOLDWYN, Invest Bhubaneswar, TIE and financial institutions has made them stand in a firm footing.

Impact of the business

G-ON and Gayatri Solar represented Odisha at Silicon Valley, USA. They have been awarded with a showcase of Odisha medal for creating awareness on energy conservation among people/organization by 37th Indian National Science Congress.

G-ON Energy Controls has participated in Confederation of Indian Industries (CII) organized Expo as a core team of the forum and was awarded as "Best small Scale Industry" since last four years.

The key factors leading to Mr. Panigrahi's achievements include:

1. Clarity of purpose, passion, perseverance and open mind; and
2. Flexibility and team approach to work

Getting acceptable in the market, which almost did not exist for solar energy, was the challenge when Gayatri Solar ventured in 1994. "Consistent product awareness, creating new milestone projects and orders led to overcome the problem of market creation. Identifying the correct market on hit &trial method took a long time initially" says Mr. Panigrahi unhappily. "Hotel Industries in and around Puri was a sizeable market for us, but we miss the bus from 1994 to 1999 and we focused it in the year 2000 – 2001 and we achieved a sizeable success; the learning's were to find out and explore the solutions within our nearby areas and talent before we go and find solution elsewhere" says Panigrahi.

Energy sector is going to play a critical role for the next 20 – 30 years. Green energy is need of the Globe; hence sustainable business model in the energy sector with different product mix is the future. The company is determined to re-define the energy services for the masses in future.

Mr. Panigrahi is passionate about young entrepreneurs entering in to the wonderland of opportunities. Being aware of the pitfalls that an amateur is likely to face, he has taken up mentorship of young entrepreneurs as a hobby.

Advices to the future entrepreneurs

He believes entrepreneurship is a natural instinct of human being. Success can come if one is passionate about his/her work and knows how to optimise time and resources. One needs to understand one's self and the power within. Risk taking and facing challenges with patience and smile makes one stronger. The future Entrepreneurs require to master these abilities.

CHAPTER THIRTY TWO

A Study on Integrity Infotech Private Limited (IIPL)

Prof. R. Pradeep Patnaik & Dr. Umakanta Nayak*
Centurion University of Technology and Management, Odisha

Unlike many engineering students of Odisha who aspired to be employees of reputed companies, Mr. Balakrushna Dixit, an electrical engineer passed out from BPUT in the year 2009, had a different vision altogether. He is born in a middle class family with no family business background dreamt of becoming an entrepreneur. The father who worked as an engineer with SOUTHCO wished his son will follow his footsteps and join any PSU and lead a comfortable life. But, Mr. Dixit with his challenging and never accepting defeat spirit could able to convince his parents and near and dear ones to be an entrepreneur.

Mr. Dixit was an average student throughout his academic career. He is gifted with keen analysis power and self-confidence. While continuing his study as an engineering student, he developed interest in web designing. Mr. Dixit accepts that this interest had a profound impact on him and kept him busy with his laptop at the cost of other subjects taught at the Engineering College. The indomitable quest to get mastery on web designing forced him to sharpen his skills in the field by spending most of his quality time as he found dearth of experts in the field readily available to him at the college days. He is thankful to counted few faculty members and friends who encouraged him.

Why Web Development Business?

Mr. Dixit analysed the business environment in and around Berhampur and found many small and medium enterprises seeking help to design and develop websites to feel their presence in the internet world. The idea of becoming an entrepreneur and providing service in the domain germinated in his mind as a student found the way to be expressed. After developing sound knowledge and skill in web designing and web development he gained experience and become an expert by developing and hosting websites for few non-profit organizations in Berhampur on voluntary basis. This resulted in developing good interpersonal relationships and contacts with many small and medium enterprises in Berhampur. He capitalised on the social capital and his indomitable entrepreneurial zeal finally culminated in establishment of Integrity Infotech Private Limited (IIPL), a premier web and software development company in Berhampur.

It provides industry-specific solutions and manages hosting for databases, server clusters, security management, data protection and more.

His success as an entrepreneur was well acclaimed by receiving awards like, IT Excellence award, Entrepreneurship excellence award, Odisha Youth Icon Awards.

Challenges faced

Mr. Dixit faced the typical challenge that every service sector faces, i.e., shortage of quality manpower for his newly established company. He was forced to stretch himself in honing the skills of newly recruited staff and provide the e-solutions on time to the clients. Besides manpower, the financial adversaries at the beginning of establishment of the enterprise were a major stumbling block. Instead of having an office space in a posh locality, Mr. Dixit started his venture from home with the laptop sponsored by the parents during college days with a mere earning of Rs.1000/- to Rs. 2000/- for web designing.

Learnings:

He learned the managerial skills in a hard way through practice. He believes in the old saying that 'a bird in hand is worth two in the bush'. Instead of looking for more deals one needs to concentrate on the quality and honour the commitment made to the clients. He espouses on the timely delivery of quality services. As new technology is invading the IT space in a rapid manner and change is the order of the day, he keeps himself abreast of the developments in the field by burning the late night lamp on many a days.

He proudly says that most companies die out of indigestion, not starvation. One has to be very careful in taking up assignments weighing the strength and weaknesses. Greed needs to have limit. It should not lead to apoplexy.

Future of the business
After getting considerable success in Berhampur, Mr Dixit has a plan to extend the business to neighbour districts like Khurda, Puri and Koraput by the year 2015.With an existing staff of seven members, he is planning to increase the numbers.

Impact of the business
This enterprise could able to provide enormous impact in the business environment of Berhampur. The important ones are:
- Providing the much needed visibility of small and medium enterprises by providing IT service in economical way;
- Serves as an excellent training ground for the web developer; and
- Promotes ethical business practices.

Advices to the future entrepreneurs
The future entrepreneurs are required to have appropriate knowledge and skill in the area before venturing into it. During the initial phase of operation an entrepreneur may get lured to another field of operation or get distracted by facing the hurdles in the field of operation. However, a successful entrepreneur requires ample concentration and consolidating the activities with full commitment.

Mr. Dixit gives outmost importance to trustworthiness to become a successful entrepreneur. The trust has to be built not only with the clients but also with the employees.

CHAPTER THIRTY THREE
A Study on M/s. Computer lab

Prof. Rabindra Kumar Mohanty & Prof. N.D. Prasad*
Centurion University of Technology and Management, Odisha

Mr. Santosh Kumar Sahoo, a budding entrepreneur from Cuttack, Odisha is a disciplined, hardworking, chivalrous gentle man with a strong conviction to provide employment opportunities to millions of rural youth. To accomplish the mission he is relentlessly pursuing activities in his Computer Lab for the last twenty years.

Mr. Sahoo was born and brought up in a lower middle class joint family consisting of three paternal uncles with their family members in addition to his own large family.Mr. Sahoo's father (an ex-service man) was the bread winner and the mother was the home maker. After retirement from defence service, his father temporarily shifted to Jaipur and engaged as a supervisor in a private company. The financial burden to sustain the large family put pressure on the two elder brothers. Being the second child Mr. Sahoo after completing his PG Diploma in Computer Science joined as an employee of Computer Lab in Cuttack. His sincerity and hardworking coupled with business acumen made him the owner of the Computer Lab.

He cherished the idea of providing one stop IT Solutions & Services to the clients nationwide, across diverse areas of business. The process of building new products and services and implementing prudent business and technological strategies which are cost efficient and ofhigh quality, has always been the objective of his Computer Lab. endeavour

The mission of Computer Lab is to be the most preferred partner for rendering IT Services to different Govt. Departments and actively participate in all e-Governance project initiatives in the State and Nationwide. His nature of business includes Bulk Data Digitization; Scanning &

Printing of Documents, Biometric Data capture, Customised Software Development, Call Centre Operations.

Why computer service business?

The IT-Services was an upcoming Business vertical in the advent of twenty-first century in India. The educational background (PG Diploma in Computer Science) coupled with employment experience had given Mr. Sahoo the orientation. The long cherished dream to provide employment opportunities to millions of rural youth, he analysed the relevance and scope of IT services and came to a conclusion that the future prospects of IT services were very bright and had potential for exponential growth for decades to come.Being knowledge and service driven vertical, Computer Lab's ROI is encouraging.

Challenges Faced

During the journey of these20 years, the major challenges faced and overcome in sustaining the entrepreneurship are:

- acquisition of projects on a continuous basis;
- acquisition of skilled and dedicated manpower resources keeping in view the high attrition of trained resources;
- cash-flow issues and timely settlement of wage & payments;
- unhealthy business practices amongst competing entrepreneurs;
- meeting expectation of highest quality services against lowest price criteria;
- complying with the restrictive eligibility and other criteria for MSME-Entrepreneur; and
- Indian IT majors venture in local market competing with small entrepreneurs due to recession in US & UK.

Future of the business

Computer Lab is looking towards becoming one of the best ethical and successful enterprises of the country by 2020. Aspiring to become a role model for the future entrepreneurs.

Learnings

One has to scan the environment on a continuous basis to see opportunities. Adopting unethical means may provide success in a short run but cannot sustain the business over a long period of time.

Impact of the business

Employment opportunities created: In the process of executing projects,Computer Labis able to create employment opportunities in rural areas over 200+ every month for over a decade and has crossed 1500+ in the last two years.

*Economic growth:*Computer Lab has continuously been growing and profit making since inception and has complied with all the financial statutory compliance requirements. The 1500+ employees generated by Computer Lab are exclusively from poor or lower middle class families, those who could not pursue higher education due to financial bottlenecks. They are providedwith decent earning opportunities at their localities with limited skills.The rural youth were enabled to avail citizen centric services through ITES culminating in bridging the gap between Govt. benefits and schemes and the common man.

Platform to interested parties: Computer Lab established itself as an ideal platform forcluster formation, conduct of conferences, seminars and spread of success stories to future entrepreneurs.

Advices to the future entrepreneurs

- Love what you do.
- Build a team immersed on your vision.
- Be creative and come up with innovative ways to solve your problem,
- Create a delightful work culture.
- Learn quickly from your mistakes.
- Never compromise with quality.

CHAPTER THIRTY FOUR

A Study on Essar Bakery

Dr. Subhendu Mishra

Centurion University of Technology and Management

The capital city of Odisha has undergone a metamorphosis in the last two decades. Once earned the fame for its rich cultural heritage and architectural excellence through its noticeable temples and obscured forts, the city is becoming a major trading centre and commercial hub because of urban sprawl with an exponential rate of growth. The city has witnessed a 30% rise in the last decade (Census 2011). Average literacy rate of the city is 93%. The city hosts a plethora of opportunities for amusement, entertainment, shopping and dining for its dwellers. At the same time the city offers a vast opportunity for the new age entrepreneurs to set up and develop their business. Such opportunities are aptlyvisualised and harnessed by Essar Bakery.

The foundations of Essar Bakery can be traced back to 1965, when the city was lush green; the streets were less congested and neat. The inhabitants of the city were mostly government employees. During that time, Mr. K. Raghvan, a dynamic, suave and soft spoken gentleman sensed the opportunity of tourism and travel in the city and the business opportunity along with that. He then established Sajitha and Choice Bakery and a South Indian Hotel. In due course he established Hotel Venus which soon became a favourite destination for tourists, travellers and vacationers. In the year 1974 Mr. K. Mohanan a young, flamboyant and ambitious boy from Kerala joined Mr. K. Raghvan who was supposed to be his maternal uncle. Mr. Mohanan soon fell in love with the city. After his graduation from BJB College in 1978, he joined his uncle's business. Mr.Mohanan had the passion and appetite to take the business to a next level. He took active interest in the bakery business and led Choice bakery at Bapuji Nagar, Bhubaneswar. In due course choice bakery was renamed as Essar Bakery.

Mr. K. Mohanan, born on 30th October 1956 at Tellacherry, Kerala married to Mrs.P.V.Sunila andhas two children Ms.Simna and Mr.Rohit. He ventured into hotel and bakery business since

1980. Mr. Mohanan is gregarious and has deep interest in watching movies, making friends, spending time with family and visiting places.

The success of Esssar Bakery resulted in coming up with another manufacturing unit to scale up business at Rameshwarpatna in 1996 and the other one in the year 2009 at Chandaka Industrial Estate. It had also opened six retail outlets to sell the products to the customers directly. The names are as follows,

- Venus bakery
- Venus Cake
- Venus Café
- Venus Hotel
- Sensation
- Venus Next

Today Essar Bakery makes several items like Breads, Cakes, Pastries, Cookies, Toasts, Patties, Sandwiches, Buns, Burgers, Pizzas, Tikkas (veg and paneer) and samosa to fill the cravings of the masses. The total annualrevenue generated is approximately at 20 million INR.

Challenges Faced

The initial yearswere full of challenges as the market opportunities for bakery items were less and there were hardly any retail outlets selling exclusive bakery items. The salesman had to sale the items door to door. The manufacturing facility was small at Bapuji Nagar and scaling up of business was unthinkable due to financial resource constraints. The recent challenges as Mr. Mohanan recollects as with higher rate of VAT (13.5% on food Items) and inflation leading to rising prices of raw materials along with competition in the bakery business is. But as it is said a smooth ocean never makes great sailors. Mr. Mohanan is focused and determined to face the odds and strived to improve upon.

Learnings

Mr. Mohanan is now experienced and realizes the competition and changing landscape of bakery market in the city. To withstand in a competitive market, one needs to be innovate in diversifying the products as per the changing choice of customers and introduce new technology to minimise wastageand reduce cost. He is optimistic about the future of Essar Bakery. With all the pressure and rigour of work, Mr.Mohanan learnt that through humility and a paternalistic approach can result into committed employees. He is a firm believer of training workers to adopt new skills. The staff describes him as a hard task master with a soft heart. Among the trust and confidence ofthousands of happy customers, retailers and supplier, the bakery has received a certificate of appreciation for participating in the Masterline cake festival.

Future of the business

Mr.Mohanan is optimistic about the future of Essar bakery. In its expansion plans, Essar Bakery is planning to start another manufacturing facility at Khurdha industrial estate. It also sensed the challenges in the form of competition from other players like Mongines, Cookies, Café Coffee Day and local bakery shops, squeezing profit margins. The impact of Government tax policy on bakery items (including higher rate of VAT standing at 13.5% on food Items) and rising inflation leading to rising prices of raw materials.

Impact of the business:

The bakery business has a large impact on the lifestyle of the people of the city and the employees who are engaged in it. It provides:
- Smiles on the faces of poor employees by providing them livelihood opportunities;
- Happiness to customers by providing ready to eat quality products to keep pace with the challenging city life.
- Building confidence for Suppliers.
- Tax Earnings for Government
- Stake holder Value Creation
- Responsible Citizenship Behavior

Advices to the Future Entrepreneurs

Mr.Mohanan believes the entrepreneurial landscape in bakery business is healthy but the young entrepreneurs must be open to technological advancement in improving operation to reduce wastages and cost.

CHAPTER THIRTY FIVE

A Study on Shree Paschimasombhu Fuels and Lubes Pvt. Ltd.

Dr. Bhagabat Barik & Dr. Pramod Kumar Patjoshi

Centurion University of Technology and Management

Mr. Shushil Kumar Sharma is a dynamic, hardworking and successful business man. Born on 4th May 1963 in a small village called Kantia in Jatni area under Khurda district. He has moved himself to be a flourishing businessman by virtue of his dedication, devotion, intuition, introspection and amicable dealings. Mr. Sharma, son of Late Dwarika Prasad Sharma, a Graduate in commerce and Law, had more than 10 years of experience in transport, grain and pulses trading business.

Shree Paschimasombhu Fuels and Lubes, established by Mr. Sharma is an outlet of Bharat Petroleum Corporation Limited (BPCL). It is located at Kantia, 10 kms away from the district headquarters of Khurda and 12 kms from the city of Bhubaneswar. Now a major junction connecting Pipili, Puri, Konark, Delang, Bhubaneswar, Khurda and Nayagarh.This location has strategic advantages and can be huge business potential for a petrol refilling centre

Why Petroleum and its Associated Business?

Petroleum and its associated business is very attractive considering the capital requirement and risk-return analysis. This business is flourishing in India and the country is obtaining rich sources of revenue out of this. One of the major reasons behind growth of this business is the rapid upsurgeof the vehicle density in India. Among the leading corporations associated in this business, Bharat petroleum Corporation Limited (BPCL) is more popular because of its customer service and product diversities. Mr. Sharma after analyzing the business opportunities ventured into this.

Bharat Petroleum Corporation (BPCL) traces its history to 1928 when the Burmah Shell Oil Storage & Distribution Company of India was incorporated in England to enter the petroleum products business in India. The business of the Company grew substantially given the international backing of Shell and it achieved the leadership position in India. In 1952, Shell and Burmah Oil Company set up Burmah Shell Refineries to set up a refinery in Mumbai. The entire operations of Burmah Shell in India were nationalized in 1976 and the refinery and Marketing Companies were merged to form BPCL. The actual name of BPCL came in 1st August 1979.

Bharat Petroleum Corporation (BPCL) is the second largest oil refining and marketing company in the country. It has bagged the fuel supply contract for Kerala State Electricity Board's Kozhikode diesel power project at Nallalam. Recently it has signed an MOU with LG Chem South Korea for a Joint Venture to set up a petrochemical plant adjacent to its Kochi refinery Complex.

Bharat Petroleum Corporation Limited is good in marketing his products. It has given much importance to its customers. It has introduced the 'smart-card' technology at retail outlets in Chennai. The company has launched 'Smart fleet', a programme for fleet owners and operators. The company has introduced 'Petro card', a customer loyalty programme, and enrolled over 2.25 lakh customers by the end of March 2001.

Challenges faced

Even after a long association in business, Mr. Sharma faced few major challenges. As the place was not a high population density area, constancy in business was not ensured with respect to customers. Now emerging as a major junction better business is expected. Frequent disruption in power supply adds to the misery of the refilling centre. As Jatni market is expanding, more competition is expected to rise. Lack of manpower sometimes worries Mr. Sharma to carry out effective day today operation.

Learnings

After more than one decade of struggles and skirmishes in number of businesses, Mr. Sharma feels happy and confident with this business. Mr. Sharma realized that adoption of modern technology and updated knowledge helpsa business to grow.With his son graduating in Business Administration, Mr. Sharma is quite hopeful to expand his business with his son be an associate.

Future of the business

Though Mr. Sharma is a promising and revolutionary entrepreneur, still sometimes He worries about thesales at the outlet. He says "the sales in outlet are positive and we are taking serious steps to keep our sales active". Leveraging on the advantages of the location, His challenge is to offer fast and efficient services to customers. He had plans   to have more no of dedicated staffs. Mr. Sharma is also planning to adopt scientific way of doing business to reap maximum benefit. Above all Mr. Sharma is very positive in handling all adverse situations in near future

Impact of the business

Some of the key impacts of this business in the immediate environment include:

- Providing the much needed access to fuels and lubricants in thesemi-urban area.
- Creating employment opportunities for the local youth.
- Providing opportunities to other business units to grow in the near vicinity.

Advices to the future entrepreneurs

- For any business, a detailed plan needs to be drawn considering both internal and external forces.
- Prior knowledge and relationship with company personnel, customers and other stakeholders are essential to succeed in the business.
- Spirit, Commitment and professionalism is the key for any entrepreneur.

Mr. Sharma is very enthusiastic about his business. His leadership quality along with local reputation has helped him to create a value added enterprise.

CHAPTER THIRTY SIX

A Study on Body Care Gym

Prof. Pooja Patnaik & Dr. Girija Nandini*
Centurion University of Technology and Management

Sunday or Monday, morning or evening, Kanti Babu is full of life and energy. Being a lively person, one will always find him on the move. Kanti Ranjan Swain, a man of dedication and determination, has a flair for sports and athletics made him choose a career option, which few people will dare. Apart from a black belt in Tycondo and winner of four gold medals at national level, He is able to prove himself as a capable boxer. Luck plays an important part in each one's life. Despite getting a golden opportunity to be a part of the prestigious Feather River Academy, California, he was unable to progress his career in Tycondo due to financial constraints. Being guided and mentored by some of the best coaches of India like Javed Khan at national level and Biswajeet Mohanty at State level, to add to his bad luck he could not make it to Olympics for Tycondo as this was not in the list of Olympics games basket. A sportsman is defined from his sportsmanship spirit and attitude. Mr. Swain is also no exception. He preferred to open a gym where he can make his dream a reality.

Mr. Swain is married and lives in a joint family along with parents and two elder brothers. After graduation, he chose to enrol for PG programme in Yoga and Naturopathy from Utkal University. Finally, his passion for sports came alive with the opening of Bodycare Gym in Bhubaneswar in the year 2001.Initially, Bodycare Gym provided workout on machines and then slowly initiated some other aspects of services like Aerobics, Yoga etc.

Why Bodycare Gym?
Unlike many sports persons aspiring for a secured government job, Mr. Swain decided to provide health care and wellness services to people by launching a Gym. The growing awareness of a sizable number of people in Bhubaneswar about physical, psychological fitness requirement in a stressful city life provided the much needed thrust to consider the business.

He was also aware of the dearth of well-equipped gym and trainers in Bhubaneswar. Kanti Babu is a perfect example having the splendid combination of Know-How and Do-How in this area. He was confident of earning a good amount from the new initiative, thus he started the business with an initial investment of 20 Lakhs. He invested 10 Lakhs from his own capital and took a loan of 10 Lakh from bank. This remind of a famous quote "Where there is a will there is a way". The Gym achieved its success due to:

- fewer competitors without having proper equipment and trained/ skilled instructors;
- Mr. Swain's proficiency pertaining to technical education on Yogic Science and Naturopathy;
- Initiation of Yoga and Dancing Aerobics for the first time in Bhubaneswar;
- Lifestyle counseling to youngsters through customer specific diet chart
- Introduction of a Special Spa and Body Massaging;
- Facilities like separate changing rooms for ladies and gents, a juice parlor inside the gym and safe racks to place helmet, key rings and mobile phones, availability of proper parking place

Challenges Faced

Mr. Swain faced considerable challenges in this business as there were lack of awareness among majority of the people regarding fitness and misconception that gyms meant for body building. Now, the increased competition and cost minimization are major challenges.

Learnings

Mr. Swain says "life is a learning process and change is the only constant". So, we have to adapt our business accordingly. But quality is one area where one cannot afford to compromise. Thus, proper strategy formulation and implementation is the key learning for this business to sustain. He very clearly highlights on four important strategies for success.

- The focus should be retaining the existing customer base.
- Introducing schemes during slack season
- Fixing price as per the service availed by the customer
- Retaining the trainers who are already groomed.

Future of the Business

The Key focus of Mr. Swain is to sustain more inflow of customers and to take the business to a higher level. He is very positive that with growing interest of people after approximately 10 years Gyms in Bhubaneswar will be successful.

Impact of the Business

Some of the key impacts of the business are-

- The gym emphasizes more on yoga and aerobics which leads to less consumption of electricity
- It provides diet chart to each of the customer so that they can understand their body requirement and eat accordingly.
- It helps to ensure holistic fitness for individuals.
- Mr. Swain provides counseling to teenagers as well as adults about lifestyle so that they can have a proper balance between professional and personal life.

Advices to the future entrepreneurs

The sole advice to the future generation is to be natural, careful and provide quality fitness service. The Gyms should focus on quality trainer. The future generation should act as eye opener and plan out strategies accordingly to make the public aware about what true fitness means. Activities like Yoga and aerobics should be given more focus as they are natural way of keeping an individual fit. As stated "Health is wealth" Gyms should not be designed for the purpose of profit rather it should focus on creating a healthy individual that in turn will create a healthy State and Country eventually. Kanti Babu feels that there is a great need for W.H.O, Health department of Government and NGOs to carry out sensitizationprogram. At the same time he suggests that the Government should make it mandatory to go for proper certification and documentation process before allowing a Gym to operate as there are many Gyms which do not have trained instructor and proper equipment.

Help yourself to become **E**nergetic, **A**ctive and feel **L**ight. Thus, it reminds me of a famous quote: "if wealth is lost nothing is lost, but if health is lost everything is lost". Your body needs an extra care! Please take care.

CHAPTER THIRTY SEVEN
A Study on Jagadamba Retail

Dr. Prashant Chopdar & Dr. Madhumita Das*
Centurion University of Technology and Management

Pradeep Agarwal seems to be very unassuming at the surface when someone sees him for the first time, but beneath that lays an assertive, confident and self-reliant person, who believes that there is no short cut to success. It only comes with hard work, dedication and honesty. He was born in the year 1968. He had a knack for doing business as academic excellence was not his cup of tea. So, after passing intermediate, he joined his uncle's garment business to hone his skills in business and later on decided to start his own business. He established "Jagadamba" family store in Jatni dealing with sale of all kinds of textiles and garments. It was conceived in the year 1991 by Mr. Pradeep Kumar Agarwal who is the sole proprietor of this business. At the beginning he was only dealing with sale of sarees. His initial investment was very less as he did not have a huge fund to start the business. Later, he expanded the business with financial support (loan) from Punjab National Bank, Jatni. He has recently added two exclusive outlets of Peter England and K-lounge to his business. His area of operations is currently limited to Jatni. Since last 10 years Jagadamba has seen a steady growth in its business with growth rate at around 10% per annum. It is dealing with all kinds of textile products like sarees, kids wear, men's wear and fabrics of various reputed international and national brands like Raymond's, Digjam, Arvind Mills, Manyavar, Peter England, Killer, Monte Carlo, Duke etc., to create value for customers and make a difference by offering genuine and branded products to customers.

Mr.Pradeep Agarwal focused on cost cutting right from the start of the business as he was not having enough funds to spend. He believed on his hard work and dedication to grow his business. He stocked merchandise according to customer's choice. He started his shop in a limited space with less rent and without any kind of support of sales staff. The business started growing year after year with capital growth and sales growth and leading to goodwill growth. His success mantra was based on variety and reasonable price which appealed to the customers at large. From a modest beginning he has taken Jagadamba to a level where it has reached now as among the top retailer in Jatni with customers flocking from nearby places. It has built a reputation of its own in the industry as well as the customers and public at large.

Why this Retail Business?

As the financial conditions of his family did not allow him to study further he joined his uncle's business. He wanted to take responsibility of his family on his young shoulders. After learning the tricks of the trade from his uncle's business, he could identify the demand of genuine and branded goods in Jatni. As it was not available in Jatni, peopleused to depend upon the

Bhubaneswar market for shopping. With moral supports from his father Mr. Jagdish Prasad Agarwal and uncle Mr. Sitaram Agarwal he decided to onset the business.

Challenges faced

From the many challenges he faced the major ones are related to:

- Finance and arrangement funds at the inception and growth stage of the business;
- Managing and coordinating with suppliers from diverse locations and honoring the commitments; and
- Creating and building a brand image of "Jagadamba" among customers and to counter competitions.

Key learning's

He learnt that honesty and complete dedication are two major pillars for success in any business.One has to be honest with all the stakeholders of the business. Proper planning and management of day to day operations has to be done with outmost care in order to create the much needed brand image. Finally, the objective has to be selling quality product at affordable price (value for money).

Future of the Business

Mr. Pradeep Agarwal plans to develop his business and network in retail and textiles all over Orissa. He wants the Jagadamba brand to grow all over Orissa. He has also plans for moving into manufacturing and developing and designing his own brands of textiles and garments which will give him a unique competitive advantage. He wants to achieve this in the next 5years from now. He has also plan to have a tailoring unit to cater to the demands of many customers.But at the heart of everything he has a desire and willingness to provide genuine products to customers and to do business honestly.

Impact of business

Jagadamba as a business house has social as well as economic impact in the sense that it has resulted in a change of mindset of people in general towards organized retail. It has provided employment opportunities to many people in the nearby area. It has also changed the mind-set of other entrepreneur in giving them the confidence that they can also achieve something like it if they work hard and with honesty. It is also helping kids by giving donation to them and helping them in their education in nearby area. That's how Jagadamba has set a shining example for others to emulate.

Mr.Pradeep Agarwal is never after any award. However, he received many awards for his excellence in business. To enumerate few

- Best management in Odisha for 3years from Odisha Textile Association
- Best seller in Odisha by Pan America brand of clothing in the year 2002
- Awards from All India Merchants Textile Association for customer support.

Advices to future generation

Mr. Pradeep Agarwal with his experience and knowledge in the field has some advices for future aspiring young entrepreneurs.

- Work with dedication to fulfil dreams in life.
- Do genuine and honest work. Nothing is impossible if you have single minded determination and focus on your work.

He is also members of various social clubs and organization in this area like the Marwari club and the rotary club. He spends his spare time contributing to various social causes. Mr. Pradeep Agarwal is a shining example of an entrepreneur who has faced so many challenges and has come out in flying colours and has made a name of his own as well as Jagadamba in Jatni and other nearby areas in the minds of the customer as well as the general public.

He is leaving a legacy of his own for others to follow and emulate. As he says in his own words "Nothing is impossible if you dare to dream and go after it with full dedication and focus"

CHAPTER THIRTY EIGHT
A Study on Bob N Harry's

Prof. Somabhusana J. Mishra & Dr. Bibhunandini Das*
Centurion University of Technology and Management

Delighting the customers with delicious bakery products, BOB N HARRY'S is known as one of the finest bakers in Bhubaneswar. It is a specialist in preparing various types of Biscuits, Cookies, Cakes, Breads and many other products that suit the taste buds of the consumers. Started in the year 1997, BOB N HARRY'S is known as one of the leading manufacturer, retailerof a wide assorted bakery items.

Mr. Hari Prasad Sharma & Mr. Biswa Ranjan Acharya aged about 43 years are friends from their school days. Both of them were engaged in different industries prior to the beginning of this enterprise. After completing their PGDM, Mr. Hari was teaching Accounts and Financial Management and Biswa Ranjan was into sales and marketing. They could not utilize their potential properly while working with different organizations. This realization germinated the seed of becoming entrepreneur in them and culminated in the creation of BOB N HARRY'S.

Why Bakery Business?

Mr. Hari said "When we thought of starting a business, it was quite a difficult task to identify the appropriate one". After carrying out quite a bit of research, they found out that essentials would be always in demand i.e.,*Roti, Kapda & Makan*. Since finance was major constraint for both them, they tried to find out a business where working capital requirement and working capital cycle would be comparatively less. They scanned the then business environment of Bhubaneswar and foundvery few players in bakery industry which had a huge growth potential as people's eating habit was undergoing change to cope up with the busy and fast moving city life. They determined to start bakery business even though they had no experience on this. Both of them did a short term course from IHM, Bhubaneswar which was a pre-requisite to sanction loan from the bank. To start this business their Parents, Bank of India, SIDBI and friends were key supporters. They started with their own contribution and some amount of loan from a bank. The mission of the enterprise is, as stated by Mr. Hari, "to serve fresh products, ensure warm environment, great value and friendly service to make the customer simply feel good".

Challenges faced

They started the business with initial investment of twelve lakhs and one employee in the workshop. They were managing the store without engaging any employee at the beginning which was a difficult and strenuous task. Mr. Hari says, "Entrepreneurship sounds glamorous but it involves a lot of hard work. It leaves one with almost no time for anything else". They had to engage themselves in the store or in the workshop from 9.00a.m. to 9.00 p.m. Another major challengeat the beginning of the business was over capitalization. They struggled a lot to overcome that challenge. After two years businessin 1999when super cyclone hit the coastal area of Odisha, the business was affected very badly. For about a year and half they suffered a lot due to decrease in sales and increase in wastage. Gradually, the business picked up.

Today the enterprise is a well-known name among the people of Bhubaneswar. The present worth of this enterprise is around 50 Lakhs and the annual turnover is approximately 40 lakhs. They achieved an annual growth rate of 15%. They have employed 3 persons in the workshop to make cakes, biscuits, breads etc. and one to assist them in the retail store.The enterprise has received many awards, among which it is worth to mention that it won 2nd and 3rd position in all Odisha bakers competition held by Institute of Hotel Management Bhubaneswar for two consecutive years 2007 and 2008.

Learnings

They had learned that dealing in low cost and high volume perishable product like bakery items, sales in time is the key factor. Hard work and determination is the key for success in business. There will be many hindrances or distraction factors since the inception of any business. But one needs to pursue the objectives and tackle the difficulties.

Future of the business

They adhere to the philosophy that "no work is small". Now, they want to scale up the business and go for franchisee model in near future.

Impact of the business

With rapid growth and changing taste of people, bakery products have gained popularity among masses. The bakery industry has achieved third position in generating revenue among the processed food sector. The business is able to carter the needs of middle income consumers who want varieties of food and an improved living standard in busy fast moving city life.It provided the much needed low price and high nutrient value products.

Advices to the future entrepreneurs

Finally the owners of this successful enterprise advise that be an entrepreneur and add value to the society by accepting challenges. Generate employment for you as well as for some others. By doing this you will help the society. You have to set clear goals and objectives when you set out with an enterprise. If those goals and objectives are not met within a set time frame then you should pull out. Entrepreneurship is about building value around a business idea.

CHAPTER THIRTY NINE

A Study on Maa Ugratara Food Products

Dr. Prakash Kumar Pradhan& Dr. Sisir Ranjan Das*
Centurion University of Technology and Management

In the year 2000, Mr. Panda at the age of 25 started his venture 'Maa Ugratara Food Products' at Badakumari, Bolgarh, Khurda in his own residential building. Initially, he was manufacturing only mixture productskeeping eye on the local market. After three years from the inception ofMaa Ugratara Food Products,Mr. Panda started manufacturing more snacks items like Mudki, Tara and Chips. Now he is having variety of Mixture products (Like *Jaae* Mixture, *Dali* Mixture, Special Mixture and Chips).

Mr. Panda born in a Brahmin family in Badakumari village of Panchagada Prangana, known for the peasant militia (*Paika*)ofOdisha, is under the Bolgarh block of Khordha district. Mr. Panda is the third child of Mrs. Haramani Panda and Mr. Nilakantha Panda. Hewas academically poor but hada passion to become a business man.That unceasing passionfor business developed in him as a child made him to be a leading manufacturer of Mixture in the block of Bolgarh and Begunia.

Currently Maa Ugratara Food Product manufactures and sells 50 quintal mixture on monthly basis. He supplies his product to local whole sellers, venders and retailers directly. The price of Mr. Panda's product is 35% - 40% less as compared to the other players like Ruchi, Saurastra and Bharata. The price of the products ranges from Rs. 60 to Rs. 90 per Kg. The turn over of the business is Rs. 50 Lakhs per month. But Mr. Panda says that he needs only Rs. 4 lakhs to stand his operation cycle in a smooth flow. The policy of Mr. Panda is not to store stocks (raw material or finished goods) in his storehouse. He is practising the management strategy of Just in Time (Toyotism). He counts each day as a manufacturing cycle, the success mantra for his venture. Now, Mr. Panda has employed 4 workers in the businessand indirectly continued to help a number of people for income generation. Mr. Santos,a vender, opined that he had been selling the Maa Ugratara Food Products for the last 5 years but never found any disturbance in supply of product.

Why Dry Food products?

Though he was not well trained or had any experience in mixture firm yet the cooking style of his mother inspired a lot to open up the venture. He found that the local mixture products available in the market were not having good taste and quality. People of the locality were not able to buy the expensive branded mixtures to satisfy their taste buds. Finding the gap of a quality product which is also less expensive, Mr. Panda started the business with an initial investment of Rs. 20,000.

His dedication to work and his parents support in the factory will be an example in our area, one of the villagers Mr. Jagdis Nayak told in his view.

Challenges faced

The main challenge faced by Mr. Panda was on seed capital arrangement from the banks.He could not avail loan from bank and borrowedthe money with higher interest rate from a private money lender to start his business. Availability of skilled manpower and modern techniques was another challenge for him. However, marketability of his product was never been a challenge to him. As big players are entering into the local markets, now Mr. Panda feels that to survive in the business he needs to adopt modern technologies to make the product cost effective.

Key Learnings

Great willpower and goodwillof all stakeholders can make an entrepreneur successful. To have goodwill one needs to be ethical in all business dealings.

Future of the business

As the market is open for all players and all products, Mr. Panda is planning to add more products in his basket,widen the area of operation and streamlining the distribution channel.

Impact of the business

- It provides a training ground for the young entrepreneurs those are interested to enter into the same field.
- It is providing directly and indirectly the employment opportunitiesfor the rural youth.

Advices to the future entrepreneurs

One has to dream and make an action plan to turn it into reality. There is not a single formula to be successful.But one has to recognise the mistakes in business and learn from it to become successful.

CHAPTER FORTY

A Study on a Horticulturist

Dr. Kshitish Kumar Khuntia & Dr. Sabyasachi Dey
Centurion University of Technology and Management

In a techno-savvy era, educated youths are moving towards the materialistic world. They are showing less interest on welfare of the people as well as development of rural sector. About 800 million people live in India's rural areas, which lack agricultural infrastructure and skilled jobs. In such a scenario in 2011 a young man, Haraprasan Nayakat the age of 31, started a horticulture nursery in the name of 'Bajrang Plant Resources and Research' in the rural area keeping in mind to provide income generationopportunities to the people. He started his project in 'Byree' an unknown village which is 20 kms away from Cuttack.

Although Mr. Nayak was born and brought up in the city, he has an emotional relation with this village. His grandfather Dr. Nagendranath Nayak, former Chief District Medical Officer, Cuttack was born in this village and spent his post-retirement life to help the poor people in the said area. He built a medical to provide free health service to the villagers.

Mr. Haraprasan Nayak is the eldest son of Dr. Chittaranjan Nayak (Cardiologist, SCB Medical College). Mr. Nayak completed his B.Sc (CBZ) from NSM City College Cuttack in the year 1999 and then joined in a course from GNIIT. After completion of his degree, he joined in a Bangalore based IT company. He worked there for 1 year and returned to Odisha and joined in a CA firm as a project manager and continued for 7 years. But his passion for agriculture compelled him to quit the job.

In his words, "I had a passion for agriculture even when I was child. I don't know how my love for agriculture started but I am always a nature lover. When I see my grandfather working in the garden, I always feel cherished".

Why horticulturist?

The passion towards agriculture found expression in the year 2011, when he took the challenge to explore his dream in the village Byree with 2 acres of semi-arid land.Having keen interest on different kind of flora prompted him to bring greenery in the semi-arid lands of the region. He found that the hilly barren lands can provide livelihood to the village farmers by growing cashew plantation. However, there was no nursery in the near vicinity to provide quality cashew plants in the area to be grown. This inspiredhim to make an initial investment of 10 lakhs to establish a nursery. The seed capital was funded by his father Dr. C.R. Nayak. Dr. Nayak said, "When I saw his passion towards agriculture, I suddenly decide to give money to materialize his dreams".

Challenges

To develop the nursery in a semi-arid land the major challenge he faced was scarcity of water. To solve the problem he depended on the groundwater. Labor problem was another challenge in this area. Frequent occurrence of natural disasters and invasion wild animals like elephants and wild boar was a perennial threat to the nursery. He never stopped his work and continuously striving to face the challenges.He says that "If one keeps faith on God and carry out the work with dedication then problems will be automatically vanished".

Now the worth of thenursery is Rs. 3 crore. "I never thought that I would earn profit from this business rather I started the nurseryto develop greenery and provide opportunities of livelihood to the rural people" Mr. Nayak says.

His nursery deals with grafting of both cashew plants and mango plants. Mr. Nayak uses the v-grafting method in his nursery. He uses healthy and vigorous root stock and scions from desirable cultivars. His method is otherwise known as saddle graft. This is like an inverted apical-wedge graft, with the rootstock forming the V shaped end (cuts 1 and 2) and the scion forming the slit for it to fit into (cuts 3 and 4). This makes it appear that the scion is sitting on top of the rootstock like a saddle. These results in a strong union as a large amount of the internal stem surfaces are united, but it's critical to make the cuts match, which makes it difficult to do.

Future of the business

Apart from this project, he is doing research on hybridizing plants with special reference to Rose. He has grown rose plants successfully from the seeds. His dream is to do the research in in-vitro propagation of medicinal plants with her sister Smitaparimita Nayak, who is doing research on medicinal plant. He has plan develop a medicinal plant nursery and orchard. He has also keen interest on photography. He is well known nature photographer in both national and international level. His amazing photographs can be seen in the website "treknature.com" with his ID- 'haraprasan'..

Impact of the business

The market demands for these grafts are high in the state. Basically he supplies to the state level nurseries and he is trying to supply to the government. "This year we will get the approval from the state government to supply the graft" he says. "My dream is to become a successful social entrepreneur by 2020" he replies to a question related his future vision. His effort could able to provide a source of livelihood and afforestation in the barren lands. Hisvision of creating more employment opportunities for the rural people is fructifying.

Advices to future entrepreneurs

"Farming is charming but the only thing that it requires is full of dedication and persistent hardwork without any leisure" says Mr. Nayak. Giving answer to a question related to advice for the future generation, he says, "You should keep faith on yourself, be a hardworking person, concentrate on your job and accept the existence of God to fulfill your dreams". One needs to understand the nutrients requirement for growth and development of plants. A fair knowledge of plant diseases and pesticides is also needed to become a successful farmer.

Not only Mr. Nayak has created niche for himself in the social entrepreneur sphere but also he became the role model for the young people in that area. Basically, he is a well hearted person and full of confidence to achieve the goal, say the friends and relatives. Through this remarkable project he can bring changes in the mind-set of the young educated youth in the rural as well as urban area.At the end we wish success in his life

CHAPTER FORTY ONE
A Study on Chapan Bhog
Dr. Monalika Rath & Dr. Anita Patra

Mr. Subrat Mohanty, a Management Graduate from Fore School of Management in 1992 developed a keen interest to be an entrepreneur while working in East-West Airlines. The Airline ceased its operation in 1997 and Mr. Mohanty returned Odisha to start a mineral water business under the banner of Green Life. The venture failed and he became bankrupt. "My father was very dissatisfied & wanted me to return back to Delhi to do a job there", says Mr. Mohanty. But, one failure could not stop Mr. Mohanty to become an entrepreneur. He rejuvenated his energy by analysing the problems faced in the mineral water business and convinced his father to start a new business in the food sector.

Why food business?

With a small survey he could find that food is the only sector where there is more chance of business survival. So, he approached his father to give his garage to start a *"Mithaii"* shop named as "Chhappan Bhog". After some inhibitions, his father allowed him to use the garage for the purpose. From the beginning his father used to warnhim that a *Mithaii* shop in the residential area wouldn't work.

"I started my business with Rs.1 lakh taken as short-term personal loan from ICICI bank with interest rate of 15%" says Mr. Mohanty. He feels that the key supporters are his customers for the growth of his business. Mr. Mohanty says "We have been recommended by our initial customers to others, due to our quality products, honesty in dealings, cordial behavior and prompt services".

Challenges faced

In this winter, while sitting on an arm chair, taking a cup of coffee & going through his memory lane, Mr. Mohanty intrigued that during the journey of these 10 years, the major challenges faced and overcome in sustaining the entrepreneurship were:

- Maintaining hygiene and procuring qualityingredients;
- Paucity of skilled and dedicated manpower resources;
- Unhealthy business practices amongst competing entrepreneurs.

Learnings

Mr. Mohanty perceives that without learning life ceases. So, he constantly keeps himself abreast of different culinary by attending seminars, conferences and training programs nationally & internationally. He learned that one needs to continuously invest in business.Accumulation of money is the major drawback for business. The moment one starts accumulating the downfall of the business starts.

Impact of business

The impact of the business can be traced by observing the employment opportunities created for many.

Future Plans

Mr. Mohanty has expanded his business by opening different branches in Bhubaneswar & opening Namkeen & dibba sweets factory in Rasulgarh. He constantly persists on providing hygienic & qualitative food to customers. Mr. Mohanty proudly says that this year he is one of the highest sales-tax payersamong the competitors. He is planning to open few more branches.

In the year 2009, Mr. Subrat Mohanty received the Entrepreneur's Award from Journalist Association for maintaining hygienic ambience, honesty, transparency& commitment in business. Mr. Mohanty believes that the key factor leading to his achievement rests on his staff members. He says, "If they are happy, they will make me happy and strive to achieve the excellence.This is where I will build my competitive advantage". While interacting with the staff members, one of the employees said, "We believe that Baba (Mr. Mohanty) strengthens oursocial security & will by providing PF & ESI to all of us. So, it becomes our responsibility to strengthen Baba's business." Chhappan Bhog's popularity can be assessed by the stories covered by, Aajtak, Zee TV& NDTV.

Advices to the future generation:

When asked to advise the future generations, Mr. Mohanty suggests, the following:

1. Always be confident, be generous to the mankind

2. Be committed, be truthful.

3. Understand the importance of time.

4. Have patience.

For future entrepreneurs, I would suggest "Do not accumulate money. It is the drawback of business." The moment you do it, the downfall of business starts, says Mr. Mohanty

Mr. Subrat Mohanty does not want to publicize himself, so he does not discuss much about his social work. According to him, God has made him efficient to help others & not to boast on it. When insisted, he could only reveal with shyness, that only, 20% of his income is spent on social work. "My family members and relatives always purchase sweets, bakery, snacks & meals (without onion-garlic) from Chhappan- Bhog due to its incredible taste & quality", says Dr. Rath, a local resident of Jayadev Vihar. "We have been offering sugar-free sweets keeping an eye on the health conscious people of the city & now, we are trying to be the top in packaging sweets in Odisha", says Mr. Mohanty confidently.

CHAPTER FORTY TWO

A Study on Rajamoni Foods

Prof. Shiv Sankar Das& Dr. Susanta Kumar Mishra

Centurion University of Technology and Mangement

Arisha Pitha, the customary "cake" of Odisha, is now a marketable commodity. It has transcended the state boundaries and finding place amongst the delicacies of other states. In Bengal it is called as '*Anand Pithe*'which is on the verge of extinction from the state, but it is somehow managed to survive in our state. It may be due to the association of this homemade cakewith every auspicious occasions and festivals in Odia culture.

Behind this lays the enduring enterprising spirit of Tara Das. For her this began as a way of tiding over her personal and financial adversities and has culminated into a proper corporate venture. "I had to sustain my family and medical expenses of my ailing husband. With no options, I decided to encase on my culinary skills, especially preparing traditional Odia cakes which I was best at" says a proud Tara.

She, along with her husband Sachidananda Das, two daughters and a son moved to Bhubaneswar from Delhi in early 1994 after her husband underwent kidney transplantation."But my husband's illness continued and his recurring medical expenses nearly milked us dry. Along with my son, I took the plunge into the business to earn some money". While Tara cooked the *Pithas* day in and day out, her son went around marketing. "Sadly we ended up earning nothing, but it did catch the fancy of some customers who tasted the *Pithas*. We began getting orders from marriage parties, families and friends," she said.

As ordered mounted, a worker from Salepur, Cuttack district was hired.Business took off and the worker strengthrose from one to three in her small makeshift factory adjacent to her house in Sailashree Vihar, Bhubaneswar. The product, labelled as 'Rajamoni', packed with five cakes was endorsed by almost every big shop selling snacks in the city.

Why this business and Success Storyline

Started with two kg of rice and two kg of jaggery, now her daily requirements of raw materials has reached to fifty kg of rice, forty five kg of jaggery and twenty litres of vegetable oil.She sells around two thousand pieces of *Arisa Pitha* on any given day. The production touches three thousand per day during festive occasions and the auspicious wedding seasons. Each *Arisa* weighs around hundred gram, and costs Rs.7/- per piece. She also prepares a special kind of *Arisa Pitha* that is made from *Desi Ghee* which costs Rs.16/- per piece. Other than *ArisaPitha*, she also prepares *Laddu, Namkins, Khira Gaja* etc. The delicacies prepared from rice powder and jaggery, can be preserved for at least one month in any season.

Das claims that it is hectic lifestyle of today's world that is stopping people from making the *Pitha*, which involves intricate and time consuming methods. "*Arisa Pitha*" has almost vanished from household in the state. People have become so busy that they do not get the time needed to prepare the dish, so I have been trying to keep the tradition alive", she said.

Residents of the city agree with Das, "I make *ArisaPitha* at home only when I get the time", said Sanjukta Misha, a resident of Niladri Vihar. "But I never manage to match Tara's preparations. She knows the secret of preparation of the most perfect *ArisaPitha*", Mrs. Mishra added. Tara started her business on August 16, 1999 on the day of Ganesh Chaturthi. After the death of her husband, her son Siddharth has been providing the much-needed support to the business. "My son has been toiling hard to market the product. I have hired four people, who are also helping me a lot in preparing *ArisaPitha* she said. My son is helping me in every walk of life", she told.

Challenges She Faced

She attributes her success to her secret method of preparing and mixing the ingredients. "In order to make the cakes taste differently from others we prepare a different mixture of jaggery with right proportion of water ", she says with great deal of satisfaction. The cakes come with more crispy and soft from inside. But fate tested her patience when workers in her factory duped her and started their own parallel business. They not only hijacked her trade secret but also marketed the cakes with the look-alike label named "Rajlakshmi" where as the original named as "Rajamoni". "It hurt me badly.We had to convince shop-owners about the duplicity of the packets", said Tara. Incidentally it was during the same time that she lost her husband. She overcame the problem when affected labours from a nearby leather factory arrived at her doorstep for work.

Impact of the Business

Today her *Pithas* have spread to almost every town of the state, as well as other parts of the country. *ArisaPitha* has gone global, "I receive orders from customers living in US, Germany and Japan. My clients include NRI's, Non-Residents Odiya as well foreigners," Das said. So well know is her *Pitha* that Das does not even have to foot the bill of sending her items by courier to her over-seas customers. Instead, it is her clients who collect Das's preparations from friends and relatives who live in Odisha. She bagged many accolades from different organizations. She has been awarded from IIM, Ahmedabad, under the tag of Shristi Samman on 29th February in the year 2007, Nehru Juba Sansthan in the month of November 2002, and she has been interviewed on many television channels.

Future of the Business

Siddharth, an MBA graduate said, "Our next step is to launch our product in the international market" with a vision to be more success and a mission to open a chain of outlets with Odia food delicacies, synchronizing with promotion tools of web, e-marketing. "But the greatest hurdle is the meagre resource"he laments.On an average they earn rupees ten thousand per day, which touches rupees twenty thousand during marriage season. With increase in cost of raw materials and labour, Tara and her son are scouting for someone who can finance their endeavour. She rues that no financial institution leave along the Government has come forward with financial assistance. "We had approached the Government to allot us a shop in Ekamra Haat where we can sell as well as promote our cakes, but the Government has paid no heed," she rued. Das is eager to participate in various food shows in foreign countries. "I would like to urge the state tourism department to help me market this mouth watering delicacy in foreign countries" Das said.

At last she urged the youth generation that "we have to work hard, work dedicatedly, and never say 'I can't, rather say I can do this work'. There will be many hurdles in each and every aspect but onehas to cross it effectively. If one wants to achieve something then he/she must do it whole heartedly".

Some Food Facts:

- Tara began her journey on 16th August 1999.
- She makes *ArisaPitha* for her clients based in India and abroad.
- Clients include NRIs, NRO's, and Foreigners.
- Das has won awards for making and reviving Odia delicacy.
- She operates from her home in the capital's Sailashree Vihar.
- Each *Pitha* weighs around hundred grams and costs Rs.7/-.
- Special *pitha* costs Rs.16/- made up of Desi Ghee.
- She sells around 2000 pieces of cakes daily.
- During Festive season, production touches 3000 pieces a day.

Tara wants to register "Rajamoni Foods" as a company and wants to open a second unit only for large scale quantity orders.

CHAPTER FORTY THREE

A Study on Bakul Foundation

Dr. Pranaya K. Swain

National Institute of Science Education and Research, Bhubaneswar

Dr. Umaknata Nayak

Centurion University of Technology and Management

Bakul was founded by Mr. Sujit Mohapatra, an activist and a researcher from Odisha. Sujit, like many other individuals had a dream of working on something that provoked him the most and that was 'cynicism', the cynicism of so what if one does not do anything, things are being done anyway. But unlike others he followed a path less chosen by others. His idea of change was to activate people so that they may put in collective effort for the social good. People should feel the need themselves and should volunteer for the effort. This philosophy has been followed in every activity of the organization where each individual feels Bakul is his/her own child. Bakul Foundation promotes volunteerism and organizes efforts towards community development. It is an attempt to pool together the small individual efforts of all the people interested in the social and cultural development of India, starting with the state of Orissa. As the first initiative, the movement has mobilized a thousand people to contribute to set up an excellent children's library and creative learning centre in Bhubaneswar on April 1, 2007. It has used interactive and interesting reading methods for inculcating the habit of reading among the children.

The tag line of the Bakul spreads a spirit of encouragement with the words:-'Alone we can do so little; together we can do so much'. To achieve the above said aim it has collaborated with UNICEF and goes places spreading the message of book reading. Bhubaneswar , the state capital of Orissa was its point of initiation.

The working mantra of Bakul is- "Making this world a better place is not restricted to philanthropists. All of us can contribute in our own way, by way of funds, time and effort, or even a 'pat on the back'! Get involved!"

Bakul attracted attention across the globe even before it was registered. Contributions poured in just around a promise. The movement was an online campaign that asked people to pledge books so that a library could be set up in Bhubaneshwar. This acted and is still acting as a constant support for Bakul.

Reasons to start the library

It is a well established fact that in India, a good number of primary school goers are unable to read clearly and efficiently. Adding to this is another truth that there is dearth of reading facilities and guidance for these children. Bakul has taken up the task from where other agencies have tailed off. It has been established to fulfill the gap so as to start up a community initiative for the betterment of India's future generations.

A community initiative

Although Bakul had been a dream for many years, it was formally launched on 1st April 2006 with the birth of the campaign, "Donate Books Build a Library". There was an online pledge campaign at www.pledgebank.com/bakul-library to mobilize a thousand people, who would contribute to set up a library in Bhubaneswar on 1st April 2007. This campaign was successful and by the deadline, 1011 people had pledged support. The library started on the promised date and was inaugurated by three children including a slum child. The entire library has been built with the small individual contributions of ordinary people without any corporate or institutional funding so far. The books are either directly donated or bought with the money donated. The Bakul Children's Library, located at 16, Satyanagar, Bhubaneswar, is already one of the best children's libraries in India with a collection of about 8000 highly valuable and interesting books and multimedia, including some of the best educational resources from all over the world (Exhibit 1). This has been largely possible due to major book collection drives at the University of Waterloo, Canada, Duke University, USA, HP, Bangalore, and BITS Pilani. The support is growing. Indian students at the University of North Carolina have just voted unanimously to support Bakul.

The wonderful infrastructure of the library has been developed and the library is being run with the contributions of the core members of Bakul. Mr Ramesh Swain, eminent architect, has built up an amphitheatre under the trees behind the library as an activity centre for storytelling sessions, theatre workshops etc. Reading inside the library is FREE and they are trying to make it the most exploited children's library in the world. The library is not only a manifestation of the spirit of volunteerism but it is being hoped that the library will be a launching pad for further initiatives for volunteerism as well.

Bakul is also trying to break the distinctions that schools create. It is providing both disadvantaged and advantaged children the same opportunities to build their own capabilities and compete with each other as equals. They have networked with some institutions working with the differently advantaged children in Bhubaneswar. For instance, Khelaghara, a school for slum children, Thakkar Bapa Hostel for tribals, Anand Ashram, an orphanage and Madhurmayee Hostel for children of jail inmates have been regularly exploiting the library. Efforts are on to network with more such institutions to get their children to the library.

Vision

The vision of Bakul foundation is of a world where everyone acts on Mahatma Gandhi's words, "Be the Change you want in the world". It wants to work towards a world where the small little contributions of people are pooled without any distinction between the benefactor and the beneficiary, where everyone is both giver and taker. It wants it efforts to lead to a world where there is equality of access and opportunity and a world that gets better each day for everybody.

Mission

The mission statement of this initiative is to lead a movement for volunteerism in India starting with the state of Orissa. The efforts aim at mobilizing thousands of volunteers (students, retired persons, homemakers, and working people) to work for community development. Community development initiatives for them are not just confined to the immediate tangible goals, but go beyond to instill and invoke the spirit of volunteerism that underlines the project.

People Involved

"We are a loose but huge group of students, retired persons, homemakers, writers, scholars, media professionals, IT professionals, and corporate guys etc. spread across the world working to make the dream of Bakul a reality" says Sujit Mohapatra one of the founding members of the Library. This is, however, a registered body in Bhubaneswar, Orissa that has an active working team. As time passed by the library grew bigger in size. Books kept on increasing in number. Each book carried a tag with the name of the donor, individual or organization, written on it. People saw this and got motivated to donate books. Local artists and painters volunteered to paint the walls of the library with children friendly pictures which gave a new look to the library.

Creating Social capital

Sujit describes how the idea of Bakul was conceived. He says that people of India and Odisha did want to give back to society at the time but there was some suspicion that people had with regards to the credibility and accountability of NGOs. Therefore Bakul took the route of engaging volunteers or what they call 'Volunteer capitalism'. At Bakul volunteers try to inspire others to volunteer and thus encourage the spirit of volunteerism. They call this phenomenon Bakulization i.e. when one volunteer inspires another to do the same they are said to be 'Bakulized'. Sujit described one of his biggest challenges to be the retention of these volunteers. He said it was difficult to meet expectations of people since not all volunteers were permanent and a lot of them kept leaving. But however short is the stay, the volunteers keep contributing in terms of ideas. Bhubaneswar being one of the major tourist destinations in the Eastern India attracts good number of foreigners. After few of them heard about Bakul visited the library and liked what was happening there. They interacted with the kids and shared the experiences from their parts of the globe. This gave birth to the idea of story-telling from around the world which went on to become an integral part of the library.

Making Reading a fun experience

Bakul aims at making reading a fun experience for the children. It therefore portrays this library as-

- A space where children can discover themselves and their interests and have the opportunities to pursue and cultivate their interests.
- An open forum that actively promotes a sensible reading culture among the children and youth. It hopes to promote this through different activities like storytelling sessions, educational workshops, film screenings, student presentations, creative writing workshops, ecological treks, and health awareness camps etc.

- A potent instrument for building people's capabilities to actualize the opportunities of a 'knowledge economy' and lessen the growing socio-economic inequalities. Through a library it is making the world of books and knowledge accessible to children and the youth.
- An institution that works towards generating the spirit of volunteerism among its users to undertake further initiatives in community development programs.
- The most exploited children's library in the world and it is working on the target of reaching out to 10,000 children from all sections of society in two years. That is why; it does not charge anything for reading inside the library.
- An opportunity for every child to grow and develop in a learning environment. Bakul has therefore partnered with *Khelaghara*, a school for slum children, Anand Ashram, an orphanage and the Thakkar Bapa Special Hostel for tribal students., a hostel for children of prisoners and B.B.C. Deaf and Dumb School The students of these institutions have been having library sessions at Bakul and Bakul is working towards bringing more such institutions working with underprivileged children to exploit the resources of the library.

Recent initiatives

Innovative ideas do not really stop at any point. Bakul's most recent activities include this unique storytelling programme through which they started involving foreigners to expose children to different cultures through stories. Another interesting initiative is its my tree campaign. Bakul pioneered this gifting of saplings on occasions like birthdays, wedding, etc. Gifting saplings send out a clear message of 'plan trees' without trying so hard or making noise about it. A sapling gifted on occasions such as child birth is always planted and nurtured for the simple reason that it has a sentimental value attached to it. Wall painting was another innovative initiative which served the dual purpose of bringing out creativity from the young minds and also beautifying the public walls in the city. One of the most amusing but effective ways is the celebration of fake birthdays where volunteers meet in a public place and fake that it is one of their birthdays. The idea is to publicly gift him/her a sapling instead of conventional gifts so that people take notice of the event.

Ongoing supportive activities

A computer lab has been started in the Bakul Children's Library. The computers have been donated by SUN Microsystems India. This was the initiative of the Bangalore Group of Bakul that was set up after the film festival at IIM Bangalore in 2008 by enthusiastic visitors to the festival. The Lab was inaugurated on 2nd October by Mr Jay Panda, the member of Parliament from Orissa. On the occasion of Gandhi Jayanti, Bakul also had an informal interaction with the renowned Gandhian Prof. Sarbeswar Das. He spoke to the 40 odd kids present about Gandhi and Gandhianism from a personal perspective. Pantaloons, Bhubaneswar placed a board at its entrance to publicize the environmental film festival organized by Bakul. The film festival has since been a regular affair that Bakul has been so passionately involved with. Pearson Education sent 200,000 books after learning about Bakul at one of its exhibitions in an American University where someone shared the story of the children's library from India.

Future plans

Online Library Catalogue :Bakul Library aims at building a state of the art Online Library system which can be accessed anytime and anywhere from the web. This online system will enable user to check the availability of books and multimedia, place a request, renew books and going forward get it delivered to your doorstep. The online system is currently under construction.

Scalability:

People actively associated with Bakul strongly feel that it is not about whether they scale up the library in terms its size or how many branches they manage to set up across the state. But it is about the inspirational value creation. People see the library and then go back to set up one miniature one in their localities. This is what they call creation of social capital, hence proving that the most scalable thing is 'hope'.

Challenges

The biggest challenge faced by Bakul is of changing the perception of the public towards the habit of reading. The present era is technology dominated with a constant inflow of modern day gadgets. It becomes very difficult to inculcate physical book reading habit among the youngsters. Bakul has taken up the challenge and is zealously working towards it. The second problem faced is of funds. Community is slowly responding to the efforts of Bakul but it is still a long way to go. Funds are just trickling in but Bakul has kept its hope high for a better response soon. Sujit recalled someone saying, it is too elitist a thing. The library in its present look does not like one for the disadvantaged, But then, an initiative for the disadvantaged does not need to look disadvantaged itself.

Innovations during Pandemic

During Pandemic, Bakul started Storytime at 9.00 pm on every Saturday on different online fora. The storytellers were engaged from all over the world. The children could able to gain knowledge on the cultures and traditions of different countries through this intervention when physical presence in the library was not allowed. A series on noble laureates and their innovations has also started for children by Bakul Foundation using online platforms. The speakers chosen by Bakul are to be reckoned in their proven field of work. These efforts on the part of Bakul to engage the children in acquiring knowledge during pandemic are noteworthy.

CHAPTER FORTY FOUR

Green Marketing as a Prospect for Green Entrepreneurs

Dr. Girija Nandini, Associate Professor,
Centurion University of Technology and Management, Odisha, India

Dr. Alaka Samantaray, Associate Professor
IBCS, Faculty of Management Sciences, SOA Deemed to be University

1. Introduction

The world is changing due to technological, economic and political changes. Also the customers' requirements are changing. Entrepreneurs those who can fulfill the customer's requirement only can sustain in the long run. Recent studies show that consumers are now more conscious about health and environment. Due to this, the concept of green market, green entrepreneur and green product is developing. So there is a big opportunity for the green entrepreneurs in future. They can choose green product and green marketing to earn huge profit in the changing world. Green marketing is also very much essential for the sustainable development of the world. Green marketing is a strategy used by entrepreneurs for reaching sustainable development. Organizations need to know buyers' attitude and their requirements, so that they can adapt new strategy. To be in the long run in competitive market entrepreneur has to understand the requirements of the customers and try to satisfy them. Green marketing is a concept which is used by the entrepreneurs for the sustainable development. Time has come to understand and implement the strategy of green marketing and green product by the green entrepreneur to save the world.

2. Green Entrepreneur

Green Entrepreneur starts its business with green product, green marketing and also green design from the starting of their business. Green means which is environmental friendly, which will not harm the environment and will be helpful for sustainable development. Green entrepreneur is a sensitive and motivated person who is ready to solve the environmental problems by doing innovation in an ecofriendly manner. Their main business activities are to solve the social and environmental problems. Their business gives a positive impact on the environment. They start their business activities knowingly to solve the social and environmental issues. They take high risk to get the profit in an ecofriendly way.

3. Green Products and Green Marketing

These products have low environmental effects. They are designed in such a way where fewer resources are used for the production. These products are durable, non-toxic and also made of recycled materials. Green or sustainable products help in economic development by preserving the resources for future generation. It is less harmful to the human health and environment. Green marketing is a process where the entrepreneurs sell their products and services to the customers by showing the benefits of green marketing to the health and environment. They show their products as environmental friendly, safe for health and also which leads to sustainable development. The objective of green marketing is to reduce the wastages, use of biodegradable materials and educating people about green products by eco-friendly message.

Phases in the evolution of green marketing

- Ecological green marketing.
- Environmental green marketing.
- Sustainable green marketing

4. Reasons for Green Marketing

- Entrepreneurs using green marketing have competitive advantage than other entrepreneurs.
- It is also required to show corporate social responsibility by the entrepreneurs.
- In some products it is required according to Government regulations.
- It is required to compete with other responsible companies those using green marketing.
- It is also required to increase the goodwill of the company.

5. Rules of Green Marketing

- **Creating awareness among customers:** The green entrepreneurs should create awareness about the benefits and requirements of green product and green marketing for sustainable development of the world. Customers should also know the benefits to their health and environment.
- **Reassure the consumer:** Customers should be convinced that they are not compromising with the quality of the product for climate. They are getting good product for the price they pay.
- **Pricing of the product:** If entrepreneurs charging a premium for products and services of ecofriendly or green products, they have to be sure that the customers will be able pay the increased price.

- **Customer expectations:** Customers expectations should be fulfilled while adopting green marketing.

Advantages of Green Marketing

- Entrepreneurs can start new ventures if they can market and bring the attention of the customers that their product is environmental friendly.
- Every one now a day conscious about the health and environment. Customers are ready to pay for green products and services. So the entrepreneurs can earn good amount of profit by doing green marketing.
- It gives competitive advantage. Customers can be convinced to pay little more for sustainable development rather than paying less for the product.
- It will increase awareness among the customers to use the products and services which is not only good for their health also good for the environment.
- It will increase goodwill of the company.
- It will save scarce natural resources.
- It will give sustainable long term growth and profit to the entrepreneur.
- It increases corporate social responsibility.

6. Disadvantages of Green Marketing

- When the entrepreneur wants to change the strategies to do green marketing it increases the cost of the project.
- Getting green certification is generally time taking and costly for the entrepreneurs.
- Sometimes the companies' charge more for the green product which actually not justified in terms of sustainable development. It means showing something and doing something else.
- It requires new technology and huge cost in research and development. Small entrepreneurs may not be able to afford this cost.
- Most of the people are not aware about green product.
- Majority of the people are not ready to pay high amount for the green product.
- Educating customers about green product is also difficult for the entrepreneurs.

Big Companies like Tata Motors, Maruti Suzuki, Canon, Toyota, Philips, NTPC and McDonald's are doing green marketing. These companies are making huge profit by using green marketing. Profit making is also one of the important aspects in green marketing. More emphasis should be given to the green marketing by the entrepreneur as it has social and environmental benefit. As the global warming is increasing, green marketing should be the normal rather than an exception or a fad.

www.ingramcontent.com/pod-product-compliance
Lightning Source LLC
Chambersburg PA
CBHW070528220526
45467CB00003B/899